D0221971

THE KALAPALO INDIANS
OF CENTRAL BRAZIL

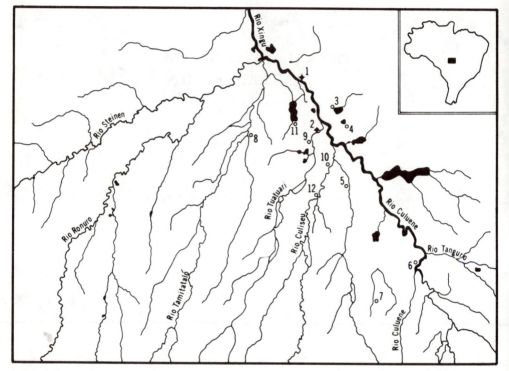

Map of the Upper Xingu Basin (insert indicates relationship of area shown to rest of Brazil). Key to map below.

● BRAZILIAN AIRFIELDS
1. Xingu (Brazilian Air Force Base)
2. Pôsto Leonardo Villas Boas

○ INDIAN SETTLEMENTS

A. *Carib Groups*
3. Mïgiyapei
4. Kalapalo
5. Kuikuru
6. Fififïtï (abandoned Kalapalo dry season settlement)

7. Kanugijafïtï (abandoned Kalapalo rainy season settlement)

B. *Arawak Groups*
8. Waura
9. Yawalipiti
10. Mehinaku

C. *Tupi Groups*
11. Kamaiura
12. Awïtï

THE KALAPALO INDIANS
OF CENTRAL BRAZIL

By

ELLEN B. BASSO

University of Arizona

WAVELAND PRESS, INC.

Prospect Heights, Illinois

WITHDRAWN

LIBRARY OF MOUNT ST. MARY'S COLLEGE EMMITSBURG, MARYLAND

For information about this book, write or call:
Waveland Press, Inc.
P.O. Box 400
Prospect Heights, Illinois 60070
(708) 634-0081

Copyright © 1973 by Holt, Rinehart and Winston, Inc.
1988 reissued by Waveland Press, Inc.

ISBN 0-88133-329-8

All rights reserved. No part of this book may be reproduced, stored in a retrieval system, or transmitted in any form or by any means without permission in writing from the publisher.

Printed in the United States of America

7 6 5 4 3 2

Foreword

About the Author

Ellen B. Basso was raised in New York City, where she was born in 1942. Her undergraduate work was done at Hunter College of the City University of New York, after which she studied at the University of Chicago, receiving her doctorate in anthropology in 1969. In addition to five years' field research in the Upper Xingu Basin of Brazil sponsored by the National Science Foundation and The Wenner-Gren Foundation for Anthropological Research, Inc., she has done work in the American Southwest and among the Fort Norman Athabascans of the Northwest Territories, Canada. She currently teaches anthropology at the University of Arizona.

About the Book

This is a case study of a lowland South American people with a surviving indigenous culture that is uniquely protected by a national reserve. Within this reserve the Kalapalo, together with thirteen other Indian groups, live isolated from national Brazilian society and economy. This unusual situation has made possible the survival of a people with a culture to a large extent unaffected by the outside world and of an economic type that was once very widespread throughout the lowland areas of South America.

This study of the Kalapalo is significant not only because it is a description of a relatively untouched society but also because the Kalapalo are distinct culturally from other people who live in similar environments in the South American lowlands, such as the Yanomamö, described by Napoleon Chagnon in another case study in this series. The reader will be instructed by reading these two case studies, one after the other, to see how different the Yanomamö and the Kalapalo are, not only in their social, political, and spiritual arrangements but most particularly in personality and in the handling of conflict and aggression.

Beyond its importance as a report on an intact, indigenous South American culture, this case study has the great virtue of being organized around certain central concepts, the most important of which is an ideal of behavior, *ifutisu*. This is an all-pervasive ideological concept that is represented in numerous ways in social life and conceptual organization among the Kalapalo. It occurs in many different behavioral contexts, such as attitudes toward the use of old village sites and the usurpation of rights and privileges held by people no longer living there, the division of public regions into distinct zones that allow individuals the option of concealing or displaying themselves, and the activities that must be performed by shamans, village representatives, and ceremonial specialists. We will leave it to the reader to find out for himself or herself how *ifutisu* permeates Kalapalo life.

Another of the special virtues of this case study is the very thorough treatment of kinship and affinity. Kinship systems and terminology are often an area of particular opaqueness to many beginning students of anthropology. Although anthropologists claim that such systems are central to social life among nonliterate peoples, they are often not explained in their behavioral settings with sufficient detail and relatedness to allow the students to understand that kinship terms are anything more than words with which anthropologists play. In this case study relationships between kinsmen, marital partners, lovers, and friends are laid out with sufficient ethnographic detail to allow the reader to understand how the system works and why they are a central part of Kalapalo life.

The Kalapalo Indians of Central Brazil is a departure from the standard case studies in the series in that it is closer to the professional ethnographic model than most. This may create some difficulties for the student who is having his or her first encounter with the discipline of anthropology, but it should prove particularly useful to those readers who already have at least a nodding acquaintance with the field. For the beginning student who will read the book carefully and who has a knowledgeable instructor to help consolidate intellectual gains as they are made, this case study will prove especially rewarding.

George and Louise Spindler

Preface

This book describes the Kalapalo, a small and isolated group of Indians who live in Central Brazil. Insignificant in terms of national Brazilian society and unknown to most members of that society, theirs is one of the few surviving indigenous cultures in lowland South America. Through no effort of their own, and indeed almost unaware of their peculiar circumstances, they have become isolated artificially from the disastrous social and economic influences that reach virtually every other Brazilian Indian people.

The prehistory of Indian tribes who live in the central regions of Brazil is generally unknown because of the absence of serious archeological investigation. With regard to language, only broad classifications have been made, and in many cases the relationships between specific local dialects and the larger South American families to which they belong remain obscure. Some languages, in fact, have yet to be described adequately and will soon be irrevocably lost with the extinction of their speakers as cultural units. Furthermore, because groups speaking languages that belong to the same major family are often dramatically different in technology and social organization, it would be extremely difficult to associate most modern linguistic families with prehistoric populations.

The Kalapalo, who speak a language belonging to the Carib family, are a case in point. Their linguistic relatives are concentrated both in Central Brazil and in the extreme northern margins of the continent. Almost nothing is known about the relationships between these local dialects, the majority of which have only recently begun to be studied intensively. As a consequence, very little can be said about the prehistoric relationships of the ancestors of these Carib speakers and even less about their geographic origins or early sociotechnical development.

The region in which the Kalapalo live, an area in northeastern Mato Grosso state called the Upper Xingu Basin, contains a number of linguistically diverse groups whose history and society pose several problems to anthropology. Despite linguistic diversity, characterized by the presence of four mutually unintelligible languages, the village groups presently occupying this area hold a number of social and ideological features in common. A reconstruction of the social integration of the historically discrete and culturally diverse groups that resulted in Upper Xingu society would be extremely difficult, considering the present state of our knowledge about the area. The means by which diverse systems of kinship classification, marriage practices, ceremonial organization, status allocation, and religious beliefs became a seemingly homogeneous set of cultural rules and social practices cannot be known without some idea of the original systems.

Another problem is the relationship of language and culture in the Upper Xingu Basin. Should we say there are four cultures or "conceptual systems" because there are four separate languages? Or is there only one culture, expressed through the media of several different languages? To what extent is communication between members of village groups that speak mutually unintelligible languages possible, and to what extent is such communication dependent upon bilingualism? Obviously, the answers to these and other similar questions await further research and the careful study and comparison of all the Upper Xingu groups.

This study focuses upon a set of concepts that can be used to construct a model of Kalapalo society. In particular, I shall concentrate on describing a system of classification by which the Kalapalo distinguish and differentiate social relationships. Central to the discussion is an ideal of behavior called *ifutisu*, a set of ethical statements by which the Kalapalo distinguish Upper Xingu villagers from all other human beings. This all-pervasive ideological concept extends into virtually every area of social life, applying in varying degrees of specificity to relationships between local groups, kinsmen, relatives by marriage, and even between men and various kinds of nonmen. Similarly, the demonstration of *ifutisu* behavior confers prestige and, therefore, is important in terms of the allocation of political power. This ideal is manifested in a distinctive behavioral and conceptual complex that distinguishes the Upper Xingu people from their traditionally surrounding neighbors.

Kalapalo society is also instructive as an example of a system wherein social units, such as the village group and households, exist only by virtue of the individuals who choose to live in them and cooperate with one another. Unlike many other non-Western societies wherein the members acquire, by birth or other means, obligation to participate in social units whose relationships to and with each other are determined regardless of the identities of the members themselves, Kalapalo social organization is characterized by extremely flexible group membership and considerable variation in the identification of individuals with specific groups. In theory at least, the options which any Kalapalo has for joining groups are many, and the choices that are made depend upon the personal relationships between individuals rather than (as elsewhere) upon such considerations as clan membership, religious affiliation, or ancestry. In particular, the absence of descent-based units makes the Kalapalo an interesting example for the comparative study of "cognatic" systems.

Several types of Kalapalo song illustrate vividly the fundamental concerns of the members of this society, and thus I have introduced certain sections of the book with English translations of choral verse. Several of these are traditional songs sung by women during group performances in the village plaza. Others are associated with a ceremony called *kwambï*, during which men dressed in ridiculous costumes dance from house to house singing about the gossip of women. In the *kwambï*, it is the intent of the singers to convey their knowledge of the opinions of others about themselves, each song being based upon something the inventor heard spoken about himself. Both *kwambï* and women's songs are replete with the themes of love affairs, jealousy, unfaithfulness, witchcraft accusations, and disputes involving close kinsmen, but they also mention humorous incidents in which the singers poke fun at their fellow villagers or admonish them to adhere to certain ideals of behavior.

Ellen B. Basso

Tucson, Arizona

Acknowledgments

The field research upon which this book is based was undertaken for approximately eighteen months during 1966–1968 in the Parque Nacional do Xingu, Mato Grosso. My research was made possible by a grant from the National Science Foundation (GS-1084) and the sponsorship and invaluable assistance of the Divisão de Antropologia, Museu Nacional (Rio de Janeiro), which was then headed by Dr. Roberto Cardoso de Oliveira. While in the Parque Nacional do Xingu, Claudio and Orlando Villas Boas, together with Marina Lopes de Lima, extended many kindnesses to me for which I am extremely grateful. In preparation for fieldwork, I benefited greatly from the advice given by members of the Harvard Central Brazil Project seminar held at Harvard University in the Spring of 1966. Professor David Maybury-Lewis, the founder of the Project, kindly took time to assist me in preparing for the field. Robert Carneiro of the American Museum of Natural History also was of considerable assistance. In Brazil, Roque de Barros Laraia, Lucia Laraia, Roberto da Matta, Julio Cesar Melatti, Roberto Cardoso de Oliveira, and Heloisa Fenelon Costa especially interested themselves in my research and cheerfully assisted me in innumerable ways. Finally, I would like to thank the following persons for their critical comments upon earlier versions of parts of this book: Keith H. Basso, Fred Eggan, Raymond Fogelson, Paul Friedrich, B.J. Hoff, David M. Schneider, and Terrence Turner.

Anthropological fieldwork in lowland South America has too often been depicted as extremely arduous, made so in part by physical conditions and also by an apparent lack of sympathy for the researcher on the part of his reluctant informants. It is, therefore, with special pleasure that I express my deep gratitude toward the Kalapalo, whose extreme generosity and unfailing good humor made my stay in the Upper Xingu Basin a particularly gratifying experience.

Guide To Pronunciation

The following phonetic symbols have been used to write Kalapalo terms. Stress and vowel length have not been indicated.

Vowels

a, as in oper*a* (low front open)
e, as in b*e*st (middle open)
i, as in s*ee*m (high front open)
ï, as in sho*u*ld (middle open)
o, as in *o*ld (middle rounded)
u, as in J*u*ne (high back rounded)
Diphthongs: *ei*, as in d*a*y
               ao, as in n*ow*
               ai, as in l*i*me
Vowel nasalization is indicated by a subscript hook, as in *ų*.

Consonants

d, voiced alveolar stop; as in English.
f, voiceless bilabial fricative; pronounced while blowing air through loosely opened, untouching lips.
g, voiced glottal fricative; as in English, but slightly farther back in the mouth.
h, voiceless glottal fricative; as in English.
j, voiced alveopalatal fricative; somewhat as in the name Na*di*a, but with more breath.
k, voiceless velar stop; as in *c*offee.
l, voiced alveolar lateral; as in English, but tongue is held slightly longer and farther back in mouth.
m, voiced bilabial nasal; as in English.
n, voiced alveolar nasal; as in English.
ŋ, voiced velar nasal; similar to si*ng*, but pronounced farther back in mouth.
ñ, voiced palatal nasal; as in Spanish ma*ñ*ana.
p, voiced bilabial stop; as in English.
s, voiceless alveopalatal fricative; as in English.
ts, voiceless dental affricate; as in ca*ts*.
t, voiceless alveolar stop; somewhat softer than *t*ooth.
w, voiced bilabial semivowel; as in *w*ent.
z, voiced alveolar fricative; as in *z*oo.
ž, voiced alveopalatal fricative; as if pronouncing *sh*oe farther back in mouth.

Where only two syllables occur in a word, stress is usually on the first syllable. In noncompound words of more than two syllables, the second syllable of the word is normally stressed. Nasalized vowels also indicate stressed syllables.

xiii

Contents

Foreword   v

Preface   vii

Acknowledgments   xi

Guide to Pronunciation   xiii

1. Introduction   1

    Contacts with Outsiders   1
    History of the Region   2
    Upper Xingu Society   3
    The Kalapalo   4
    Living among the Kalapalo   5

2. Relationships with Human Beings and Nonhumans   9

    The Model of Upper Xingu Distinctiveness   9
    The Origin of Human Beings   10
      Ifutisu Behavior   12
    The Classification of "Living Things"   14
    The Use of Cosmological Labels   17
      The Structure of the Paradigmatic Set   17
      The Possession Indicator   19
      Kalapalo Models of the Categories Ordered in a Paradigm   20

3. Subsistence Practices   27

    The Upper Xingu Habitat   27
      Seasonal Variations   28
    Subsistence   29
      Manioc   30
      Piqui   34
      Other Cultivated Plants   36
      Salt   37
      Fishing   37
      Hunting   39

4. Village and Household Structure   43

  The Village   43
     Public and Private Areas   46
     Privacy of the Household Area   47
  The Plan and Organization of a Kalapalo House   48
     Structure of the Household Group   49
  The Household and Village as Economic Units   52
  Village Specialization   55
  Death and Burial   56
     Village of the Dead   58

5. The Opposition of Men and Women   60

  The Kagutu   60
  Spatial Distinctions   62
  Sexual Contact and Pollution from Body Fluids   63
  The Ritual of Childbirth   64
     The Boys' Ear Piercing Ritual   65
     Steps in the Ritual   66
  The Development of Social and Economic Responsibility   71
  Puberty Seclusion   71

6. The Network of Kinship and Affinity   74

  The Relationship of Kinship   74
     The Otomo or Kindred Category   75
     Kalapalo Filiation   75
     Kalapalo Siblingship   78
  Categories of Kinsmen and Kinship Relationships   78
     Parent–Child Relationships   81
     The Sibling Relationship   83
     Filiation and Siblingship in Relation to Illness   83
     Relationships between Potential Affines   84
     Relationships between Persons of Alternate Generations   85
     Naming   85
     Kinship and Affinity   87
  Marriage and Affinal Relationships   88
     Brother–Sister Exchange Marriage   88
     The Marriage Arrangement   90
     Categories of Affines   91
     Relationships between Ifotisofo   92
     Relationships between Ifametigï   94
     Itsahene   97
     The Marriage Ceremony   97
     Widow Remarriage   98
     Divorce and Remarriage of Ajo   99
     Effects of Depopulation on Marriage Practices   100

"Spouse," "Lover," "Friend"   102
   The *Iŋiso–Ajo* "Continuum"   106

7. Specialists and Authorities   107

   Prestige and Influence   107
      Control over Relatives   108
   Ceremonial Sponsorship   110
   The Acquisition of Ifi *Status*   112
   Fuati: *Shamanistic Curers and Diviners*   113
      Curing Rituals   114
      Divination   118
      The Use of Curing Payment   118
   Factions   119
   A Man of Prestige and Influence   121
      Prestige and Influence: Summary   124
   Witchcraft   124
      Becoming a *Kwifi Oto*, or Witch   125
      Motivations for Witchcraft   126
      Defining a Case as One of Witchcraft   127
      Accusations of Witchcraft against Individuals   128
      Flight from Witchcraft Accusations   129
      Revenge Magic   131

8. Relationships between Groups: The Role of Village
   Representative   132

   Inheritance of Anetu *Status and Succession to Office*   133
   Activities of Anetaw *in the Village*   134
      Children's *Uluki*   137
      Household *Uluki*   137
      Anetaw and Intervillage Ceremony   138
   Anetaw *Ceremonies*   138
      The *Tiñi*   139
      The *Egitsu*   140
      The *Uluki*   147
      The *Ifagaka* Ceremony   152
   Summary: The Village Representative and Upper Xingu Society   153

Glossary   154

References   156

1 / Introduction

CONTACTS WITH OUTSIDERS

Near the geographic center of Brazil, in the state of Mato Grosso, lie the headwaters of the Xingu River, a major northward flowing tributary of the Amazon. The land encompassed by these headwaters, known as the Upper Xingu Basin, or more simply, "the Xingu," is the traditional territory of several village groups which to this day remain isolated from national Brazilian society and economy.

Unlike many other major Amazonian tributaries, the Xingu River has never been a significant route of expansion into the interior for settlers, missionaries, or laborers in extractive industries (such as rubber collectors, nut gatherers, or diamond prospectors). This is partially due to the numerous falls and rapids which make navigation difficult beyond the lower range of the river, and also (until quite recently) to the presence of hostile, often unknown, tribes (Carneiro 1956–1957). To the southeast and east of the basin itself, the presence of bellicose tribes of the Gê linguistic family (especially the Shavante and Kayapo) were a deterrent to settlement and exploration as late as the 1950s.[1] By the end of the last decade, however, most of the formerly hostile groups had been removed by one means or another from the line of frontier expansion, and Brazilian adventurers had already begun to penetrate the extreme southwestern and eastern margins of the area. Most recently, the inroads of national society have been marked by the building of the Trans-Amazonia highway, a system of dirt roads which in part cross territory formerly occupied exclusively by Indians.

In 1961, after considerable political debate (for there was pressure to open the land to commercial speculation), an area of approximately 22,000 square kilometers (8,530 square miles), which includes much of the Upper Xingu Basin, was set aside as a reserve for Indians under the name *Parque Nacional do Xingu*, "Xingu National Park" (see frontispiece map of the Upper Xingu Basin). Non-Indian settlement, missionary activity, commercial exploitation of the natural resources, and even casual tourism were prohibited, preserving a remarkable society whose entirely pacific nature otherwise might have prevented it from surviving the disruptive influences of an aggressively expanding Brazilian frontier. In recent years

---

[1] See Maybury-Lewis 1967 for an excellent account of Shavante contact.

1

the Xingu National Park has on several occasions served as a refuge for tribes flee-ing Brazilian incursions into their unprotected territory to the west. Thanks to the administrators' policies, it is probably unique in allowing indigenous people the free pursuit of their own traditionally defined goals. Tragically perhaps, at the very time when the success of these policies is dramatically demonstrated by the sad situation of Indians elsewhere in Brazil, the Park's existence is threatened by the presence of a new road. At the time of writing, the Trans-Amazonia highway passes through the northern section of the Park. This road severely threatens the autonomy and cultural integrity (if not the very existence) of the Xingu tribes as well as effectively reduces the reservation territory by nearly one half its area.

HISTORY OF THE REGION

The first historical records of a visit to the Upper Xingu Basin are those of the German ethnologist Karl von den Steinen, who, in 1884, traveled overland by mule from Cuiaba, the capital of Mato Grosso, to the Batovi River (which flows into the Xingu), and from there by canoe to the upper reaches of the Xingu itself. On a second expedition von den Steinen explored the Culiseu, another major tributary of that river. Subsequent publications of von den Steinen and of another German ex-plorer–scholar, Hermann Meyer, present the first descriptions of the inhabitants wherein the authors stress the linguistic complexity of the area in contrast with an apparent racial and social uniformity.

Although a number of later expeditions entered the region, it was not until the 1940s that serious efforts were made to establish permanent contact with the Indians. During that period, expeditions were organized by the *Fundaçao Brasil Central* (Central Brazil Foundation), a government agency that was created to ex-plore and develop the unknown regions of Central Brazil, and the *Serviço de Pro-teção aos Indios* (Indian Protection Service), another official body whose responsi-bility was to peacefully contact and incorporate Brazilian Indians into the national society.

An airstrip was cleared at a site on the Culuene River, and a temporary camp set up further north at Jacare, from which exploration could proceed. The early base at Culuene served as a refueling station for air force planes flying to the north of Brazil during the opening of the interior, and in 1968 this (and service as a head-quarters during military maneuvers) remained the essential function of a new base called Xingu, located near Jacare. Eventually a permanent administrative post was built at a point along the Tuatuari, a small affluent of the Culuene. Today, this site is known as Pôsto Leonardo Villas Boas, named for one of a group of brothers, formerly employees of the Indian Protection Service and leaders of the Xingu-Roncador expedition across Central Brazil, who were important figures in the fight to establish the Xingu National Park. Two surviving brothers, Claudio and Orlando Villas Boas, are now official park administrators. Their policy has been one of non-intervention, provision of medical treatment, and the deliberate maintenance of the population's isolation from national society. The result of this policy has been the continued cultural vitality of a basically healthy population, in many important respects unchanged from the time von den Steinen first visited them.

UPPER XINGU SOCIETY

Since von den Steinen's and Meyer's pioneering efforts at linguistic classification in the Upper Xingu, ethnographers have recorded the presence of four mutually unintelligible language families and at least eight dialects. Three of these families represent major South American linguistic stocks: Tupi, Arawak, and Carib. Today the linguistic diversity is such that seven of the eight villages which have survived represent unique speech communities. The following list indicates the villages present in 1968, together with their linguistic affiliations.

1. Arawak speakers: Waura; Mehinaku; Yawalipiti
2. Tupi speakers: Kamaiura; Awïtï
3. Carib speakers: Kuikuru; Kalapalo; Mïgïyapei (formerly members of the Jagamï and Wagifïtï village groups).
4. Speakers of Trumai, an isolated language, once lived in several villages of their own. Today they are represented by a few survivors living at Pôsto Leonardo.

Most residents of a single village are associated with it by birth, and share a common speech dialect. The majority of Upper Xingu villagers are monolingual, but because dialects within each major family are mutually intelligible, they are able to understand the speech of the members of two or three village groups. It should be emphasized, however, that individuals frequently join groups other than those into which they are born—through marriage, in flight from accusations of sorcery, or upon the destruction of their own villages because of severe depopulation. For these reasons, each local group contains speakers of more than one dialect, and several who speak more than one language. A few individuals are truly multilingual, having been born of parents who speak mutually unintelligible languages, then subsequently living in a village where a third tongue is spoken. This kind of situation is rare, however.

It might be thought that linguistic diversity of this sort is necessarily accompanied by major cultural and social differences. In fact, however, the situation in the Upper Xingu Basin radically contradicts such an assumption. Despite the variety of languages, members of Upper Xingu villages participate in a complex set of relationships associated with several institutions that crosscut village boundaries. Local groups participate in a common ceremonial system, share a large group of myths, and engage in a mutually supportive system of trade based on village specialization. Individuals trace kinship ties and often marry across village boundaries, hold a general set of normative expectations about the conduct of social interaction, and maintain in common a set of dietary restrictions by which people of the area are defined as distinctive. Practice and familiarity are required to distinguish members of different village groups by appearance, for there is an impressive uniformity in dress and technology throughout the area. In short, although

Upper Xingu villages are spatially autonomous and linguistically discrete, they are united in a single viable system through social, religious, and economic relationships.

THE KALAPALO

The Kalapalo are one of three Carib-speaking groups presently a part of Upper Xingu society. They numbered about 110 in 1968, and were thus the second largest village group in the area. Today they live in a village called Aifa (meaning "finished"), located far to the north of their traditional territory, about three days' canoe travel downstream. The Kalapalo moved to the present site after the park boundaries were established, at the same time that outlying groups were encouraged to move closer to the Post in order to control contact with outsiders and provide medical aid in the event of epidemics.[2]

Among Carib speakers in the area, the Kalapalo are named after their present village, being called *Aifa otomo*, "people of Aifa village." The term Kalapalo is the name of an old village site, abandoned about 50 years ago, but it is now common usage in the literature about the Upper Xingu Basin. Non-Carib speakers who visited the original group later applied the name to their descendants even after the village was abandoned.

It is uncertain when the village group known as Kalapalo was first contacted by outsiders, although individuals identified with that village were measured by Meyer during an anthropometric study of Upper Xingu tribes. In 1920, Major Ramiro Noronha of the Rondon Commission surveyed the Culuene River and made the first recorded visit to the Kalapalo, Kuikuru, and Anagafïtï (usually spelled "Naravute") villages. In 1925, Colonel P. H. Fawcett, an eccentric Englishman searching for the remnants of the elusive Lost City of Mu, disappeared somewhere in the Upper Xingu Basin. Despite several attempts to piece together the circumstances of his disappearance, Colonel Fawcett's true fate remains a mystery. Unfortunately, the Kalapalo have been accused of murdering Colonel Fawcett and his party over a dispute about payment for their services as guides (see Cowell 1961). Although the names of the allegedly guilty Kalapalo cited by Cowell are indeed those of persons who were alive around the time of Fawcett's disappearance, modern Kalapalo emphatically deny any knowledge of this incident and judge it to be the slander of other Indians who wished to provide overanxious information-seekers with anything deemed worthy of payment. Indeed, during the period of my own research, I met several persons visiting the Upper Xingu who were willing to pay for information about Colonel Fawcett. This was particularly true of Englishmen seeking to solve the mystery which apparently still is alive (at least in some circles) in Great Britain.

It is worth mentioning here that the Kalapalo themselves tell a story about their first contacts with non-Indians. This story suggests that the Upper Xingu Basin may have been at one time the target of slave raiding by Brazilians living far to the south of the present settlements. In fact, the site of an incident in the tale was

---

[2] For a demographic history of the area see Agostinho da Silva 1970.

pointed out to me by the Kalapalo when we were visiting their old village territory, suggesting some foundation in historical reality.

These old village sites are regarded by the Kalapalo with great sentiment and interest. Many of their myths refer to identifiable sites, and significant historical events are associated with nearby landmarks. While living with them at Aifa, I was encouraged to travel to their abandoned village Kanugijafïtï, so I could see for myself the many splendors of the area. I was taken to the old summer village, Fïfïfïtï, close by the Culuene River, where the Kalapalo had fished during the dry season. Here an old woman showed me the graves of the victims of a measles epidemic that occurred in the summer of 1954, recalling exactly who was buried there. The residents of Aifa are constantly reminded of the tragedy of this epidemic by an unusual number of orphans, and this in turn brings to mind the life which they led in the old villages, a subject of frequent reminiscences.

LIVING AMONG THE KALAPALO

Unlike the experience of several other anthropologists with lowland South American Indians, most notably those of Allan Holmberg (1969), David Maybury-Lewis (1965), and Napoleon Chagnon (1968), my work among the Kalapalo took place under what can only be described as nearly ideal field conditions. At a superficial level, but nonetheless one which was certainly conducive to a sense of well-being, this was due to the physical conditions I encountered in the Upper Xingu Basin, for this area has been up to now fortunate to have escaped most of the serious diseases that are endemic throughout much of Brazil. Coupled with this general condition of health is the fortunate attitude of the Kalapalo towards cleanliness, which encompasses their food, houses, and physical persons. During the time of year when manioc gardens are being prepared for planting, or when gourds are being harvested and made into containers, it is not uncommon, for example, to find the Kalapalo bathing three and even four times a day as they conscientiously cleanse themselves of the grime from these activities. Soap and shampoo are prized possessions—used not only to wash the body and hair but to cleanse ornaments and cooking vessels. At times, the Kalapalo's attitude towards cleanliness approaches the excessive preoccupation of some Americans in our own society.

Much more important, however, was the acceptance of my presence in their village, a willingness on the part of the Kalapalo not only to feed and house me, but to speak about any and all things. In part, the peaceful relationships with park personnel have resulted in this lack of suspicion towards non-Indians, but the attitude also derives quite explicitly from related Kalapalo ideals of generosity and peaceful behavior (described in Chapter 2) which stand in marked contrast to the aggressiveness and violent expression of individual power over others so characteristic of the Shavante and Yąnomamö, for example. The Kalapalo reject such behavior as entirely inappropriate for human beings and instead embrace an ideal of pacificity that includes not only suppression of anger and of violence but a passive tolerance of the behavior and opinions of others with whom one does not agree. Although this is by no means a society without disputes or jealousies, I was impressed by the mutual cooperation and respect shown by the members of the Kalapalo village towards each other, and the way in which people are incorporated into a cycle of reciprocity that has its most fundamental and ideal expression in the exchange of presents "given with a smile." It was this very ideal of generosity, however, which gave me the most trouble.

While I was perfectly willing to be generous with those men and women who told me stories, taught me genealogies, and explained why the Kalapalo did things in certain ways, or who allowed me to live with them in their communal houses, I could not refrain from thinking of my gifts to them as rewards for acts favorable to myself. Although "payment" is a perfectly straightforward Kalapalo concept in itself, generosity and sharing are other matters: They are acts which should be performed for their own sakes, but which are, in truth, performed on the basis of several contingencies. Whereas the Kalapalo continually distinguish between "payment" and "just giving," I did not make such a distinction and hence was regarded as stingy.

Although they value the ideal of generosity, spontaneous gift giving is not in itself characteristic of Kalapalo behavior, for sharing takes place only along the lines of prior relationships (such as those of kinship, friendship, or membership in the same household). A person does not normally ask for a gift from someone he cannot reasonably assume will give it to him; it is also considered improper to make such requests of certain kinds of relatives—especially older persons to whom one is related by marriage—and of unrelated persons in households other than one's own. Finding out just who will exchange or who will give freely for the asking is one object of a young person's self-education and a means of assessing one's personal prestige and influence over others.

As a guest in the Kalapalo village, I was continually aware of the many subtle and coercive means by which people acquire gifts, especially of food. Unfortunately, I was sometimes the unwitting tool of their efforts. For example, in the beginning of my research, I found myself being asked by members of the household in which I was living to beg food from other households which had been lucky to receive large quantities of fish or wild fruit on a particular day. I was urged to hurry to so-and-so's house, in order to receive some food that so-and-so was very anxious to give me. When I suggested that someone accompany me, I was refused. After two or three instances of this, I noticed that I was the only adult among a crowd of children who clustered near the doorway of the lucky house while food was being distributed. Although no one refused me fish or fruit, the donors were always curious to know who had told me of their good fortune. Finally, after several embarassing episodes, I realized that only children were actually permitted to beg in this fashion and that adults were expected to wait inside their houses until an invitation was extended to eat in the benefactor's household. The people with whom I lived, however, were for a short time taking advantage not only of my naïveté but also of the generosity of their fellow villagers which they were certain would be forthcoming to me, a visitor.

A common reaction of visitors to the Upper Xingu Basin is that the inhabitants "have no idea of the value of things," or more bluntly that they are "shameful beggars." This is because the outsider first enters the system as an unknown figure without relationships to individual members of the society, and therefore must be continually tested in order to anticipate his or her willingness to participate in it. During the first year of my stay with the Kalapalo, I was inundated with requests for articles of clothing, cooking vessels, food, magazines, and other of my possessions, as well as for presents that I was exhorted to buy in Rio de Janeiro. Most of these requests were put in the strongest language possible for a Kalapalo—that is, in the form of demands for immediate action—in order that I respond with appropriate alacrity. As a variety of persons requested specific objects and were denied or given them according to my judgment about whether they deserved them or not, my relations with individual Kalapalo took on character, including attributes of relative friendliness, deference, or equality, and more or less in accordance with Kalapalo expectations about how kinsmen, friends, or affines act toward one another. At this point, I began to be treated as a kind of relative by several persons, especially those with whom I lived and those who were my instructors, and thus I came to be called "mother," "grandmother," "older sister," "daughter," and "sister-in-law" by specific Kalapalo men and women. After being classified in this way, I then learned to act toward these people in ways which they could anticipate and which they considered appropriate. In this manner we could properly show what the Kalapalo call *ifutisu*, respect for one another.

Most Kalapalo, however, regarded me as a nonrelative and therefore felt no compunction to show me respect or, especially, to reciprocate with goods or services in exchange for my presents from Rio. I was, in short, caught in the middle, being unable or unwilling to request specific gifts myself, yet continually obligated to bestow them upon my putative relatives. At the same time, I was expected to be generous to those who did not care to consider me any kind of relative or who never assisted me in my research.

Unfortunately, the presence of unopened boxes, a locked trunk, or even an odd sack of salt left tied to the houseframe near my hammock tempted a number of persons who were unwilling to ask for presents from me and who had no older relatives (such as parents or older siblings) who were able to provide them with gifts. The only recourse to this kind of theft (which affects the Kalapalo as well as the visitor) was to steal back the missing items whenever possible. In order to avoid this situation, as well as the continued barrage of requests for gifts, I soon learned to give away everything I brought with me, except for the essentials. This way, I achieved some measure of peace for several months before I paid another trip to the coast. It soon became apparent how superfluous was the excessive load of "equipment" I had brought to Aifa. Reduced to a few tattered changes of clothing, medical supplies, hammock, camera, notebooks, pens, and a tape recorder, I had finally achieved some measure of freedom from the materialist cravings of the people around me, and indeed from my own concern with protecting the collection of unnecessary and often nonworking odds and ends over which I had needlessly worried since my arrival in Brazil. Knowing that I had nothing left to give (except after trips to Rio de Janeiro or São Paulo), the Kalapalo were finally able to see me as someone other than the owner of unlimited wealth.

It would be extremely unfair, however, to condemn them for this materialism. In the first place, the craving for European goods has been the result of repeated donations of gifts over the years by visitors to the area. From the Kalapalo point of view, the visits of many of these individuals have been for no other apparent reason than to give away large quantities of material items. Indeed, for many Kalapalo, the government personnel in their territory exist for the sole purpose of distributing largess.

These gifts have resulted in important innovations in such areas as subsistence and manufacturing techniques, and the care and decoration of the body. In other words, a need has been created for metal tools, beads, fish hooks, razor blades, and ammunition, and the way in which this need has been satisfied in the past has naturally led the Kalapalo to anticipate its continued satisfaction.

Furthermore, although the leaders of the house in which I lived knew of my tendencies to hoard a few tins of sardines on occasion and to keep candy and salt at the bottom of my duffel bag for special trips, they consistently included me in the daily distribution of food, even during the worst month of the rainy season. This kind of generosity was difficult for me to accept because I had no way of adequately reciprocating and I knew they were under no real obligation to feed me. Yet as a continuous resident, I began to take on the role of some long-term guest from another village who was expected to return the hospitality shown her, if in the future the Kalapalo should be able to visit her. By offering food and by asking for presents, the Kalapalo were trying to establish a relationship of alliance with me that included an obligation on my part to reciprocate, an obligation which could appropriately be fulfilled at any time in the future.

2 / Relationships with human beings and nonhumans

THE MODEL OF UPPER XINGU DISTINCTIVENESS

Before the establishment of park boundaries and permanent contact with Brazilians, the ethnographic situation in the Upper Xingu Basin was complicated by the fact that a number of aggressive tribal groups surrounded this territory (see Villas Boas and Villas Boas 1970). Relationships between members of Upper Xingu society and some of these groups were occasionally amicable, but accusations of witchcraft murder and revenge killings by groups on both sides took place more frequently. To the north were the Juruna (Tupi speakers), a group that exchanged hostilities with the Kamaiura (see Oliveira 1968), and the Suyá (Gê speakers), dreaded by the Trumai because of their raids on villages (see Murphy and Quain 1955). To the west were the Txicão (Carib speakers) who attacked the Mehinaku, Jagamï, and Waura frequently enough to cause relocation of those groups on several occasions (see Galvão and Simões 1965). Living to the east of the Culuene River, beyond the tributary stream known as the Tanguro, were the Yaguma, an extinct group of Carib speakers with whom the Kalapalo were on uneasy terms. According to the latter, the two groups exchanged women and established trading relationships, but the Kalapalo feared them because the Yaguma occasionally killed men who ventured into their territory.

Thus, the residents of the Upper Xingu Basin found themselves surrounded by Indians whose aggressive attitudes contrasted sharply with their own ideal of peaceful behavior. Despite the fact that many of these hostile groups are now living within the boundaries of the Park and have ceased their overt aggression against members of Upper Xingu society, they are considered a distinct kind of human being whose behavior precludes their incorporation into that society.

The Kalapalo refer to these formerly hostile tribes — or, more generally, to any Indians who are not part of Upper Xingu society — as *angikogo*, "fierce Indians." This category of "human beings" is conceived primarily in terms of a kind of behavior labeled *itsotu*, which refers to unpredictable anger and violence. *Itsotu* behavior is often explicitly contrasted with a concept mentioned earlier, *ifutisu* (peaceful, generous behavior), which is one important distinctive feature of the category "people of Upper Xingu society."

The Kalapalo conceive of themselves and other Upper Xingu villagers as a unique people, different from all other "human beings." Both categories, "human beings" and "people of Upper Xingu society," are labeled by the same term, *kuge*.

9

The Kalapalo model of Upper Xingu distinctiveness, which includes definitions and interpretations of the possible kinds of relationships between men and nonmen, is examined in this chapter.

THE ORIGIN OF HUMAN BEINGS

> I come up the river like a Suyá man.
> I come up the river like iñikogo.
> I come up the river to kill many people.
> With war clubs, with bow and arrow drawn,
> I come up the river like a Suyá man.
> I come up the river like iñikogo.
>
> (*Kwambï* Song)

A large group of myths told by the Kalapalo relates the adventures of twins who are believed responsible for the invention of certain technological practices, as well as the creation of several natural features of the world, including various bodies of water in the Upper Xingu Basin, certain natural species, and some astronomical phenomena. One twin is called Taŋgi or Giti ("Sun"), the other Awlukuma or Ŋune ("Moon"). In a story telling of the twins' birth and subsequent exploits (briefly told below), the Kalapalo describe the creation of human beings, an event caused by Taŋgi, the older twin. The activities associated with this creation serve to justify the present relationships which the Kalapalo have with other Indians, and with non-Indians.

A prehuman "grandfather" named Kwatïŋï went to the forest to gather materials with which to make a new bowstring. There he encountered Nitsuęgï, the black jaguar, who was hunting with members of his village. Seeing that he was surrounded by dangerous animals, Kwatïŋï promised Nitsuęgï his daughters in marriage, in exchange for being allowed to return to his own village in safety. When Kwatïŋï returned home and told his daughters of his promise, they began to weep, begging their father not to send them to a husband they feared would eat them. Moved by their pleas, but unwilling to break his promise, Kwatïŋï went to the forest and cut five lengths of *weigufi* [a hardwood], from which he carved women's bodies. He then decorated these with various natural products to form hair, eyes, and teeth. Then he asked the tapir to have sexual intercourse with them so that they would have vaginas. When the five images were completed, Kwatïŋï placed them in seclusion in order that they would grow. Some time later, he took a cotton belt and beat them until they cried out; he then knew they were alive, and sent them to Nitsuęgï.

On their way, the five women encountered a weasel who gave them food in return for which he asked one of them to have sexual intercourse with him. Continuing further, they met a kingfisher who did the same. Then the sisters came to a lake, from which one of them began to drink. The water was poisonous, however, and so she died. The four remaining women continued on, until they came to a tapir. He also gave them food and, like the weasel and kingfisher, asked for sexual intercourse. One sister agreed to his request, but she was split in two by his enormous penis, and so died. The three remaining sisters went on, until they met the hairy armadillo. Once more they were given food, but when the armadillo tried to have intercourse with one of them, he was unable to have an erection. The three continued their trip, commenting upon how the creatures they had encountered had wanted sexual intercourse with them. "Let us put on burity palm ribs between our legs," one sister said. "With this on, no one will be able to have sexual intercourse with us."[1] She then climbed up a burity palm but she fell and impaled herself upon one of the shoots. Now, only two sisters were left.

When they finally came to Nitsuęgï's village, they were shy because they did not know what he looked like. They waited near the bathing place until someone should come. Soon the sariema bird appeared, carrying a large gourd on her head. As she filled this with water from the stream, she talked to herself, remarking on how beautiful her legs were. Seeing that the sariema really had long, skinny legs, the two sisters began to laugh. This caused the bird to drop her water gourd and hurry back to the village, where she told her husband, the maned wolf, that Nitsuęgï's wives must have arrived. He, wanting them for himself, came to where they were hiding, and when they asked if he was Nitsuęgï, replied affirmatively. The two women followed the maned wolf back to his house, but seeing that it was small and unpainted (unlike that of a real village leader) they realized he was not the man Kwatïnï had promised them to.

Shortly thereafter, Niesuęgï discovered he had been deceived and arranged a ruse by which to capture his wives. First, he organized a hunting trip, during which all the men of his village were to be present. On the day of the trip, he put a thorn between his toes and pretended his foot was injured, making it impossible for him to travel. Asking that he be excused from the hunt, he appointed the maned wolf to take his place as leader of the hunters. Then, when he returned to the village, Nitsuęgï shot two arrows which landed at the feet of the two sisters, who had been watching from the doorway of the maned wolf's house. When the jaguar came to retrieve his arrows, he discovered the women and brought them to his own house.

One sister, named Isanisegu, became pregnant quickly. When she grew heavy and unable to work in the gardens, her sister, Sakufenu, and Nitsuęgï their husband left her at home when they went to gather manioc. One day, the pregnant sister was sitting in the house spinning cotton while her mother-in-law swept the floor. At the same moment the mother-in-law emitted a loud fart, Isanisegu spat out a piece of lint she had removed from the length of string she was spinning. Thinking her daughter-in-law had insulted her by expressing disgust, the mother-in-law ripped off one of her claws and threw it at the young woman, killing her.

When Nitsuęgï and Sakufenu returned from the gardens, they saw the dead woman's body alone in the house, for the mother-in-law had fled from the village. Nitsuęgï sent for a leafcutter ant, who was told to crawl into the body to see whether the unborn child was completely formed; in fact, there were two children, not one. Then, at Nitsuęgï's direction, the leafcutter ant cut open his wife's stomach, revealing the twins. After they had been removed, their mother's body was hidden at the top of the house.

The twins grew very quickly, much faster than normal children. One day, they were stealing peanuts from a partridge's garden. When she remonstrated with them, and they threatened to kill her, she told them of their mother's death.

[1] Upper Xingu women wear fiber belts joined together over the pubic bone by a piece of bark (tyi) folded in triangular shape. When they dance in ceremonies, a long strawlike rib from the burity palm leaf is tied to this piece of bark, passed through the legs and left to shake from between the buttocks. Although this ornament draws attention to a woman's genitalia and is a powerful erotic symbol in Kalapalo culture and art, it is designed so as to preclude sexual intercourse when worn.

"The woman you call 'mother' is your mother's sister, not your real mother. She is hidden on top of the house where your father put her," the partridge said. To take revenge, the twins had to first kill their grandmother, who had gone to live by herself in a house far from the village. There she lived surrounded by many kinds of stinging insects, who prevented anyone from hurting her. Taųgi directed several species of birds who eat these insects to come where the grandmother lived and eat them all, after which he and Awlukuma set fire to her house, killing her. Then, Taųgi and Awlukuma decided to take revenge on Nitsuęgï, because he had concealed their mother's death from them.

Pretending he had lost or broken his weapons, Taųgi went each day to his father, asking for new bows, arrows, and war clubs, which he then hid in the forest. When he had collected an amount he thought sufficient, he went to his mother's sister, Sakufenu, who was sitting by the door of the house spinning cotton. Taųgi placed a long arrow before her, and asked her to step over it. When she did, she immediately became pregnant. Taųgi then sent her to the forest, near the place where he had hidden the weapons.

For many days, Taugi visited Sakufenu in the forest until at last she gave birth. From her body came many men, the grandfathers of human beings who live in the world today. To the grandfathers of the Upper Xingu villagers (kuge), Taųgi gave bows and arrows; to angikogo, "fierce Indians," he gave war clubs; and to kagaifa, "non-Indians," he gave guns and metal knives. That is why angikogo are angry with the people of the Upper Xingu, and why kagaifa have those good weapons.

When angikogo were given their weapons, they began to fight, causing the creatures of Nitsuęgi's village to flee by rising to the sky. Seeing that Nitsuęgi was about to run away, Awlukuma directed angikogo to attack him, and thus the black jaguar also escaped to become a figure in the sky, where he may still be seen. Only the agouti [a creature resembling a guinea pig] escaped, for he was able to dodge through the feet of the fighting men.

A more optimistic informant ended his version of this myth in the following way:

> Each received weapons from Taųgi: war clubs to angikogo, guns to kagaifa, bows and arrows to kuge. That is why we Upper Xingu people are peaceful, why we don't get angry with other human beings. When we are angry, it is just with our mouths, because we are all brothers, we have all come from one mother, we have ifutisu for other human beings.

Ifutisu Behavior

In a most general sense, ifutisu can be defined as behavior characterized by a lack of public aggressiveness and by the practice of generosity.[2] Each of these elements can be interpreted, according to context, in a more specific way. The first characteristic can mean simply that a person refrains from physical or verbal abuse, as when the Kalapalo speak of their unwillingness to argue in public. Ifutisu also refers to the unwillingness of a Kalapalo to intrude into a situation where he will make others uncomfortable. For example, young Kalapalo men and women who have no relatives in villages speaking languages other than Carib refrain from visiting these places without a reason, because, they say, of their ifutisu for the people who live there. Again, it is considered wrong to publicly call attention to a theft, for that would embarrass people, as the following incident illustrates.

---

[2] The state of ifutisu, "having ifutisu," is referred to by the term ifutisunda.

Waiyepe, a bachelor living in the house of his brother-in-law, missed a bar of soap that he had carefully hidden in a cloth sack tied to the houseframe near his hammock. Upon realizing the soap had most likely been stolen, Waiyepe began complaining in a loud voice in front of the other residents of the house, "Alas, where is my soap? It seems as if someone stole it." Although other members of the group were sympathetic to his loss, Waiyepe's actions prompted another man to remark, "That man should not talk that way; he should remain quiet, not say anything, even though he liked that soap. If you think some person is a thief, then when you say something, other people listen and are sad. It is as if he is angry with all of them."

The second defining characteristic of *ifutisu* is generosity, which refers in more specific terms to behavior characterized by hospitality, a willingness both to part with material possessions and to assist others when called upon to participate in work groups, and acceptance of those who ask to be one's lovers.

The ideal of hospitality is well expressed in the treatment of strangers who visit the Kalapalo. Upon their arrival in the village, individual visitors are immediately presented with food and asked to hang their hammocks inside one of the communal houses. Even in situations in which fear or resentment preclude amiable sentiments toward a guest, the overt gestures of the hosts convey goodwill.

The ideal of generosity is manifested in the acceptance of the claims of others upon one's personal possessions. Individuals who have managed to acquire unusual items find others coveting them and soon give them away. For example, one of my informants asked me to bring him a blanket from Rio de Janeiro. When I returned from a trip to that city, I gave him a particularly large and vibrantly colored one, which contrasted with the small, worn-out scraps other Kalapalo had managed to save from similar gifts presented years earlier. The blanket was clearly given in payment for his assistance to me, and it became a kind of symbol of my client relationship to him. One night several months later, when the blanket had become a uniform dull red from the paint with which my informant repeatedly decorated himself, he came to me and sat without speaking beside my hammock for several minutes. Finally he said, "Ellen, would you be angry with me if I gave away your blanket? Sindu has asked me for it, in return for something of his." When I replied that I would not mind, and asked what was offered in return, he said, "Something not very good, those cotton knee bindings of his. They are ugly, but I have *ifutisu*. I can't say no. Sindu is stingy; me, I am generous. He asked me and I want to give the blanket to him, even though what he gives me is nothing."

Although the practice of generosity often results in hardship, the Kalapalo believe it is necessary to conform to this ideal, for in their view society's viability depends upon it. Most difficulties associated with the continual giving away of wealth are temporary, for generosity in turn causes others to reciprocate. A person who is stingy with his possessions or his person causes others to become "sad–angry" (*otonunda*), and in such a state the disappointed are likely to leave the group and live elsewhere. This kind of anger (distinguished from *itsotonunda*, or the state of unpredictable violent anger) is typical of children who are denied food by their parents, persons who cannot find spouses or lovers, and individuals whose few kinsmen do not care to support them during disputes. The desire to leave the group, to wander alone in the forest, or to desert the Upper Xingu Basin to live with Brazilians is really a kind of suicide from the society's point of view, for those who leave and do not return are effectively treated by the Kalapalo as if they have died.

The second important means by which the Kalapalo distinguish *kuge* from other human beings is a set of dietary practices that reflect *ifutisu*. The most significant aspect of this is a system in which "living things" are classified according to whether they are eaten or not eaten by people of the Upper Xingu. The Kalapalo recognize that many of the animals they reject are eaten by both *angikogo* and *kagaifa*, so the rejection is not based on a belief that the species in question are inedible. Rather, it is said these things are simply unfit for ingestion by the Kalapalo and other Upper Xingu people. Coupled with this rejection is an explicit definition of other kinds of living things as "eaten by Upper Xingu people." To understand how these categories are distinguished, it is useful to look at the general principles underlying the Kalapalo system of classification of "living things."

THE CLASSIFICATION OF "LIVING THINGS"

The Kalapalo classify certain items in their experience according to a set of categories that are arranged in a *hierarchy*, or a sequence of more or less inclusive units (Figure 1). Each category is defined in terms of a few specific attributes which the Kalapalo consider distinctive and which are thus used to differentiate things placed in one category from those placed in others. All the referents of these categories together are known as *ago*, or "living things."

At the most specific levels of their taxonomy, the Kalapalo make use of such readily observable attributes as body morphology, eating habits, and habitat to distinguish different kinds of natural species. At more inclusive levels, however, the criteria used to differentiate categories of living things are distinctly nonempirical.

The category *ago* is first divided into several general categories, of which the most important are: *kuge*, or "human beings"; *itolo*, or "birds"; ŋ*ene*, or "land creatures"; *kaŋa*, or "water creatures"; *eke*, or "snakes"; a number of unlabeled categories into which insects are placed; and *i*, or "upright standing plants." All of these groups are further differentiated into more specific units, many of which do not have names. At the most specific level of the hierarchy are categories which contain only one item; that is, which refer to what are, in the main, natural species or varieties of plants and animals. Figure 1 illustrates how these categories are ordered in a hierarchic relationship, and shows in some detail the internal differentiation of those classes of "living things" that are significant for an understanding of the Kalapalo dietary system.

The category ŋ*ene*, or "land creatures," includes several more specific units, among them felines, deer, rodents, armadillos, tapir, monkeys, cayman, molluscs, lizards, and bats. Whereas many groups surrounding the Upper Xingu Basin prize meat, the Kalapalo and other Upper Xingu villagers regard virtually all land animals or ŋ*ene* as disgusting and refuse to eat them. The two exceptions are monkey and

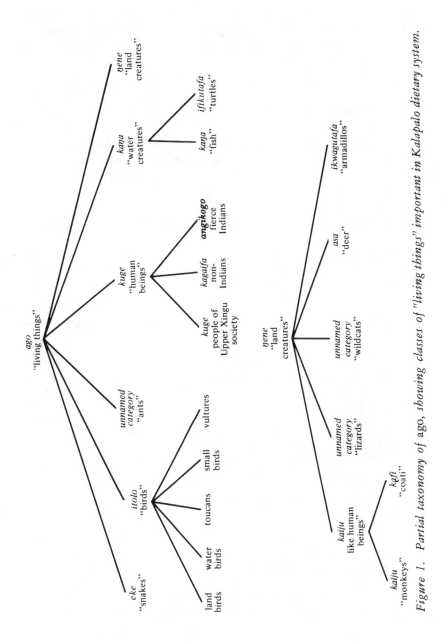

Figure 1. Partial taxonomy of ago, showing classes of "living things" important in Kalapalo dietary system.

sometimes coati, which are classed together in a subcategory of ŋene called *kaiju*. (The same word is also used to refer specifically to monkeys.)

In contrast, "things that live in the water" (*kaŋa*) are highly prized as food. This group includes fish, turtles, the stingray, the Surinam toad (but no other frogs or toads), and sometimes the electric eel, giant catfish, and red piranha. Because of the value placed on *kaŋa*, fish alone account for nearly the total amount of protein consumed by the Kalapalo.

Birds (*itolo*) are divided into several categories, only a few of which are defined as "eaten." The most important are parrots and a group defined as "birds that walk on the land." The latter group includes doves, partridgelike species, and a group whose members resemble the wild turkey. The Kalapalo reject all other kinds of birds, including water birds (such as herons, terns, storks, kingfishers, and spoonbills), owls and nightjars, vultures, birds of prey, toucans, and a multitude of small birds. The duck may or may not be eaten, depending upon whether it is considered a "water bird" or a "land bird."

All the previously described categories of *ago* are in the context of discussions about proper dietary practices, divided by the Kalapalo into three groups:

1. Things no one eats (*afïtï kugefeke teŋetakola*). Ŋene is explicitly defined in this way, but the group also includes any other categories of *ago* that are not explicitly defined as "eaten." This is a category of *generally* tabooed items—subject to the expletive *kïtsï*, meaning "disgusting, avoid it!"
2. Things everyone eats (*kugefeke teŋetako*). This group includes *kaŋa*, "land birds," parrots, and *kaiju*. Some informants called this group *kuge otu*, "people's food."
3. Things some people eat (*iñalu kotote teŋetako*). The few species in this group (electric eel, red piranha, giant catfish, duck, coati) are those which are ambiguously classified, sometimes falling within a group which is eaten, at other times being placed with things that are not eaten. This ambiguity of classification is consistent, in that the same things are always the subject of different assignments. There is no general agreement among the Kalapalo as to what they "really" are. Whether they are to be eaten or not is therefore questionable. Apparently, how any individual classes them is a matter of personal preference, based on the question whether it is necessary at the time to demonstrate one's "Kalapalo-ness." Sometimes, Kalapalo classify an item as "eaten" when they are hungry, but otherwise consider it unfit to eat. They should not be eaten under any circumstances during ritual events, nor when other groups are present and assessing the appropriateness of their hosts' behavior. In this way, some boys in puberty seclusion (who were supposed to be careful about what they ate) often ate duck when there was nothing else available, but when there was a quantity of fish in the house, they said they could not eat duck because it was "not food"; that is, not eaten by the Kalapalo. In private, and hidden from the critical eyes of dominant relatives, the same persons who stressed the importance of their avoidance of land animals ate pieces of deer meat which I occasionally cooked away from the house.

I noted above that those items in the group, "things that no one eats," can be considered objects of a *general* taboo; that is, they are *never* eaten. Those in the second group, "things everyone eats," are the subject of *specific* taboos; that is, they become temporarily prohibited for individuals in specific situations. First, all birds that are normally eaten are prohibited for young men in puberty seclusion just before they wrestle because this food is believed to make their bones brittle. Similarly, the flesh of birds is also avoided by parents with young children who have not yet been weaned, for the eating of this kind of food influences the growth of the child's bones. Second, kaŋa are prohibited to persons in some kind of physical danger, especially "bleeders" (women after childbirth, menstruating women, boys whose ears have just been pierced), and to seriously ill individuals, their parents, siblings, and offspring. Third, monkey is prohibited only to boys who have just undergone ear piercing. However, this prohibition is part of a general fast, during which their diet is exclusively vegetarian. After a period of eating manioc and fruit, monkey becomes the first nonvegetable food eaten by these boys.

The first category of tabooed items, birds, is prohibited as weakening for persons who are in critical periods of growth: adolescents and young children. This association can be considered "sympathetic," in that there is a direct association between the subject and object of the taboo. Weak bones are caused by eating the flesh of brittle-boned birds.

In the second set of taboos, those centering on the eating of kaŋa, the association is a "negative" one between that category of items and persons who are in physical danger, though it is not clear, nor can the Kalapalo say, why there is such a correlation.

The third taboo, that on kaiju, only appears on a single occasion, when it is part of a general fast. Thus, monkey can be considered the supremely edible item in the Kalapalo diet, a kind of food that is acceptable in all circumstances but one. A clue to why this is so lies in the Kalapalo justification for eating monkey in the first place, even though it is classed in the generally prohibited ŋene category. The Kalapalo say, "ago eat monkeys because they are like human beings." Some of the ways in which the Kalapalo speak of different kinds of "living things" helps to explain this statement, and to these I will now turn.

THE USE OF COSMOLOGICAL LABELS

The category ago, "living things," can be thought of as a member of a paradigmatic set[3] in which four categories are defined in terms of two intersecting dimensions. Each one of these categories, taken alone, represents a specific model consisting of several defining attributes. The use of a term labeling such a category draws attention to a behavioral attribute or relationship of an item to man based upon Kalapalo experience. These attributes and relationships can be thought of as crucial features of a general model of "Xingu humanity" or "Xingu distinctiveness," for they contribute to conceptualizations of the possible relationships between men and nonmen.

The Structure of the Paradigmatic Set

The four categories that comprise the paradigmatic set (see Figure 2) are ordered through the intersection of two dimensions: (1) the "human metaphor,"

---

[3] See Paul Kay 1966 for a discussion of the formal properties of paradigm and taxonomy.

and (2) the suffix indicating "possession." The paradigmatic organization of these categories is an analytic structure devised by the anthropologist, for the Kalapalo do not explicitly compare the categories with one another, nor can they make general statements about the two dimensions. The importance of these dimensions is demonstrated, however, by their continual appearance in speech.

I have used the phrase "human metaphor" to subsume a set of descriptive phrases and terms that refer to physiological and social phenomena, and that are used when speaking about items called *ago*, "living things," or *itologu*, "pets," regardless of

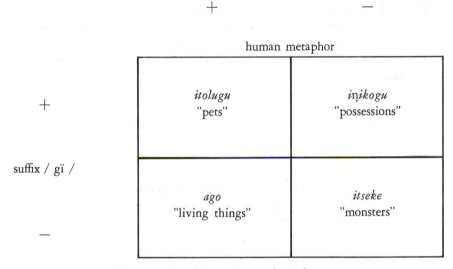

Figure 2. Paradigm of cosmological terms.

the subcategories into which they are placed. In many cultures, including our own, human beings are often distinguished from nonhuman beings by the use of different descriptive terms and phrases. For example, in English the offspring of a human being is called a "child," but it is considered inappropriate to use this term in reference to animal offspring. Similarly, in an Athabaskan language of Northern Canada, the track or path of a human being is called *beikeilu*, but the track or path of an animal is called *beitene*. These kinds of distinctions are not made by the Kalapalo, however, for in general the terms used when speaking about physiological and social phenomena are identical, regardless of the hierarchically arranged categories into which various kinds of "living things" are placed. Although the human models are considerably more detailed than models of similar phenomena among nonhumans (for example, the presence of an elaborate set of human kinship terms, as opposed to only a few used when speaking of nonhumans), it is safe to say that a significant number of phrases and terms appear in both human and nonhuman contexts to justify the claim for a very general set of principles in operation. Even though the terms are those most often applied to human beings, they are acceptable for speaking about nonhumans as well. The following are examples of this "human metaphor" used by the Kalapalo.

1. Terms for physiological processes:
   a. growth (*atukulu*) and death (*apïŋgulu*).
   b. offspring (*itijïpïgï*) and parents (*oto*).
   c. names for parts of the body.
2. "Mental" states:
   a. *ifutisu*: In the special sense of "retirement from public activities," this term can refer to the untamed behavior of an animal, for example, a turtle withdrawn into its shell.
   b. *itsotu*: Unpredictable anger or unreasonable rage.
   c. *awïnda*: "To speak falsely," as an animal who makes humorous loud noises of apparent protest although undisturbed.
3. Social relationships:
   a. Many species classed as *ago*, "living things," are referred to as having village representatives (*anetaw*), villages (*etu*), and followers of *anetaw* (*otomo*). Similarly, they are said to have wives (*efïtsaw*) and husands (*iñoko*); frequently, they have kinship relationships as well.

The use of human metaphor is a means of explaining certain relationships. By speaking of nonhuman beings in terms normally associated with humans, the more general relationship of nonhumans to humans is made explicit by the Kalapalo as one of closeness, admitting of possible intimacy. This potentially intimate association often becomes realized in specific mythological incidents, where humans and nonhumans engage in sexual relations and produce offspring.

The Possession Indicator

The second dimension of the paradigm refers to the suffix / gï /, indicating "a thing or attribute possessed."[4] It must be affixed to any term for an object or thing whose possession is indicated during the course of the utterance, and is found as part of the structure of names for certain classes of items which can be considered "normally possessed." For example, terms for material objects take the suffix when occurring in a possession context. The term for "canoe," *efu*, becomes *efugu*, "a canoe which is property," in the context of "ownership," as in the sentence, "*Ande Kafukwigi efugu*," "Here is Kafukwigi's canoe." Items in one group normally taking this suffix, regardless of context, are names for body parts (for example, *igï*, "tooth"; *tefugu*, "stomach"; *tapïgï*, "foot"). Those things which are called *itologu* ("pets") and *iñikogu* ("property") inevitably have the possession suffix attached to their names.

In summary, the paradigm containing the categories *ago*, "living things"; *iñikogu*, "property"; *itologu*, "pets"; and *itseke*, "monsters," is formed by the dimension, "presence or absence of the human metaphor," and the dimension, "presence or absence of the suffix indicating possession." The resulting four categories are discussed below.

1. *Itologu*, "pets"   The Kalapalo make use of the human metaphor when speaking of "pets," and attach the suffix / gï / indicating possession to their names.

---

[4] Allomorphs are / gï /, / gu /, / sï /, / su /.

The term derives from *itolo*, meaning "bird," hence the literal meaning, "a bird which is property."[5] Like their wild counterparts, "pets" are metaphorically associated with man, but the association has reference to the parent–child relationship among humans. As we shall see, this reference goes somewhat beyond metaphorical association.

2. *Inïkogu*, "property"   Human metaphor is not applied to items referred to by *inïkogu*, but the possession indicator is always used. Included in this category are things which are normally possessed, such as payment (*fïpïgï*), water in a container, harvested crops, and material paraphernalia such as fish hooks, arrows, hammocks, baskets, ceramics, and feather ornaments.

3. *Ago*, "living things"   *Ago* are all spoken of in terms of the human metaphor, but do not take the possession indicator. The term itself labels the highest level taxon in the hierarchy discussed earlier, but also connotes features not made explicit in Kalapalo definitions of that category (see below).

4. *Itseke*, "monsters"   Human metaphor is not applied to items referred to as *itseke*, nor do they take the possession indicator. The category includes celestial phenomena, which are not included in the taxonomy of "living things," and items that are of monstrous shape, mixing morphological features of more than one category in the *ago* hierarchy. The Kalapalo consider *itseke* potentially malevolent beings, but this aspect of their nature is only made apparent when they discuss the relationships between *itseke* and humans, and cannot be derived from the paradigmatic criteria.

The use of these four "cosmological" labels often appears contradictory, since, despite the fact that they mark categories defined in terms of specific and mutually exclusive behavioral attributes, they are often applied to the same specific items. This apparent anomaly is easily explained, however, by considering that these attributes are only meaningful in specific situations. The situations themselves are those in which some kind of relationship with or behavior toward a human being is observed; that is, something that can change or cease to exist in another situation.

Kalapalo Models of the Categories Ordered in a Paradigm

> Where is Tima'na, he ate my pet.
> He ate him, my pet.
> He ate him, my pet.
> (Women's Song)

As I have already noted, the distinctive features of the Kalapalo model of Upper Xingu uniqueness refer to ideals of behavior or relationships. These include *ifutisu*, or polite, generous, peaceful behavior, and the observance of a set of dietary restrictions.

In addition to the classification of "living things" into groups according to whether they are eaten or not eaten, Kalapalo dietary practices include another rule, perhaps more important for explaining how the four terms in question are

---

[5] Traditionally, birds, monkeys, and turtles were the only wildlife kept as pets, though immature animals, such as fawns, young cayman, and peccary were occasionally captured and briefly held in the village. Dogs, which the Kalapalo also refer to as *itologu*, are said to be a recent introduction to the Upper Xingu Basin (note the Xingu Carib term for dog, *Katsawgo*, and the Brazilian equivalent, *cachorro*).

used. This is the rejection of animals classed as "eaten by Upper Xingu people" when they have become *itologu*, "pets."

The *itolugu–oto*, "pet–owner" relationship is characterized on the human side by nurture and protection within a household, and on the avian side by lack of *ifutisu* (in the sense of shyness), in other words, by tameness. This relationship is particularly interesting because the distinctive features are also those which define the filiative relationship, or that between human parents and their children. Children and pets alike are ideally supposed to be fed, reared, and kept protected within the confines of the house. Often pets are secluded like human adolescents "to make them grow beautiful," especially when the animal is a young bird able to provide its owner with valuable feathers as it reaches maturity. Although *itologu* may be members of species generally defined as edible in the dietary system, they themselves are never eaten, nor are they supposed to be killed. Ideally, such animals are supposed to be buried when they die, rather than be discarded or fed to another pet. Upon their deaths, both unnamed children (such as stillbirths or infants who die during postpartum seclusion) and birds are buried near the hammock of the parent or owner. Pet birds are the only animals held to have a village of the dead. As men who die travel to the village of dead men located to the east where the sun rises, so dead birds go to *their* village of the dead located in the direction of the sunset. Thus men are buried with heads facing east, pet birds with heads facing west. The *itologu–oto* relationship is therefore not only a special emotional relationship between humans and nonhumans, but is associated with life-crises–related symbols of great importance in human ritual.

Despite the significance of such symbols, *itologu* are considered possessions, or *inikogu*, of their owners. A person who is *oto* (owner) has acquired the items in question through some form of exchange, including payment to mark social relationships (such as that given to a widow's brothers upon her remarriage, to a ceremonial performer by the ceremony's sponsor, and to gravediggers by kinsmen of the deceased), personal buying and selling, and the *uluki* or "trade ceremony."[6] The transactions in each of these instances are legitimate means of exchanging wealth. Although different items may appear in each kind of exchange, they are referred to generally as *fipïgï* or "payment." In addition to these kinds of wealth transfers, a person may of course manufacture something himself, or as is often the case with a "pet," capture it in the wild. In all of these situations, the resultant relationship is one of property–owner. Ceremonial paraphernalia, including ceremonial trumpets, flutes, masks, and headdresses made for particular performances, are not considered *inikogu*. Such items are conceived as belonging to the village, much like public structures are, and therefore are nonnegotiable. On the other hand, similar objects which are commissioned by non-Indian outsiders can be bought and sold.

Itseke are characterized by potential malevolence towards men, and are therefore beings who are both physically dangerous (*tekotiñi*) and violent (*itsotu*). They are believed to cause harm in several specific ways: (1) through *kwifi* or invisible

---

[6] Dole has described these forms of exchange in detail in several interesting articles (see Dole 1956–1957; 1956–1958; 1966).

darts that are projected into a victim's body, (2) by capturing the shadow (*akuagï*),[7] and (3) by merely presenting themselves to the sight of a human being. For example, the following story relates how the sudden death of an ostensibly healthy man was attributed to his frequent sightings of *itseke*:

> Nakï's wife kept nagging him because he had many lovers and had just arranged to marry a second, much younger wife. One day, he decided to get away from her by going on a long fishing trip by himself. On the river, Nakï saw a school of fish and drew his bow in order to shoot, but as he did so, the fish changed into human shapes.
>
> Another time, Nakï left Aifa before dawn to fish, accompanied by his daughter and his wife's son by another marriage. As they walked in single file, Nakï leading the way, the little girl, who was in the rear, said, "Father, who is that following us? I hear someone's feet on the path." They stopped and listened, but saw no one. A second time, the girl heard footsteps, but again they saw nothing. The third time, just as Nakï turned around, he saw a human figure on the trail far behind them, but as he looked, it vanished.
>
> Another time, Nakï went out at night to play the ceremonial trumpets (*kagutu*), which are kept in a small house in the center of the village. He went inside this house and began to play in such a way as to call other men to join him. As he sat waiting Nakï noticed a strong light coming from outside, so he walked outdoors to see what was happening. The moon had become very large, and its light filled the entire sky. As he watched, the moon grew bigger and bigger, until the darkness had completely gone and it seemed like daytime. Frightened, Nakï ran inside the trumpet house to try once more to call a companion. Shortly thereafter Taguwaki arrived, but by that time the moon looked normal again. Nakï told Taguwaki what he had seen, and they both became worried, because it meant Nakï would probably die soon.

Although relatively few persons become victims of such catastrophies, several common minor illnesses are attributed to the inadvertent antagonism of *itseke*. A number of plant species, including many used for herbal remedies, are believed to be owned by snake *itseke*. If a Kalapalo harvests a plant the snake owner does not wish to be destroyed, there is danger that the latter will shoot *kwifi* into the human being's body, thereby causing a skin rash. Similarly, fish *itseke* are believed able to cause stomachache and diarrhea if they do not want to be killed on the day a fisherman happens to shoot at them.

In addition to their harmful powers, *itseke* are characterized by their unusual and shocking appearances. Some are known for their ability to transform themselves or, like the moon seen by Nakï, are considered *itseke* because they suddenly appear to be different from normal phenomena. In some cases, *itseke* appear in strange shapes, mixing morphological attributes of different categories of "living things," or simply appearing in abnormal size. Thus the names of many *itseke* take the form of (1) the name for some ordinary low-level taxon in the *ago* hierarchy, plus (2) the suffix / *kuegï* /. The latter is an affix with the implication of "potential malevolence,"

---

[7] The Kalapalo believe that inside each living thing and some material possessions (arrows, guns, shell ornaments, some feather headdresses) is a "shadow," a duplicate, yet invisible image of the thing or person. The shadow (distinguished from that cast upon the ground) can leave the body, when it may become visible to the owner. When the shadow of a living thing leaves the body, it results in sickness (especially unconsciousness) that can soon lead to death.

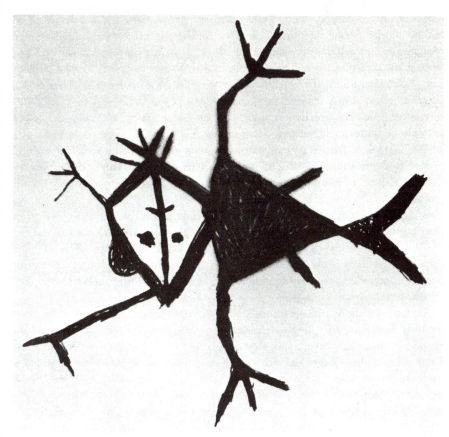

Figure 3. Tufulei's drawing of an itseke.

which thus indicates "monstrosity." Examples of *itseke* names are: Safundukuegï, "monstrous bass fish," Itaukuegï, "monstrous women" (who live beneath the water of deep lakes), and Tïtsahakuegï, "monstrous giant kiskadee."

Having now specified the Kalapalo models associated with each of the four categories, I would like to turn to specific examples of contextually varying classification to illustrate how these concepts are symbolized by the use of terms in Kalapalo speech.

As I noted earlier, the relationships of parent–child and pet–owner are defined in terms of similar normative behavior. These similarities are the basis of a metaphorical use of the word *itologu* to refer to a child who has come under the nurture and protection of a nonrelative. Although adoption (wherein a child is jurally considered offspring of someone other than its real parent) is unknown among the Kalapalo, fosterage is quite common. In the latter case, a child is raised by a relative of a deceased parent (usually a sibling) but in no way is this considered a parent–child relationship. Most important is the notion that kinsmen of a deceased person have an obligation (because of *ifutisu*) to care for orphaned children. When a nonkinsman, for no apparent reason (that is, who has no prior obligation based on *ifutisu*) has taken charge of such a child, the latter is called *itologu* of the person supporting it. This special use of the term indicates the recognition of a relationship similar in behavior to that between owner and pet, since it includes nurture and protection of an immature being, performed without any prior relationship of obligation. Since a child is of course also considered a "human being" and is referred to as such when the speaker wishes him to be distinguished from another living thing, the use of *itologu* in this way is another example of contextually varying classification.

The Kalapalo often refer to animals as both *itologu* and *iṇikogu*. When wishing to specify the relationship of "pet," the former term is used. This is often the case when the speaker needs to stress the fact that the animal in question is not an ordinary *ago*. For example, if a person wants to kill and eat an animal he sees roaming the village, another can refer to it as *itologu* of a specific individual, thus denying the suitability of such an idea. For example, one day Bïjïjï cooked and fed to his dogs his daughter's small parrot which had been found dead. When Tiṇone discovered her father had disposed of her pet in this unseemly manner, rather than burying it according to Kalapalo custom, she berated him for not remembering the bird was her *itologu*.

For an example of the situationally varying classification of birds, I draw upon my own experience of trying to raise a burrowing owl. The bird had been traded to me for some cloth by a young woman whose brother had found it in the scrub forest outside the village. At first, the members of the household with whom I lived were interested in my attempts to tame it, and occasionally helped me to capture cockroaches with which to feed it. It soon developed that this owl was quite reluctant to be kept as a pet. Not only was it extremely difficult to feed (for it refused to become accustomed to the presence of humans), but it would make successive nocturnal flights over the hammocks of people trying to sleep, all the while making raucous cries that awakened them throughout the night. Finally, Ugaki, exasperated by the disruption to her household, suggested I let the bird go, explaining that owls were unfit for pets. "They are not like humans," she said. "They are *itseke*, they fly at night." Ugaki's use of the term *itseke* to refer to this owl was a means of explaining why it was unsuitable for *itologu* status. Whatever the specific justification ("they fly at night," in this case), she considered owls unlike humans and therefore unable to participate in a relationship modeled on that between parents and their children. On the other hand, when Ugaki and others listed names of birds for me, owls were always included. When considered in the context of "kinds of birds," owls are thus classed as *ago*, "living things," but when rejected in terms of their possible relationship to human beings as pets, they are termed *itseke*. The use of the term *itologu* therefore appears to be a special reference to a certain kind of social relationship which can occur between men and "living things" who are nonrelatives. The latter may or may not be human beings. When the Kalapalo want to emphasize that an animal is someone's possession—that is, when wishing to specify the dimension of "ownership"—the term *iṇikogu* is applied. For example, this use of the term occurs when individuals are enumerating their possessions.

A similar set of symbols is associated with the *itseke* category. The use of this word appears to be related to a situational denial of the humanlike attributes indicated by the use of the human metaphor. The example of owls has been given above. Another is the mythical association of morphologically human heroic figures (such as Taugi and Awlukuma) and other beings in humanlike relationships and situations, who are nonetheless referred to as *itseke*. In such instances, the term symbolizes the association of these characters with nonhuman attributes, which are in a real sense "unnatural" and therefore awesome. Mythological characters have the ability to change their shape, engage in fearful destruction, and perhaps most importantly, change or invent things. The latter attribute was most vividly impressed upon me on one occasion, when a Kalapalo man requested that I explain to him how paper is made. After describing the process as well as I could, he suggested that *kagaifa* were monsters rather than human beings.

In addition to monsters of humanlike form, there are others which are monstrous in a physical sense. Among these are certain "machinelike" beings who are said to be owned by witches. One example of this is a kind of monster likened by several informants to an airplane. Decorated with red parrot feathers, but unlike birds sleeping in underground burrows, it flies around the countryside where it can be captured by a person having witch's power. Once struck down in flight, the "witch's airplane" is kept underground by the owner, who can call it out on request in order to fly from village to village causing sickness and death. When considered in the context of such an association, this being is often referred to as *inikogu* (as in *kwifi oto inikogu*, "witch's property"), but when considered as a free, unowned being, it is called *itseke*.

As with *itologu*, items which are normally eaten are rejected if they are labeled *itseke*. An incident which took place in Aifa during a period of scarcity illustrates this quite nicely. During the month of February, at the height of the rainy season, fishing is extremely difficult because of the extensive flooding and silting of lakes and streams. At this time of year, Kalapalo men, who are normally avid fishermen, become reluctant to continue this activity. Only the most persistent individuals, usually those who are obligated because of their newly established marriages to seek food for a household group, continue to fish. On one occasion, such a man brought a single fish weighing about three pounds to the members of a household with whom I was living. This fish, of a species known as *wagiti* (*matrincha* in Brazilian Portuguese), is highly desirable as food in normal circumstances because of its tasty flesh and high fat content. Naturally, during a period of scarcity people regard themselves as particularly fortunate to eat it.

When the fisherman returned, all the men of his household group were seated in the center of the village with men of other households, as is customary in Upper Xingu villages during periods of relative inactivity. His single catch was given to the women inside the house to prepare for distribution among the entire household, which numbered twenty-six persons. The fisherman's mother-in-law began to clean the fish, removing the stomach and intestines prior to boiling it with manioc flour. Noticing something unusual in the stomach, she removed the contents and discovered a half-digested water rat. The women's delight and anticipation of a good meal turned to consternation. Quickly giving the fish's stomach to her young son to dispose of in the garbage heap behind the house, the older woman con-

LIBRARY
OF
MOUNT ST. MARY'S
COLLEGE
EMMITSBURG, MARYLAND

tinued to prepare the fish for eating, cautioning her kinswomen not to speak of the incident to the men. When the food had been prepared, the men were called inside, and all twenty-six household members were given a share of fish porridge spread on manioc bread. After we had all begun to eat, the young boy told the men of what had been found in the fish's stomach. Several threw the remains of their food away, and one actually became nauseated. When I asked why they had rejected this excellent food at such a bad time of the year, the men replied that the *wagiti* was in fact not food (*otu*) at all, since it was not *kaŋa* but rather *itseke* and therefore inedible. The presence of a water rat in the fish's stomach demonstrated this fact. When I then suggested that fish occasionally were found to have such things inside them, the men assured me that only monsters would eat ŋene. The proper diet of fish was defined as other fish and plant materials, according to the species.

The incident illustrates how items normally classed as *ago* are considered *itseke* on the basis of attributes which are considered antithetical to human behavior. In this case, a decision was made to classify something normally considered fish as a monster on the basis of a dietary practice considered improper according to Kalapalo rules about eating. At this point, we can return to the question of why the Kalapalo justify their eating monkey by the statement, "it is like human beings." Both this example and the one given directly above serve to illustrate the following generalization: Kalapalo cosmology contains principles whereby things in the universe which incorporate humanlike behavior (eating things Upper Xingu people should eat and acting peacefully) are idealized, and things behaving otherwise (eating anything indiscriminately and acting violently) are avoided. Such behavior is defined as the antithesis of that considered proper for human beings, namely the practice of *ifutisu* and the adherence to a carefully restricted diet.

3 / Subsistence practices

With the important exceptions of the Bororo and Caraja, the majority of tribes living until recently in central Brazil were seasonally transhumant hunter–gatherers with limited dependency on cultivated plants. In contrast with such groups as the Shavante, Kayapo, Nambikwara, and Mundurucu, the residents of the Upper Xingu Basin are settled agriculturalists and fishermen, an adaptation which can be ascribed in part to the environmental peculiarities of the region. Equally important, however, are the dietary practices which, as I have shown in Chapter 2, restrict the number of hunted species to a very few. In contrast to their Tupi- and Gê-speaking neighbors, who place positive value on eating meat, the pursuit of hunting, and an aggressive masculinity associated with that pursuit, the members of Upper Xingu society reject these values and adopt the opposite moral code: Fishing and agriculture, rather than hunting, are the proper male subsistence activities, and pacificity and generosity are the ideals of behavior.

THE UPPER XINGU HABITAT

The natural environment of the Upper Xingu Basin is a transition zone between thickly wooded, high scrub plains (called *cerrado* or "closed country" in Brazil) located to the east and south, and tropical rain forests (known as *mata*) to the north and west (see Askew *et al.* 1970). The upland *cerrado*, which in many other areas of central Brazil is poorly watered, is in the Upper Xingu Basin modified by a geologically ancient riverine system, characterized by numerous swamps, oxbow lakes, and large expanses of relatively low rain forest (called *galeria*) which are flooded during the rainy season. The *galeria* is found along water courses, and is the classic "impenetrable jungle" of traveler's tales. Seen from the rivers, the *galeria* does appear inhospitable, for where the sun is able to reach the lower levels of the forest, vines and small saplings grow in profusion beneath the taller trees. Slightly further inland, however, where the canopy of tall trees blocks out the sun, undergrowth is almost nonexistent, making it easy to walk through the *galeria* during the dry season. During the rainy season, when this same forest is flooded as much as four or five feet, a person traveling by canoe can take short cuts through it, to avoid the wide meanders of the larger rivers. These routes bring the fisherman into less turbulent water, where fish are more plentiful at that time of year, and to

27

places where he can easily hunt capuchin monkey and numerous species of birds whose habitat is the low forest. Because of such heavy flooding during the rainy season, the *galeria* is not suited to manioc cultivation.

Adjacent to the *galeria* zones, on slightly higher land which may nonetheless be flooded during the rainy season, is the *campo sujo*. Here the flora consists of small scrubby trees and extensive patches of coarse grass. This zone merges with the higher *cerrado* where termites build their mounds and denser stands of trees thrive. Deer, armadillo, and to the south, the rhea or South American "ostrich" are typical animals. Whenever necessary, the Indians burn the *cerrado* to clear the taller grass, thus keeping the view open and the area "clean," as they say. Consequently, the *cerrado* near villages and along trails is usually denuded of everything but the more fire-resistant trees.

In addition to flooding, which often occurs during the rainy season (but never as heavily as in the *galeria*), at least two other factors preclude agriculture on the *campo sujo* and the *cerrado*. First, the soil types are extremely poor, lacking the humus of the heavily forested areas and containing large amounts of clay. Second, the lack of a dense plant cover, which results in especially heavy leaching of the soil, would, under cultivation, result in heavy erosion during the rainy season. By contrast, where the stumps of trees can remain in the area under cultivation, erosion is minimal. Only the intermittent high forests, which are less extensive than either *cerrado* or *galeria* in the Upper Xingu Basin, can be used to cultivate manioc, the major subsistence item. Thus, the geographical situation limits the location of village sites to broad strips of land between, and well away from, the major rivers.

Seasonal Variations

The climate in the Upper Xingu Basin is characterized by a clearly delimited dry season, falling between the months of May and September, and an equally distinct rainy season, which occurs from the end of October through early April. During the dry season, no rains fall at all, except briefly during June. At this time, the days are extremely hot, with temperatures soaring into the 100s. At night, however, the air is quite cold, and the Indians light fires beneath their hammocks to fend off the chill. The dry season is a period of intense subsistence activity. At this time, new gardens are prepared and manioc is harvested. Fishing, the major nonagricultural activity, is particularly good, for the rivers are low and the water relatively clear. At the end of the dry season, during the latter half of August, large numbers of turtles come to lay their eggs on the white sandbars exposed by the receding waters of the rivers. These eggs are gathered and eaten in large quantities, and are an important dietary supplement during that time of year.

The period of transition between the dry season and the rains, which occurs at the end of September and in early October, is a time of great intervillage activity. Throughout the dry season, people have been cultivating and processing manioc. When the new gardens have been completed and various expeditions such as salt-plant-gathering parties have returned, whole village groups, temporarily freed from subsistence tasks, travel to major ceremonies in other settlements.

The rainy season is welcomed by the Kalapalo because of the ripening of various species of wild and cultivated fruits. As the rains increase in intensity,

TABLE 1.   KALAPALO SEASONAL AND CEREMONIAL CALENDAR

Month	Subsistence Activities	Ceremonial Activities
January	corn harvested; piqui, wild fruits eaten	local ceremonies held
February	height of rainy season; water at highest level	no ceremonial activity
March	last year's manioc nearly depleted	
	begin to harvest manioc and gourds	
April	DRY SEASON BEGINS	
	new gardens cleared	
May	water lower; fishing parties for ceremonial food payments	trade ceremonies begin (held through June)
	manioc harvests (until September)	
June	two-week rainy season; gardens weeded	harvest of trumpet sponsor's manioc; trumpet ceremonies
July	cold nights	
	burning of new gardens; clearing of burned materials from new gardens (through August)	
August	turtle egg gathering; manufacture of salt; fishing parties for ceremonial payments	
	manioc planted	
	new cornfields prepared, planted	
September	RAINY SEASON BEGINS	
	fishing for ceremonial food payment; fish poisoning expeditions	anetu ceremonies held (through October)
October	last year's piqui depleted	
November	piqui harvest begins (through December)	
December	wild fruits begin to be collected; piqui processed	

however, this period becomes one of markedly decreased subsistence activities. As a result, the height of the rainy season, which occurs in February and early March, is a time of real scarcity. Because the rivers are flooded and heavily silted, fishing becomes exceedingly difficult, and people are forced to rely on a depleted supply of stored food, collected fruit, ants, and grasshoppers, together with what little game they have acquired by hunting. This is a period of lethargy and malaise. With the end of the rains, men and women become active once again, as renewed efforts are made to accumulate large quantities of food. Once more major ceremonies are held during which enormous distributions of manioc and fish are made to the participants.

SUBSISTENCE

Kalapalo technology is, in certain respects, quite primitive, for the number of items produced is limited (under 200 items of manufacture) and stereotyped both in form and ornamentation. Traditionally restricted by the absence of metal and stone tools (except ground axes, which were traded into the area), they made extensive use of bone, tooth, and wooden implements. The most impressive examples of the skill shown by the Kalapalo in the face of limited technical resources are associated with their subsistence activities. The techniques for processing a number of raw materials are extremely sophisticated, for they result in an almost complete utilization of the harvested products, permitting storage of important subsistence items for up to half a year.

These elaborate food processing ventures are collective enterprises in which the Kalapalo spend considerable time during periodic seasons of intense activity. In fact, participation in group subsistence activities—be they the preparation of gardens, extended fishing trips, or the processing of manioc, piqui, corn, and salt— is a critical means of marking one's viable relationships with other Kalapalo.

Manioc

The major subsistence item is bitter manioc (*Manihot esculenta*), a root crop the Kalapalo call *kwigi*. The following legend tells of the circumstances under which ancestors of the Kalapalo first cultivated manioc.

> Before human beings knew about manioc, they lived on roots which they found in the *cerrado*. One day, Taugi and another man went fishing with their wives, who were sisters. Accompanying them in the center of the canoe was a third, younger sister, who was not yet married. Towards the end of the day, as the men paddled the canoe towards home, a tern flew overhead, swooping low over the craft. "What a beautiful bird," exclaimed the younger sister. "I want him for my husband." Upon hearing this, the bird flew away.
>
> That night, in the form of a young man, Tern appeared before the woman, saying he was the one to whom she had called that afternoon. "Now you must marry me," he said. "Yes," she replied. "I will tell my mother." They went before the woman's mother. "Mother, this is Tern, who is my husband." "Good," answered the older woman. "You will be my daughter's husband."
>
> After several months of living with his new wife's family, Tern began to feel homesick and asked his wife to accompany him to his own village, so that she could meet his mother and sisters.
>
> Tern and his wife traveled to the river, and then, rising in the air, plunged beneath the waters, where Tern's village was located. Upon their arrival, Tern's mother and sisters were busy processing manioc, and at night they offered their new affine strange food, urging her to eat and drink. At first, she was afraid this was poisonous, but her sister-in-law laughed and said, "This is good food, it is called manioc." The daughter-in-law tried it and found it delicious. She stayed in Tern's village a long time, eating manioc. Finally she asked Tern to take her back home, since she wanted to see her own mother once more. Her husband agreed and told his mother they were about to leave. She in turn instructed her son to bring manioc to his female relatives.
>
> At the wife's village, the manioc was distributed to the men, who began to plant it. The gardens were first cleared by Tern with the aid of a magic axe, which he could instruct to cut down the forest overnight. Then, he caused the manioc to be planted very quickly. Every day, the men went to their gardens to wait for signs of new growth. Finally, Taugi visited his garden one day and saw that the stalks, planted in the ground, had begun to sprout leaves. After waiting only a short time longer, he returned once more and dug up the manioc. Tern's wife then taught her kinswomen how to process the root.

Every year, Tern prepared the gardens with his magic axe, and the manioc harvest was bountiful even though the men did not have to work at weeding or planting. Nor did they have to wait long for the roots to mature. One summer, when the manioc was being harvested, Tern planned to seduce the youngest sister of his wife, who was in puberty seclusion. She lived in a large basket, suspended from the ceiling of the house by a rope, one end of which was attached to the side wall. One day, when everyone had gone to collect manioc, and Tern had stayed behind, pretending to be ill, he untied the rope, lowered the basket, and seduced his sister-in-law. Each day, pretending to be unable to work because his stomach hurt, Tern had sexual relations with the girl, until finally her mother became suspicious. Examining her daughter, she discovered traces of red paint on the girl's body. Then the youngest sister confessed that Tern was her lover. The mother-in-law, enraged, began to chastize her son-in-law, who became extremely embarrassed and declared he would leave forever. Despite his wife's pleadings, he took his axe and destroyed the manioc gardens. Then be began to walk to the river. The wife, following behind, urged him to take her with him, but he refused. In pity, however, he threw her a few manioc stalks, saying, "Now men will make their own gardens, and will have to work hard. Men will wait a long time to dig up the roots."

Today, manioc is planted each year in large, well-kept gardens. The root is elaborately processed to obtain several kinds of flour, used to make large flat cakes which are the stable food.

Towards the end of the rainy season, around April, every adult male Kalapalo enlists the aid of his fellow household members and male affines to prepare a new manioc garden. The men first cut down the smaller trees and kill the larger ones by ringing the bark. When the trees have dried sufficiently, the newly cleared gardens are set afire, until most of the underbrush and cut wood has burned. The area is then cleared as much as possible by hand, usually for a week or two, but remains crisscrossed with the fallen trunks of the largest trees, some of which measure as much as eight feet in circumference.[1]

Manioc is planted by men. A small area of earth is mounded up with a machete, and into this loosened soil several stalks are inserted at a steep angle to eventually form a cluster of new plants.[2] The choice of these stalks is determined by the quality of the previously harvested tubers, as well as the variety, for the Kalapalo grow at least twenty-three separately named types of bitter manioc. Some of these types are desired for the size of their roots, while others are grown for the sweetness of the soup which can be made from them.

Throughout the dry season, manioc from older fields is continuously harvested and processed. Towards the beginning of the rainy season, the fields which have been depleted are replanted, but those which have yielded two crops are allowed to become fallow. During the rainy season, the roots in the newly planted fields are

[1] The heavy bark from these charred trunks, which has burned on the outside but which still remains damp and fibrous on the inside, is an excellent source of fuel for household fires. Several months later it has been almost entirely removed by the young girls and women who collect it during the late afternoon; then the men are urged to cut down some of the dead trees left in their gardens, in order to replenish the fuel supply.

[2] The knowledge of digging sticks, which are illustrated in von den Steinen's publications, has become lost, although today they are said to appear in a ceremony which, however, has no present connection with manioc.

Manioc Processing: (a) Kufagi (left) scrapes manioc roots on a palm thorn grater, while Kafundzu squeezes the mash in a mat strainer placed over a large ceramic tub.

(b) Processed manioc drying at edge of plaza prior to storage. In the foreground are balls of coarse mash and pieces of sediment which have been removed from the bottom of the processing tub. In the background is a drying rack on which sediment has been crumbled; when completely dry, this will be stored in a silo inside the owner's house for use throughout the next six months.

left to increase in size until the following year's harvest. Because the Kalapalo usually weed their fields diligently to prevent competition from other plants, they are able to keep them productive for two years and to harvest the crop almost in its entirety. Such high productivity allows them to maintain a reserve of flour in the house, as well as a reserve of unharvested roots in the ground. This way, a loss of even a great quantity does not create hardship.[3]

While I was with the Kalapalo, the Txicão, a formerly hostile tribe which was harrassed by Brazilian incursions into its traditional territory, were encouraged to settle within the Park by the administrators. Unable to survive on the meager dole received at the Post, they were forced to travel from village to village begging food. The Kalapalo, remembering how they were obliged to do the same when they moved from their own traditional territory, freely gave large quantities of their reserve flour and unprocessed roots to about twenty Txicão. They were able to retain an adequate supply for themselves, although it happened to be the rainy season, during which manioc is not processed.

During the season of manioc harvesting, a household group leaves early each morning for the fields, each woman with her unmarried daughters going to a field planted by her husband or unmarried brother. Digging up the roots with machetes, the women place them in shallow rectangular baskets, which when full are carried on their heads back to the house. After bathing in the lake, the Kalapalo women return to their houses to begin the long process of converting the day's harvest into food.

It has been frequently asserted that the aim of most elaborate techniques for processing bitter manioc in South America is to extract the toxic fluids (prussic acid) which make the raw root inedible, although Dole (1960) has refuted these assertions in an article reviewing techniques of processing manioc found over a wide area of South America. As far as the Kalapalo are concerned, the methods used are clearly not designed simply to make the root edible, but to obtain specific end products. The roots are first scraped with pieces of tin cans or river oyster shells to remove the tough outer skin. Each woman then places a board, set with palm thorns, on a large ceramic vessel, and, leaning one end of the board against a house post, firmly scrapes each root while bracing her stomach on the other end. The resultant mash, usually watery and somewhat fibrous, is then scooped into a mat constructed of the stiff, strawlike ribs of palm shoots, which is lain over a second large vessel. After pouring water over this with a gourd dipper, the women then squeeze the mash between the mat, allowing the liquid to accumulate in the pot below. Depending on the variety of manioc being processed, the mash may be discarded or rolled into balls to be dried in the sun. The liquid squeezed from the mash is allowed to settle for most of the day. In the late afternoon, it is carefully scooped out of the processing pot and placed in a large cooking vessel, where it is boiled for several more hours to make a delicious, nut-flavored soup called *kwigiku*. The sediment left at the bottom of the processing vessel is removed and dried in the sun. It then becomes a very fine flour which can be stored in large indoor silos. Although it is usually depleted after six months, it could probably be safely stored

[3] See Carneiro's discussion of Kuikuru agricultural practices (Carneiro 1961).

for a longer period of time. Mixed with the coarser flour, which has been preserved in sun-hardened balls, manioc in this form is made into *kine*, large tortillalike flat bread, and *telisiñi*, a drink made from water into which very thin toasted *kine* has been crumbled. Without *kine* and *telisiñi*, the Kalapalo consider themselves unfed, though they may have fish, fruit, and game at hand.

Piqui

Second in importance to manioc as a subsistence crop is piqui (*Cayocar brasilensis*) or *intse* in Kalapalo, a cultivated fruit rich in vitamins and oils. The Kalapalo say that piqui trees first grew from the stomach of a dead cayman, as told in the following myth.

A man discovered that he was being deceived by his five wives. Seeking to learn the identity of their lover, he followed them to the manioc gardens. There he saw them having intercourse with a tapir. The next day, he followed them again and while they were waiting for their lover to appear, he climbed a nearby tree. When the tapir arrived, the husband shot him from above and killed him with an arrow. The wives mourned their lover and buried him in the manioc garden. From his eyes, nose, mouth, and ears grew trees which today provide the Kalapalo with wild fruit.

The women soon found another lover, the cayman. One day their husband followed them as they went to the river to bathe. There he saw them engaging in sexual relations with the animal. After the women had left, their husband shot the creature from a tree with his bow and arrow, leaving the body by the riverbank. The next day, the five wives again went to the river to meet their lover. Discovering the body, they buried it, then threw off their belts as a sign of mourning.

The husband, upon their return, was pleased with himself, and began to laugh at them. "Why are you mourning like that?" he said. "You have killed our lover, the cayman," they said.

Some time later, the women returned to where their lover was buried. From his stomach was growing a tree on which were many fruits. These they decided to prepare for food, but they had no idea of how to go about this. First, they dried it in the sun, but it tasted like dust and made them thirsty. Then, they buried it in the ground, but it became rotten. Finally, the youngest said, "Let's go to Taugi." When they came to Taugi, he said, "My sisters, you come to see me?" "Yes," they said, "we have this fruit, but we don't know how to make food from it." "Where did it come from?" asked Taugi. "From the cayman, our lover, out of his stomach," the women replied. "Then," answered Taugi, "because this fruit comes from the water, it must be returned to the water." He explained how the women must soak the fruit in water to ferment it, in order to preserve and eat it. That is how women know how to make *intsene*, the piqui drink.

The processing of piqui is laborious, but, like that of manioc, results in several important products and almost no wasted materials. From the fruit the Kalapalo obtain a fragrant oil used for repelling insects and for decorating the body and material objects, a sweet, jamlike substance, seed kernels (which serve as a dietary supplement shortly after the piqui harvest), and, most important of all, a fermented pulpy substance which is the basis of repeated ceremonial food distributions that are crucial for subsistence during much of the rainy season.

Piqui seeds are planted in fields where manioc is still growing, the quality of last year's fruit determining which seeds are selected for cultivation. By the time

Men returning to Aifa with a piqui basket that has been removed from a nearby stream. The piqui will be donated to performers of a ceremony sponsored by Sagama, in whose household these men live.

the trees bear fruit, the fields in which they were planted have been abandoned for many years. For example, the trees which presently bear fruit are those which were planted by the parents and grandparents of persons who are today adults. In places where settlement has been continuous, groves of piqui trees extend for several miles around the village sites, still bearing fruit as much as fifty years after planting. The Kalapalo repeatedly burn the underbrush in these orchards to make harvesting the fallen fruit easier, so that a parklike aspect is created around old villages.

The right to harvest specific piqui orchards (which are named according to some prominent feature of the fruit of the trees, or after an event which took place near where they are planted) is inherited by the descendants of the original planter (normally men), but female relatives are the ones who actually gather the harvest; in good years there is more than enough for every woman to keep busy processing piqui over a period of two or three months.

Although piqui is often eaten raw or roasted (in this form it provides an important source of vitamin A), the bulk of the harvest is processed for long-term storage. The fruit is first boiled in ceramic vessels, then the pulp scraped off the large seed and packed in cylindrical baskets made of woven bark lined with huge leaves. These baskets often weigh over 100 pounds. They are placed in a shallow stream where they can be kept for nearly a year. The fruit begins to ferment under water, but remains nonintoxicating, as the alcohol is dissolved in the water. When needed, the baskets are removed and split open. The pulp is taken out and mixed with water or manioc gruel to produce an excellent cold soup (*intsene*). The Kalapalo prize the fermented piqui pulp, since the vinegary taste is a welcome change from their usually bland diet.

From the inner piqui shells men manufacture ankle rattles worn during trumpet playing and other ceremonies. The many tiny spines on these inner shells (which make eating the raw fruit somewhat hazardous) are burned off, leaving blackened husks that are strung, twenty or more together, to make the ornaments.

Other Cultivated Plants

Corn is the third major foodstuff grown by the Kalapalo, but, although of crucial subsistence importance during January and February, it is only cultivated by a few individuals, who are obligated to make food distributions in payment for the performance of certain major ceremonies. Most corn is eaten roasted directly off the ear; sometimes cornmeal is made into small flat cakes or thick cylindrical buns called *ijalifïgi*, "tapir's penis."

Aside from these three major food plants—manioc, corn, piqui—the Kalapalo cultivate several kinds of beans, sweet manioc, and sugar cane, as well as two varieties of peppers. All these are minor foods, being planted by only a few individuals who have taken the time to protect them from leafcutter ants and small children.

Although the Kalapalo are familiar with a number of Brazilian cultigens, like papaya, bananas, rice, tomatoes, oranges, and limes, all of which are grown by the workers at the Post, they are not interested in seriously adding these to their diet. This is so despite the fact that the items in question are all well liked and eaten whenever available. Occasionally, someone plants one of these introduced crops, but little care is taken in seeing that it reaches maturity. The traditional crops, especially those upon which the Kalapalo depend, seem to be uniquely suited to the conditions of soil and climate (as well as the insect infestations they must withstand), and none require the care needed during early growth as do those cultivated by Brazilians.

In addition to subsistence crops, the Kalapalo cultivate a number of other plants. One of the most important of these is cotton, which, together with burity palm fiber, is used to make hammocks. The planting and harvesting of cotton is exclusively male work, but women are responsible for spinning it into thread. When not used for hammocks, this is wound into large balls and presented to husbands, brothers, and lovers, who use it for decorative knee and arm bandages and for belts.

Another important cultivated plant which is found in old gardens is urucu (*Bixa orellana*), grown for its pigment-bearing seed pods. From the many small seeds and fibrous material inside these pods, the Kalapalo prepare a brilliant red body paint they call *mïŋi*. By leaching the seeds and boiling down the resulting liquid, they obtain a sticky substance which, when mixed with piqui oil and shaped into balls, is easily applied to the body for decoration and protection against sunburn.

Although urucu is invariably used for ceremonial ornamentation, the Kalapalo frequently use it to paint themselves on ordinary occasions. After long feasts (for example during a particularly successful fishing season) when the Kalapalo have gorged themselves for a week or more, they bathe thoroughly, then apply *mïŋi* "to become beautiful again." So common is the practice of painting with urucu, almost every household item, including hammocks, clothing, baskets, and the houseframe itself, is stained a dirty brown from the substance.

A cultivated plant of considerable economic utility is arrow cane. Since this plant periodically sends out new shoots, the Kalapalo are able to harvest the cane in areas which were planted at a considerable time in the past, often beyond memory of persons presently living. In fact, the planting of arrow cane seems to occur only when a new village site is chosen for occupation. Since the original planter of a stand of arrow cane is often unknown, the harvesting of it can become a free-for-all, as the men of the village vie with one another to procure the most and straightest specimens.

Gourds are cultivated extensively for containers. After their harvest in early March, they are dried, then split open. On the inner surface a black lacquer made from plant juices and pot black is applied and highly polished, then urucu rubbed on the outside surface. Thus, Kalapalo gourds make unusually effective dippers, ladles, and water containers, which are greatly valued. Light in weight and relatively unbreakable, they compare favorably with ceramic vessels for purposes other than cooking.

Kalapalo who are shamans grow tobacco behind their houses. This is used to make cigars which are smoked during the curing rituals conducted by these men (see Chapter 8). Otherwise, hallucinogens, as well as intoxicating beverages, are unknown. Finally, a very few women cultivate a small agavelike plant, from which a fiber is used by them to make their belts and by men to make net bags.

Salt

The manufacture of salt (*agafi*) is another excellent example of the ingenuity in preparing food from raw materials which is displayed by the Kalapalo. A variety of water hyacinth is gathered in the swamps, where the plants are hung up to dry for several days on racks. The dried plants are burned and the ashes repeatedly leached to get rid of impurities. For this purpose, a large funnel-shaped, basketlike container, about three feet high and two feet wide at its mouth, is made of bark strips and vines. Lined with leaves, this is used as a sieve. The ashes are placed at the bottom of this container, and water poured over them. The resulting saline solution is allowed to drip into a cooking pot, in which it is later boiled to evaporate the water. The resulting substance is dried on the floor of the house in pyramidal shapes several inches high. When completely dried, it is packed into small baskets made of bark strips. Several grades of this salt (technically, potassium chloride) can be made in this way, depending upon how often the ashes are leached. The most desirable is a nearly white substance which is served mixed with hot peppers to form a spicy sauce, usually eaten during the few weeks of exceptional scarcity when fishing is poor.

The only other wild plants presently exploited for food are those which bear fruits. During the rainy season, wild pineapples, burity and macaiuva palm fruits, three kinds of "wild cherries," wild cashew, and several other small fruits are important supplementary foods, yet are relatively unimportant compared with piqui and corn.

Fishing

Fishing is the most important subsistence activity performed away from the village, and provides the greatest amount of protein in the diet. The Kalapalo are interested in fish more than any other animal, and most men can name over eighty distinct categories of fish, describe the feeding habits of each, tell how best to catch them, and in the majority of cases, specify where they are usually found. The Kalapalo employ a number of fishing techniques, including bow and arrows, hook and line, nets, baskets, sieves, weirs, and poison. Because each particular method is especially suited to a type of situation and a special need of the fisherman, the Kalapalo are able to exploit virtually every habitat in which fish are known to live.

The large rivers and deeper lakes can be exploited most successfully by hook and line fishing, a method which has been introduced indirectly by Brazilians. This is presently the most commonly used technique next to shooting with bow and arrow. The hook is baited with fruit or raw fish (never with worms or insects—that is, things the Kalapalo would not eat themselves). Hook and line fishing at present does not make use of poles. Instead, following the custom of interior Brazilians, the baited end of the line is thrown like a lariat into the water, while the other end is secured to a four inch piece of wood held on the floor of the canoe by the fisherman's foot. Hook and line fishing is most often practiced from a canoe in deep water, or where the prey cannot be easily seen. The species caught by this method range in size from tiny minnows to three or four foot specimens which are usually shot with arrows after being drawn to the side of the canoe.

Bow and arrow fishing is used extensively where the prey can be seen, as from a canoe in shallow water. It is also used in close situations, for example, to shoot the four foot long *tañc* (in Brazilian Portuguese, *trairão*), which makes its home in holes along the banks of lakes and small streams.

Fish poisoning usually takes place at the beginning of the rainy season, when fish are beginning to spawn and the waters are still low. First, a group of men select a small oxbow lake or other body of water with few outlets. If there is a current, a dam is built to prevent the fish from escaping the poison. Then one of several kinds of woody vines or lianas is chopped in the water, causing a white, foamy substance to be discharged, which causes the fish to suffocate. After approximately a half hour or less, the smaller fish begin to rise to the surface, where they can be collected by hand or in small basket sieves (used by women). The larger species, often stupified but not dead, can be easily shot with bow and arrow. Fish which have been caught by poisoning are completely edible.

The Kalapalo also make use of several kinds of fish traps. The most common type is a large funnel-shaped basket (*utu*) designed so that a fish swimming into it cannot escape. Several of these baskets are placed in openings made in a small dam built across a small, but swiftly flowing stream. They are particularly effective during seasons of the year when large schools of fish migrate to spawning areas. A very small type of fish trap is sometimes used to catch minnows. This is in the form of an inverted funnel, which is placed in a shallow stream or lake. A small opening under water is baited with a bit of cooked manioc flour, and a piece of cotton is attached to the tip protruding above the water. When the fish enters to eat the bait, the fisherman sees the cotton tassle move, and quickly retrieves the trap.

Nets are sometimes used when a large quantity of fish is needed for ceremonial payment. However, the Kalapalo do not own any nets of their own, and must borrow them from the Park administrators. Because the frequency of net fishing has not been properly adjusted to the conditions of the area, overfishing has already occurred in some streams, particularly those in the territory of the Yawalipiti, a group which lives close to the Post. Although net fishing can be dangerous because of the inevitable presence of stingrays, caymans, and electric eels in Upper Xingu lakes, the Kalapalo are not reluctant to use this technique because of the high yield which results from it.

The most common fishing procedure is for two men of the same household group to spend a day together in a canoe. The day before, they discuss where to go, and assemble the equipment they are to take with them. A wife or mother of one of the fisherman is informed of the trip, and she prepares manioc bread and a pot of telisiñï that evening for them to take along. The more ambitious men, or those who must feed a large number of relatives, often borrow or buy special items, such as a particular type of fishing line, basket traps, spoons, and finely made fishing arrows, in order to procure those species of fish which they expect to encounter on a particular day. Often men are obliged to borrow essential equipment, including hardwood bows, canoes, and paddles. Usually these items are lent by fellow household members, but sometimes a man must ask a person living in another household to lend his possessions. Such a request cannot be refused, though not infrequently a man claims he has given away the object sought after if he does not want to lend it.

The men who have agreed to fish together rise before dawn to walk to the canoe landing, and are often fishing by daybreak. If they are lucky, they fish until the early afternoon and return to the village well before dusk. Not infrequently, however, men spend the entire day on the river and its tributaries, having explored several possible fishing sites without much success. This is especially true during the rainy season.

When two men fish together from a canoe, the elder of the two is usually defined implicitly as the leader. This man is the one who has suggested to the other that the trip be made and who has thus prevailed upon the other to assist him. Although both men fish during the day, the leader is more or less continuously engaged in this pursuit, standing in the bow of the canoe while the assistant paddles from the stern. Men who fish together in this way are usually brothers-in-law, brothers, or a father and son. Thus the activity is not one of marked coercion on the part of the leader, but rather a cooperative venture which is pleasurable to both individuals. Indeed the success of the expedition depends upon the goodwill between the two men.

A man sometimes takes his wife upon such a trip, especially if he has no male companion available or if he is suspicious of her having too many affairs. Although women do not actually fish on these trips, they paddle the canoe while their husbands fish from the bow, and usually help them carry the catch back to the village.

Hunting

Because of their self-imposed taboos against eating most animals, hunting is a minor activity among the Kalapalo. An expedition undertaken specifically for hunting game is rare and usually occurs in one of two situations. During the rainy season, men who are unwilling to fish sometimes go on hunts, but they seem to be motivated by a desire to escape the boredom resulting from continual idleness, rather than by a desire to eat meat. Otherwise, hunting is only performed as part of

Fishing Techniques: (a) Fishing with hook and line from the stern of a bark canoe on the Culuene River.

(b) Utu *being placed in a dam.*

(c) Kaluene waits to shoot any fish that have escaped the dam.

(d) After a successful fish poisoning expedition, Ugaki wraps smaller catch in leaves, prior to steaming them over coals. Somewhat larger fish in foreground will be distributed uncooked to members of her household. The largest fish are already cooking on a grill or being made into fish porridge.

a ceremony which consists in the killing and eating of capuchin or howler monkeys (see pp. 54–55, Chapter 4). More often, however, animals are hunted if they are encountered during some other activity, for example, on a fishing expedition or when a man is seeking some natural product or hunting birds for their feathers.

Traditionally, hunting was performed with bow and arrow, but firearms have begun to take their place in this activity. However, the skill of hunting monkeys and birds with bow and arrow has not been lost, for men must still be good marksmen in order to catch fish. Furthermore, the Kalapalo must depend upon the generosity of Post officials and casual visitors to the Park for ammunition, and thus frequently find themselves unable to use their firearms.

Traditional Equipment and the Dependence on Modern Tools

Since their earliest contacts with non-Indians, the residents of the Upper Xingu Basin have received from time to time lavish presents of Western goods. It has become common practice for administrators, anthropologists, filmmakers, and others who spend some time in the area to bring with them metal tools, firearms, ammunition, fishing tackle, glass beads, cotton thread, cloth, soap, razor blades and the like, either for payment in return for special services or more commonly, simply as gifts. These sporadic and unpredictable windfalls have created a limited dependence on and need for objects of Western manufacture.

The Kalapalo have incorporated several types of modern tools into their subsistence practices, in some cases to the exclusion of more traditional equipment. For example, because there is almost no stone available in the area, stone axes were formerly traded from the Suyá Indians who live in the north of the Basin. Today, metal axes have completely replaced the stone tools, and the traditional relationship has vanished. Similarly, as I mentioned earlier, the machete has superseded the digging stick, which is now unknown among the Kalapalo. The efficiency of hook and line fishing under conditions formerly unexploitable during certain times of the year is well recognized, and thus fishing tackle is highly desired. All these things can only be acquired through pressure on visitors or Park officials, and many Kalapalo recognize that this pressure, which takes the form of continual begging, is distasteful to non-Indians and often unsuccessful. However, they are accustomed to a scarcity of important equipment, and thus fortunately their new needs have not placed them in a desperate situation.

It is the rare individual who owns all of the critical subsistence tools. Almost every man and woman must borrow some of these things from time to time and must depend upon the generosity of their fellow household members and other relatives for hardwood bows, canoes, paddles, manioc processing pots, clay griddles, and fish traps. Western equipment, such as steel axes, machetes, knives, firearms, and fishing tackle, is similarly shared, for, whatever is needed, there is a customary reliance upon other persons for the successful completion of essential subsistence tasks. In the chapters that follow, I will examine the bases for this reliance.

4 / Village and household structure

The two most important social units in Upper Xingu society are village and household groups. Although each type of unit exhibits considerable variation in internal organization, both are typically characterized by a sense of autonomy and solidarity among the members, especially in the context of relationships with individuals belonging to other units of the same order. Both the village and the household can be considered "corporate" in that each controls rights to territorial resources, acts as a unit when performing certain economic and ceremonial activities, and under these circumstances, is considered internally undifferentiated by outsiders. For example, members of the Kalapalo village group have exclusive rights to the resources of the territory in which Aifa is located. They alone can clear land for manioc fields, harvest arrow cane, collect wild fruit and other plant products, and exploit aquatic resources. Members of other village groups cannot exploit Aifa territory, unless they are living with the Kalapalo and thus have implicit permission to do so.

Similarly, members of a household group are obliged to distribute food which they accumulate among themselves; although every adult is responsible for contributing continuously to the food supply, a Kalapalo is assured of a share even when he does not, or cannot, contribute. However, the obligation to share food is not extended to include the general membership of other households, and it is considered extremely impolite to exploit the goodwill of persons outside one's own group who are under no obligation to provide one with food.

Despite this corporate organization, membership in villages and households is constantly shifting, and there is considerable movement of persons from group to group. A Kalapalo man or woman may participate in the corporate activities of several different groups by taking advantage of relationships of kinship and affinity throughout the Upper Xingu Basin, and thus it is not unusual for a person to have been active in several groups throughout his lifetime.

THE VILLAGE

The unity of the village group depends upon the historically inherited rights of its members, which are dependent upon birthplace. Among the Kalapalo, for a person to be considered a member of *Aifa otomo* ("people of Aifa"), he must have

43

been born either at Aifa or in the abandoned village of Kanugijafïtï. Regardless of parental affiliation, children who have been born and raised in Aifa are considered *Aifa otomo*. It is therefore not unusual for parents and children to be associated with different villages. Consider, for example, the case of Nikumalu and Kejupala, brother and sister born into the Wagifïtï group. Nikumalu and her two sisters were married to a Kalapalo man, and lived with him in Kanugijafïtï. Kejupala, Nikumalu's younger brother, married a Kalapalo woman and lived with his brother-in-law. The Wagifïtï siblings had several children, all of whom were considered *Kanugijafïtï otomo*, that is, members of the Kalapalo group. After the sisters' husband died, Nikumalu and one sister remarried other Kalapalo men. The third sister then married Saṇafa, a Kuikuru man, who came to live in Nikumalu's new husband's household. Later, a young Kuikuru woman was eventually married to Kejupala, who had become a widower. The children of these two Kuikuru–Wagifïtï marriages, because they were born among the Kalapalo with whom their parents were living permanently, are considered Kalapalo, that is, *Aifa otomo*. Figure 4 illustrates these relationships.

Village affiliation is important because rights to important resources found around old village sites—piqui trees, trees which yield bow wood, fishing sites, arrow cane planted many years before, shells from land and water molluscs, and land suitable for cultivation—are extended to the former residents and their descendants. Although individuals may never actually make use of these privileges, as long as there

Figure 4. Village affiliation of members of a Kalapalo household.

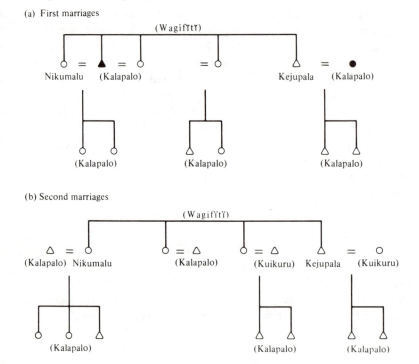

(a) First marriages

(b) Second marriages

are some members of a defunct village group still alive, others do not exploit their territory. During my stay with the Kalapalo, a neighboring village group made plans to gather piqui at old Trumai village sites which lay close to their own territory. The Trumai are presently reduced to a few individuals living at Pôsto Leonardo. Although these few Trumai apparently never visited their old sites, and there was little chance of their ever regaining sufficient members to form a new village, the feeling among the Kalapalo was that their old village sites should be left alone, until the time when there would be no Trumai left. It was said the people who wanted to gather Trumai piqui had no *ifutisu* for those Trumai who were still living.

The Kalapalo village, like all those of the Upper Xingu Basin, consists of a circle of oval-shaped houses (looking much like elongated hay stacks) which open onto a cleared plaza called *fugombo* (see photograph below). Slightly off center in the *fugombo* is the *kuakutu*, a small houselike structure in which are stored wooden trumpets and other paraphernalia used by men in various ceremonies. In front of the *kuakutu* is a peeled log, about 15 feet long, upon which men sit and gossip when they have nothing else to do. At approximately the center of the plaza are located unmarked graves, where those who have died since the village was built are buried.

A wide, well-cleared path, called *tagiñu*, lined with piqui trees, leads into the village from trails which wind through the *cerrado* and surrounding forests. The

Aerial view of Aifa, October 1966. The broad swath in center of photograph is an airstrip, cut in dry season to accommodate the Post airplace used to distribute medicines. In the forest to the rear can be seen a clearing, in which manioc has been planted. The tagiñu *(formal entrance path) is the trail leading into the village circle from upper left. An unfinished house is clearly visible in lower part of the village.*

tagiñu is the formal entrance path, upon which visitors to the village enter in ceremonial procession. Less open trails encircle the ring of houses and lead to the rear entrances, gardens, and bathing areas. Beyond the house circle are more piqui trees, indicating the sites of abandoned garden plots, and further on are newer gardens which border on the uncleared high forest.

Public and Private Areas

The Kalapalo village can be formally divided into "public" areas, used by members of all household groups, and "private" regions almost exclusively used by individual household groups, who are said to "own" them. These "private" areas, which include the houses, gardens, and a few adjoining paths, contrast with the "public" zones in that they are normally unapproachable by nonowners without some formal announcement of intent. The public regions, including the trails leading into the village, bathing areas, the plaza, and the trails encircling the village, can be further divided into two types: (1) *ifutisu* areas, that is, those used by persons who are *ifutisunda*, or remain socially unapproachable and isolated from public activity (such as mourners and adolescents in puberty seclusion), and (2) non-*ifutisu* areas, that is, those used by members of the village group who are willing to show themselves publicly. The non-*ifutisu* areas are given over to ceremonialism and men's communal gatherings, as well as personal display. The *ifutisu* areas are regions where people may move without having their presence formally proclaimed, even though they are often visible from the plaza or the houses. In these *ifutisu* regions, the Kalapalo can avoid confrontations with persons with whom they are in conflict, or during such time when they are expected to be withdrawn from normal activities (see Gregor 1970 for a study of the responses of the Mehinaku to these situations).

In contrast, when in the public non-*ifutisu* areas men and women greet and joke with one another. Here a Kalapalo is constantly bombarded with rhetorical questions and greetings which must be answered politely, whether or not he is on good terms with the speaker. Even the most intimate errands must be acknowledged, as in the following typical exchange: "Where are you going?" "I am going to defecate." "To defecate?" "Yes." "Do so." Needless to say, a person making use of the public, non-*ifutisu* regions of the village is under constant surveillance, and thus finds it impossible to conceal his actions or his destination. Therefore, when Kalapalo wish to avoid such scrutiny, yet must leave their houses to perform necessary chores, they have the option of using *ifutisu* areas where they can move about relatively freely. For example, there are three bathing areas close to the village, two of which are considered *ifutisu* regions. The main, non-*ifutisu* bathing area is directly connected to the village circle by a wide, easily visible path. In contrast, the other two are small clearings along the shore of the lake which are hidden from the village and which can be reached only by poorly cleared trails winding through the dense *galeria* forest growing along the shore. One of the *ifutisu* bathing areas is used by a man who is the political rival of the senior *anetu* or village representative (see Chapter 8) in order to avoid their coming into contact more than is necessary. The other is frequented by persons who are temporarily *ifutisunda*, especially recently divorced persons and those who are in mourning. For example, Kajagi, a young woman who had recently divorced her husband and promptly remarried, bathed and drew water in this *ifutisu* area for several months. In so doing, she was sure not to come into contact with her ex-spouse or his mother.

The paths around the village circle are frequently used by women when they must walk from one house to another or when they go to the lake to draw water. They do this in order to avoid the ribald comments of men seated in the *fugombo*. Since all unused spaces between houses are kept clear of underbrush, women are clearly visible when they walk in these areas, but they are not called to in greeting, nor are they subjected to raucous male commentary.

Successful hunters and fishermen return to Aifa by the *tagiñu* and approach their houses by walking through the *fugombo*. As they enter the village circle, the casual group of men sitting before the *kuakutu* cheer them with a special cry reserved to mark a successful male food-gathering enterprise. After they have been recognized in this way, the men who have brought food into the village are expected to share some of it with the idlers in the plaza. During the height of the rainy season, men sometimes jokingly parade through the *fugombo* carrying only the few small fish they have spent all day catching, and they are properly cheered in turn. However, when the season is far advanced and the Kalapalo feel underfed, what little catch a fisherman manages to obtain is surreptitiously brought into his house from the rear entrance to avoid persons outside the household who might claim a share of it. Similarly, men and women who have returned to the village with honey almost always avoid the *fugombo*, since this public display would necessitate a subsequent distribution of the highly prized substance to the village group at large.

The areas of *ifutisu* which cannot be easily seen are frequently used by lovers. A woman may invent the excuse of having to draw water or to defecate, in order to meet her lover waiting in the bushes behind her house. A man who has made plans to meet a woman on her way to collect firewood may pretend to start out in the opposite direction, then double back along one of the many concealed paths which wind through abandoned gardens and piqui groves.

In summary, the division of public regions into *ifutisu* and non-*ifutisu* areas allows individuals the option of concealing or displaying themselves. In this small village, where scrutiny by others is constant both inside the unpartitioned houses and outdoors in the non-*ifutisu* areas, a person can gain some measure of privacy and secrecy by making use of the zones defined as those of concealment.

Privacy of the Household Area

The inviolability of the Kalapalo house as a private region is such that no one enters without a definite reason for doing so, unless he is accompanied by a member of that household group (someone who is classed as his "friend" or *ato*, for example) or unless he is a kinsman of some member of the group. For this reason it is common to see Kalapalo men and women speaking from outside a house to someone within, making use of a small opening in the thatch. Persons who do visit for a specific purpose—such as adult kinsmen, shamans who have been asked to cure a sick person in the house, or village representatives who enter for the trading ceremony (*uluki*)—are formally greeted by the adults of the household, as in the following example of a senior member greeting a kinsman who has come for a casual visit.

"Apihu." (The visitor's name is called out by the host.)
"Oh." (A response to being called)
"What is it?"
"Just so. I am here." (Some other, more definite statement of the visitor's purpose for visiting may be given in other situations).
"Do so, stay here."

At night, the houses are shut tight with large doors fastened from the inside, which are placed over the front and rear openings. The Kalapalo are fearful of thieves, witches, and men who come to seduce their wives, all of whom make use of the dark to conceal their movements. The attitude of concealment and protectiveness which Kalapalo men in vain try to engender among their household group, and which is manifested in locking up the house in the preceding fashion, is often violated by their wives. While a husband is in the plaza playing the *kagutu*, his wife's lover will slip into his house and quietly extinguish the fire beneath her hammock before lying down beside her. Women also commonly wait in the darkness beside the rear door, where sexual relations often take place, so that they can admit their lovers into the house. In other situations, too, household members assist outsiders in betraying their fellows. For example, on one occasion a young man agreed to help his friend, who lived with another group, steal ammunition from a fellow household member who was notoriously stingy and who had himself been accused of stealing from the revengeful thief.

THE PLAN AND ORGANIZATION OF A KALAPALO HOUSE

Location of houses within the village circle is largely fortuitous; houses are not located near one another according to the relationships of persons who live in them. Since the villages are sufficiently permanent to allow rebuildings, these entail the eventual movement of entire household groups to areas of the circle that were formerly unoccupied, or that have become cleared by the purposeful destruction of a house. When the circle has become completely closed, a new house is built in front or to the rear of one which is presently occupied.

The Kalapalo house is built with the cooperation of the entire village group. First, the future male occupants select trees whose logs will be used for the center post and surrounding oval foundation structure. These trees are cut and stripped of branches, then carried to a point just outside the village, near a path leading from the gardens to the circle. When enough logs have been collected at this place, the household leader requests the men of the village to help carry them to his house site. Then the basic foundation is completed by the household leader and his group, after which they cut a large number of saplings (each approximately 15 feet long) to form the framework. Once again the villagers as a whole help to position these, tying them in place with vines and bark strips so as to complete half of the house frame. The other half is then finished by the men who are to live in the house, and these persons are also responsible for the thatching, for which purpose a tough grasslike yucca (bear grass) is used. From the first cutting of the house posts until the thatching is completed, the entire process can take more than six months. After approximately six years, the main posts begin to sag dangerously, and the owner must start to build a new structure.[1]

At each end of the house is a living area where the residents sling their hammocks and store personal possessions. Several stout poles are placed along the inner periphery of this area, so as to allow hammocks to be slung between them and the outer wall. Members of a nuclear family, or two unmarried men, usually share a single pole. Fires built near each cluster of hammocks, where small quantities of food are prepared for an individual's or nuclear family's meal. These fires also provide warmth at night. Personal possessions are kept along the wall, stuck in the thatch or tied to the framework.

The house is divided by a large central platform, called *ogo*, on which is stored manioc flour in large silos and sun-dried manioc mash kept in men's carrying baskets. Smaller, more carefully made women's carrying baskets are also kept here, as well as firearms and bottles of piqui oil. Masks, flutes, and headdresses (considered village property) are often suspended above the *ogo* if the sponsor of associated ceremonies lives in the house. Except for these ceremonial items, most of the objects piled on and tied over the *ogo* are considered private property, but can be used by all the members of the household.

The main fire area, always located in the back of the house opposite the rear entrance, is used for preparing major meals. Here manioc soup (*kwigiku*) is boiled, large quantities of fish are grilled, and manioc bread is made. Each procedure requires a large space to accommodate various kinds of cooking utensils, including large ceramic vessels (*afukugu*), ceramic griddles (*ulato*), and wooden grills (*ogo*). Also in this area is a pestle, used for pounding dried manioc mash, made from a section of hollow log set into the floor near the doorway. During the dry season the main fire is built outdoors to the rear of the house.

The open space in front of the central platform, from which the plaza can be seen, is used as a communal work area. Here men and women can work on individual tasks, such as spinning cotton, making arrows, or weaving baskets, and at the same time see what is going on outside. When a person desires privacy, a small work area is cleared near his hammock, and a small opening is made in the thatch to allow light to enter.

Structure of the Household Group

The dual division of a Kalapalo house reflects an ideal structural relationship: that between two nuclear families which together form the "core" of a household group. This "core" consists of persons who were originally instrumental in persuading relatives to form a new social unit within the village. The relationships between members of the core and their ties to the rest of the household group can

---

[1] When a house is intended as a temporary structure, or the future occupants have only a few men to assist them, it may be built in the square Brazilian style, with mud walls and thatched roof.

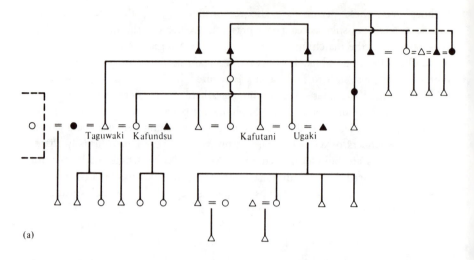

(a)

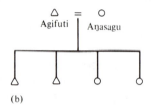

(b)

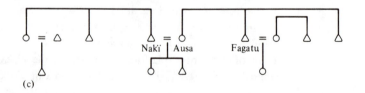

(c)

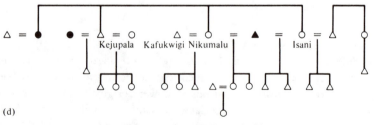

(d)

Figure 5. Kalapalo households.

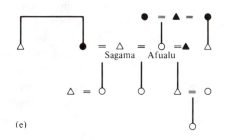

(e)

Bïjïjï

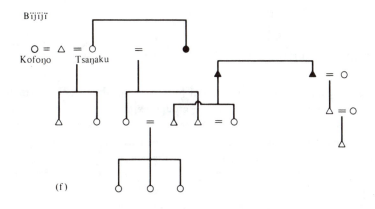

(f)

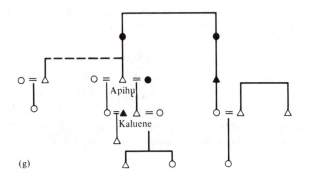

(g)

vary considerably, to the extent that almost any combination of kinsmen and affines is possible. In general, however, all household groups are composed of members of bilateral kindreds, who are all related in some way to the core, but not necessarily related to one another.[2] To illustrate the variability of Kalapalo households, diagrams of seven such groups which were present in Aifa during 1966–1968 are given in Figure 5. The core in (a) consists of persons in a sibling-exchange relationship (Taguwaki, Kafundzu, Ugaki, Kafutani); (b) is a single nuclear family household (Agifuti, Aṇasagu); (c) consists of two brothers-in-law (Nakï, Fagatu); (d) of a set of siblings (Nikumalu, Kejupala, Isani); (e) of a single couple (Sagama, Afualu), who have kept their children and children's spouses together; (f) of a man and his wives (Bïjïjï, Tsaṇaku, Kofoṇo); and (g) of a man and his son (Apihu, Kaluene). In all of these households, except (b), noncore members include sons- and daughters-in-law, unmarried siblings and offspring, and brothers-in-law. In Chapter 6, I will discuss the nature of these and other kinds of kinship and affinal relationships, and then return to the implications of such ties for residence patterns.

THE HOUSEHOLD AND VILLAGE AS ECONOMIC UNITS

The joint preparation and distribution of food is one of the principal symbols by which members of household and village groups express their solidarity. During most of the year, there is a continuous exchange of food between individuals and household groups, to such an extent that it is never necessary for all adult men and women to engage in subsistence activities simultaneously.

The Kalapalo household can be seen as a unit organized to perform certain subsistence activities. Persons who move away from a certain household are not expected to participate in the subsistence activities of that group, but must participate in those of the new one. The products of these activities—including manioc, fish, piqui, and to a lesser extent, corn, beans, salt, peppers, and game, as well as non-subsistence crops like gourds, cotton, and arrow cane—though recognized as belonging to the individual or nuclear family collectors or cultivators, should be shared among everyone in the household whenever possible.

The head of the household expects every adult male member to cultivate a manioc garden,[3] and suggests to men who have not contributed recently to the food supply by fishing that they do so. Men who are married fish often and consistently, but they tend to take turns so that usually not more than four (and often only two) men from a single household are away from the village on a particular day. Unmarried men do not fish as frequently, because they have neither wives nor parents-in-law to whom they are obligated as food suppliers. Often their fellow household members become exasperated and someone, usually a woman, angrily tells

[2] The Kalapalo kindred category term, *otomo*, discussed in Chapter 4, is not used to refer to the household group, for which there is no special word.

[3] It is the manioc which is planted, not the land, that is owned. Fields of household group members are contiguous since the men of a single household group help one another to clear the land.

them to go fishing. If they are still recalcitrant, the male household leader suggests they accompany him on his next fishing trip. Men usually do not refuse this subtle request for a contribution of labor, for to do so, the Kalapalo say, indicates their desire to move to another household.

Because most women are married, there is usually no ambiguity about their subsistence obligations. They are required to process the harvest of their husbands' fields (or those of their fathers and unmarried brothers) and to cook the fish and game which has been given them. During the manioc harvest, women of the same household assist one another with the preparation of manioc soup and flour, and similarly, they help one another collect and process piqui. Women also contribute to the food supply by gathering quantities of wild fruit, but this is considerably less important and only takes place during the few months of the rainy season when they are freed from manioc and piqui processing chores.

During periods of scarcity, when fishing is difficult and the resources of manioc flour which have been stored during the dry season have run low, food distributions are still carefully made within the household. However, any food which does come into the house is jealously guarded from outsiders who, during these periods of scarcity, beg from persons other than those in their own households. At such times, the obligations of kinship—which include food sharing—are exploited fully, and the Kalapalo attempt to be included in food distributions in houses where they have such relationships. Usually household groups react to this situation by becoming more secretive about their food supply, restricting drastically those with whom they share. In contrast, during a time of repletion ostentatious displays of food gifts, both within the household and between kinsmen in different households, become frequent.

When a large catch of fish or a harvest of some rare item, such as corn, honey, or wild fruit, is brought publicly into the village by members of a particular household, every other group hurriedly sends its children to receive a share. A household is then obliged to give all the children who come a portion, regardless of their relationships to the donors. Unlike the sharing between kinsmen, where adults freely solicit food from one another without embarrassment, it is considered unseemly for adults to ask for food under such circumstances, that is, "without reason." Because it is considered wrong to refuse food to children, it is permissible for them to ask for it when a household obviously has collected more than it can consume.

When a man is successful in fishing, he presents the group of casual loiterers in front of the *kuakutu* with some of his catch. Men who are married usually reserve part of their share and later return to their households where they distribute it among their wives and children. In this way, men who have not fished on a particular day receive food not only from persons in their own household groups who have, but also from fishermen of other groups. Similarly, a man who has killed several game birds will usually donate at least one to the men's group, sometimes all if the hunter himself is prohibited from eating them because of the extreme youth of his children.

Food is also distributed among women. When a large quantity of fish is boiled in a house and every member of the group has received a portion, the woman who has prepared the meal—normally the wife, sister, or mother of the fisherman—goes from house to house distributing the remainder to other women. Often, she is unable to present each woman of households other than her own with a portion, but she keeps track of those who have not received fish, and includes them in her subsequent distribution. On many occasions, these gifts are counted on by people in households where men have not been fishing that day or when they have been unsuccessful.

There is another kind of distribution which results in the circulation of food between households. This is payment given for the performance of ceremonies, donated by the men or women who sponsor them. Sponsors are mainly assisted in their accumulation of food payment by fellow household members, although they often must also draw upon the aid of relatives outside the group.

The distributions of food made in payment for important ceremonies (in other words, those performed several times a year or which involve the repeated performances of the entire village group for an extended period of time) are of such a quantity that each contributes substantially for several days to the subsistence of everyone. In some cases payment is made continuously throughout the year or for several months at a stretch, and under these circumstances the donations of food are actually necessary for survival by the recipients. For example, men or husbands of women who sponsor ceremonies which are continually performed throughout most of the year (as the *kagutu* or *ndufei*), or those who sponsor a number of ceremonies (and who are therefore responsible for several major food payments) are the only persons who plant corn, a critical subsistence item during the months of January and February. In 1967–1968 only five persons had corn fields. Similarly, kinsmen of a deceased village representative must pay their fellow villagers for the performance of a variety of ceremonies which continue throughout the year after the death. For this purpose, the deceased's relatives must accumulate vast amounts of piqui, depended upon during the rainy season.

So far I have spoken about food distributions which are explicitly identified with specific individuals or groups of kinsmen who are recognized to be the donors. There is another kind of ceremony, consisting solely in the production, redistribution, and consumption of food products, where the accumulation of food itself is treated as a collective ceremonial endeavor. For example, one such event known as *kaiju* ("capuchin monkey") was sponsored by Tufulei, a young man in whose house I was living. The evening before the ceremony, Tufulei walked to the center of the plaza and announced that the next day the men were to hunt monkeys. The following morning, men of each household group started off together in the direction of the forested area closest to their respective houses. Upon their return at the end of the day, they presented the monkeys they had killed to Tufulei, who had spent the afternoon preparing a large grill inside his house, upon which to roast the meat. The hunt that day was extremely successful, for with one exception, all the households had managed to kill from four to six monkeys. After cleaning the animals, Tufulei gave them to his wife Ambo, who placed them on the grill, before which she sat tending the fire. Toward evening, when all the men of Aifa had returned from hunting and the meat had been well cooked, Tufulei cut each carcass into several pieces. After distributing a good portion of the meat to the members of his own household, he brought the rest of it before the *kuakutu*, where men from other households were awaiting their share. Here Tufulei distributed a portion of meat to each man, according to the size of his respective family, after which he returned to his house. Similarly, the men who had just received food left for their own houses, where they gave part of their portions to their wives and children. This ended the ceremony.

During *kaiju*, game which had been originally killed by specific individuals and donated in concert by the men of specific household groups became undifferentiated and indistinguishable. The roasting of meat in the sponsor's house, the subsequent redistribution of the divided carcasses, and the final consumption of the animals by all members of the village in their respective houses took place in such a way that there was no means of distinguishing the game, let alone the cooked meat, in terms of who originally killed it and brought it into the village. There was, in other words, a lack of identification of food with individuals, and the final meal was considered the result of a communitywide endeavor from which everyone benefited.

To summarize, food distributions are an extremely important expression of solidarity among members of the Kalapalo village. Although food is normally shared between persons who are relatives, there also are formal mechanisms for sharing among nonrelatives. Furthermore, though a gift of food may on some occasions be insignificant in size, in other situations the well-being of the village as a whole may depend upon it.

VILLAGE SPECIALIZATION

One important symbol of a village's distinctiveness is the right of its members to manufacture a specialized commodity. Persons who marry into a village group may continue the specialty of their natal village, but do not teach their offspring this specialty. Similarly, these persons do not learn the specialty of their new village.

In some cases, a group's specialty can be associated with the unique occurrence of a natural resource in that village's traditional territory, but in other cases specialization takes the form of an intensive production for trade of something members of other groups manufacture for internal consumption only (see Table 2). Although both kinds of items are freely bought and sold by individuals, there are differences in how they are circulated in more public situations. Those things which are resource specialties—that is, based on territorial differences—are included in a set of objects used as social prestations, in other words, as markers of newly established social relationships. In contrast, those items which are production specialties—that is, intensively produced by particular villages—are not so used, but circulate most often in the *uluki* or intervillage trade ceremony (see Chapter 8). Because members of all village groups have access to every kind of specialty as a result of these methods of exchange, no group has a monopoly on the distribution of its own specialty, though it may have a monopoly on its production. Thus, no village group benefits economically from the right to produce a special item. For this reason, the prime significance of village specialization seems to lie in its value as a symbol of local group autonomy as it is expressed in territorial prerogatives.

TABLE 2. VILLAGE SPECIALIZATIONS AND THEIR MEANS OF CIRCULATION

Linguistic Group	Resource Specialties (social prestations)	Production Specialties (trade ceremony items)
Carib villages		
Kalapalo	belts and necklaces of *iñu* shell[1]	gourds
		piqui oil
Kuikuru	necklaces of *iñu* shell	gourds
Mïgiyapei	necklaces of *iñu* and *oïke* shell[2]	
	belts of *iñu* shell	
Tupi villages		
Kamaiura	hardwood bows	
Awïtï		cotton
Arawak villages[3]		
Waura	large cooking vessels and zoomorphic ceramics; ceremonial ceramics	urucu, salt
Mehinaku	zoomorphic vessels	cotton
Gê villages[4]		
Suyá (via Trumai)	stone axes	
Kayapo	red parrot tail feathers	
(Txukahamae group)		

[1] A land snail
[2] A water snail
[3] Note the Yawalipiti are not presently specialized.
[4] Although these Gê-speaking groups are not presently part of Upper Xingu society, their specializations are (or were) included in the system of exchange, and thus are indicated in the chart.

DEATH AND BURIAL

In addition to food sharing and the manufacture of specialized goods, members of a village group express solidarity by participating in a series of rituals which take place upon the death of one of their members.

When someone in the village dies, the entire community becomes closely involved in the funeral and its preparations. Kinsmen crowd into the house of the deceased, wailing the terms which mark their relationship to him and embracing the survivors who had lived with him most intimately. As the mourners sit on the ground weeping, nonkinsmen also enter the house to show their sympathy for the survivors and to assist, if asked, in preparing the corpse for burial. In contrast with the mourners, these persons stand near the doorways or sit on the hammocks slung inside the house. After several hours of wailing, the body is prepared for burial. Two persons of the same sex as the deceased wash the corpse, decorate it with ornaments found in the deceased's possession, and paint it with urucu. It is then placed in the hammock and covered with manioc processing mats "to keep the dirt off the face." Lastly, the hammock is wrapped around the body and tied securely. It is now ready for burial.

The grave is dug by nonrelatives in the center of the plaza,[4] after which the

[4] See Chapter 8 for differences in the burials of village representatives and persons who do not hold this status.

corpse is carried to the grave and lowered into place. The main mourners (kinsmen who had lived with the deceased) then ask to embrace the corpse for the last time, and are themselves lowered into the grave. The Kalapalo believe that the shadows of the living are embracing the shadow of the deceased, prior to the journey of the latter to the village of the dead. Cotton strands are removed from the deceased's ornaments by the gravediggers in response to requests from the mourners. Other less closely connected relatives who have earlier presented ornaments for decorating the corpse (if the deceased was found not to have had them himself) now request them back, for it is enough that the shadows of these objects have become attached to the body. Finally the gravediggers begin to fill in the hole. At the last moment, nonrelatives request dolls made from *kejite* leaves which they have placed on the corpse during the preparation for burial, together with soil from the grave itself. These are used in curing feverish children, who are washed with water in which dolls or dirt have been soaked.[5] After the grave has been completely filled in, most of the onlookers return to their houses while the kinsmen continue to wail over the grave until sunset.

The next morning these kinsmen again return to the grave carrying arrows which are shot into the air, signifying the movement of the dead person's shadow from the grave to the village of the dead. The shadows of these arrows are supposed to carry the shadow of the dead person to the sky. Later that day the spouse or a parent of the deceased burns the latter's personal possessions over the grave.

If the deceased was married, the surviving spouse has his or her hair cut off, close to the scalp, by a sibling of the dead person who is of the same sex as the spouse. After this ritual, the spouse must enter mourning seclusion, which is also true of a parent whose child has died, or a sibling who shared at least one filiative tie with the deceased. In any case, for one or two months the entire village group undergoes the obligation of mourning. During this time, no ceremonies are held, and people refrain from painting themselves and wearing ornaments. The continuous wailing of bereaved kinsmen, who are in complete retirement and who make use only of the areas of *ifutisu*, remind the villagers of their duty to refrain from jocularity and the decoration of their bodies.

The release of the village from this mourning period is formally proclaimed by the deceased's kinsmen through the senior village representative. In the morning, stools upon which the bereaved sit are set out in a line before the *kuakutu*. Specialists who are acquainted with songs for this occasion stand behind them, chanting verses which today are unintelligible to the Kalapalo.[6] When they are finished, the senior *anetu* selects individuals to wash the main mourners. These washers are usually nonkinsmen of the mourners, but persons related to the *anetu* himself. Men wash men, women wash women, and *anetaw* are supposed to wash *anetaw*.

The ritual of washing consists in the washer throwing a pot of water over the mourner, who then quickly rubs himself briskly as if to cleanse the body. When all

---

[5] There seems to be no concept of grave pollution whatsoever; on the contrary, certain kinds of contact such as the present one are considered beneficial to children.

[6] It is said these songs were invented by Bat, who sang them during a ceremony in the village of the birds. Beyond this, however, nothing more is known about their significance.

the mourners who have been seated in the plaza have been washed, the *anetaw* then directs the washers to other, less closely related kinsmen of the deceased who have been watching the event from the doorways of their houses. These persons must come out to the plaza and be washed as well. They in turn wash the original group of washers. Finally, any other members of the village group who care to can also ask to be washed. Ultimately, the majority of villagers participate in this ceremony. In return for being washed, they are obligated to publicly present payment to the washers, which is usually given in the form of arrows, beads, or feathers.

The entire ceremony, known simply as "washing" (*itsongitsa*), is designed to release the village from mourning. Washing is an event which prepares the Kalapalo for body painting. Thus the ceremony does not imply that pollution has resulted from contact with death, but rather that the villagers have not decorated themselves for a long period of time, and now wish to do so since the mourning period has been declared ended by the grieving kinsmen.

Village of the Dead

The Kalapalo believe a person's shadow travels upon death to a village located in the sky, far to the east near the point where the sun rises. After the body has been buried, that night the shadow visits the grieving family for the last time in their house and consumes food which the family has prepared for him. The next day he leaves the village and travels to the east (in the direction of the sunrise) until he reaches the sky. Still traveling east, the shadow approaches the entrance path to the village of the dead. Here he first encounters a side path leading to a smaller settlement. The shadows who live in this village always try to persuade the newly deceased to join them, and if the traveling shadow turns to look at them as they call to him, he is compelled to live in their village without ever seeing the main one.

If he is successful in avoiding this detour, the shadow then comes to a stream, over which are placed logs covered with a thick layer of moss. The shadow has difficulty walking over this slippery bridge and must be met by a deceased relative (frequently a parent or a sibling) who assists in the crossing. Finally, the shadow is conducted to the plaza of the village of the dead, where he is seated on a stool and presented to Sakufenu, out of whose body all men originally came. Sakufenu has one breast swollen with milk (some say she has only one breast, the other having been cut off by her creator, Kwatïŋï). The newly arrived shadow drinks from her breast or from a gourd dipper into which the milk has been squeezed. Then, a seclusion chamber is built, and the shadow enters for as long as it takes to grow strong again. During this period of isolation, the male shadows are visited by Sakufenu, who has sexual relations with them. Female shadows are visited by the men of the village. Finally, when the soul is strong once more, he or she joins the rest of the community in continual ceremonial dancing and singing. Sakufenu, rejecting the newly strengthened shadow, takes as her lover the next newly deceased man who arrives. The people of the village of the dead are able to spend all their time singing and dancing in ceremonies, for they do not have to cultivate manioc. In the center of the village is a large manioc silo, filled with flour, which never becomes empty. Although the village is very large, consisting of several concentric rings of houses, no one ever goes hungry because of this magical silo.

From time to time, Kalapalo who are still alive visit this village of the dead, but it is said that those who do so will soon die. The Kalapalo tell the following story of a shaman who had this experience.

We know about the village of the dead because Kofi's father, who was a great shaman, once visited it. He died a little [that is, became unconscious] one evening, and when he was alive again, he told us of how he traveled there and what he saw. The night he died, he heard someone calling his name, outside in the plaza where there were no people. He went out and saw a man decorated with red parrot feathers, sitting on a stool. Kofi's father was very much afraid, but the man said, "I am Taŋgi, I came here to take you to the village of the dead." "No," answered Kofi's father, "If I go with you then I will die." "You won't die," said Taŋgi. "I just want to show you the dead people and what they do." So they both went up to the sky. That is how Kofi's father knew about the village of the dead. When he came alive again [that is, regained consciousness], he did not die, but lived until the measles came.

A myth relates what happened to a woman whose husband died before her.

A widow cried all the time because she missed her husband. He, in the village of the dead, heard her and decided to come down to see her. When he came, he asked her to return with him to the village of the dead, and she agreed, but only for a short time. After staying with her husband for a while, she asked to return to her own village. But she lived only one more day when she returned. At night she rose from her hammock to urinate. As she crouched against the house wall, a spider bit her on the vagina, and she died. The spider was really her husband, who wanted her to return and live with him again.

5 / The opposition of men and women

The structure of Kalapalo village and household relations cannot be fully explained without reference to a fundamental cultural distinction—that between men and women. This opposition is not only conceptualized at the level of physiological, social, and economic relationships, but is manifested in the spatial arrangement of the village, the management of internal household affairs, and the community's treatment of the individual as a member of one or the other sex group.

In most societies the distinction between men and women is primarily focused on sexual differences defined in terms of physiological and morphological features. This commonly recognized opposition is usually further elaborated by criteria which refer to other, nonphysical distinctions. In some societies, for example, the sexual contrast is symbolized by a rigid physical separation wherein women live in one part of the settlement or household, men in another. Similarly, modes of dress, dietary practices, and economic divisions of labor are common means by which men and women are further marked and opposed.

In the Upper Xingu Basin, men and women go entirely naked, and sexual dimorphism is so obviously apparent as to be almost taken for granted as a means for distinguishing the sexes. Nonetheless, among the Kalapalo as elsewhere, several specific nonmorphological features are used to elaborate this opposition. One of the most important means by which men and women are distinguished is the complex of activities associated with what I will refer to as the "trumpet cult."[1]

THE KAGUTU

In the center of every Upper Xingu village stands a small building in which are kept hardwood trumpets (which the Kalapalo call *kagutu*[2]), played by men and forbidden to the sight of women on pain of mass rape. The *kuakutu*, as this house is called, is also used as a storehouse for certain ceremonial paraphernalia worn by men (although not necessarily avoided by women), but it is primarily a place where men congregate to gossip among themselves, to paint one another before a cere-

---

[1] I do not use the word "cult" to imply any special kind of ritual observance directed at some supernatural being or for some specific end, but merely to designate in a convenient way the complex of activities associated with ceremonial trumpets.

[2] The *kagutu* are large, heavy instruments which are usually played three at a time; to play them well requires considerable skill that is only developed through long practice.

mony, and to receive payment for ceremonial performances. Presence of the trumpets precludes women's entrance into the *kuakutu*, and at the same time justifies the designation of the plaza as "owned by men." When the trumpets are not stored in the *kuakutu*, as during periods of mourning, women sometimes enter, but only when there is a man inside with whom they must speak urgently. For example, when a Waura ceremonial messenger who did not speak Carib arrived at Aifa, he remained inside the *kuakutu* until the senior representative to whom he was required to convey the message had returned from fishing. A woman who could speak his language went to sit with him inside the *kuakutu*, where they gossiped for several hours.

In the Kalapalo village, several individuals are designated *kagutu oto*, by virtue of having been cured by the playing of trumpets during a severe illness (see Chapter 7 for more details concerning ceremonial curing). These persons are responsible for announcing when the trumpets are to be played, seeing that there are men to play them, keeping the *kuakutu* in repair, making payment to both players and specialists, and storing the trumpets in their houses when they cannot be played.[3] Because of these responsibilities, the sponsor must periodically give payments of food to a great many persons, and thus cultivates an enormous manioc garden with the assistance of all the men of the village.

One of the two *kagutu oto* in Aifa was Kaluene (son of Apihu, the senior village representative), who, in June, 1967, called for the assistance of the village in processing manioc which the men had planted for him the year before. For approximately two weeks, adults and children alike hurried at dawn to the large field in order to dig up as many roots as could be managed and return to the village before the *kagutu* began to sound in the plaza. As soon as everyone had returned from the field, the houses were shut from the front, and the women and girls retired to the rear outdoor area in order to process the harvest without seeing the trumpets. For the entire day, with a break at noon and one in the early afternoon when they bathed and drew water from the lake, the women worked at processing Kaluene's manioc. The men were either fishing or playing the trumpets in the plaza. At first, the women enjoyed the excitement of participating in this communal ceremony, but as the days passed and the work became tedious, they began to complain of the confinement. It was difficult for them to remain inside the house or behind it during the hottest time of the year, unable to bathe at their leisure or to engage in sexual liaisons on the periphery of the village.

When all the manioc was finally processed, the women gave the finest flour to Kaluene's wife Meku, keeping the by-products (soup and sun-dried mash) for themselves. Meku dried the flour on several mats placed on the ground in front of her house while her husband built a large silo inside for its eventual storage. Throughout the following year she was to use this flour for making manioc bread and *telisiñi*, which Kaluene would give from time to time to the men who played the trumpets.

The other *kagutu oto* in Aifa was Afualu, a woman who many years before had

---

[3] When a *kagutu oto* dies, the trumpets are buried with him. Later, new ones are made under the sponsorship of surviving *oto*.

been cured of a severe illness by the trumpets. Because she was unable actually to see the trumpets (she would be shown them, however, upon her deathbed), the responsibilities of her *oto* status were transferred to her husband, Sagama. In this way, the latter was also able to derive the prestige inherent in acting out this very important social commitment. In no way, however, was Sagama considered the real *kagutu oto*; this label was always applied to his wife.

Twice a year the *kagutu oto* is supposed to organize special fishing trips which last over a week, during which large quantities of fish are caught, dried, and stored in baskets. When these parties return to the village the trumpets are played and the women retire to their houses. Later the same day the houses are opened once more on the plaza side, and the fish are distributed to men and women alike in payment for their earlier assistance in harvesting the *oto*'s manioc garden.

For several reasons the *kagutu* can be considered a symbol of masculine distinctiveness and a means by which men are consciously opposed to, and separated from, women. Although men and women benefit equally from the *kagutu oto*'s organized activities, only men are allowed to participate in the special expeditions which prepare the manioc gardens, gather materials for building the *kuakutu*, and catch fish for the biannual food payments; finally, of course, only men may actually see the trumpets. Furthermore, although the playing of *kagutu* is thought to be vaguely beneficial to the community (but not any more so than most other cere-monies) and is definitely associated with vitality (hence played during a ritual beating of adolescents in puberty seclusion, but not played during a mourning period), there is no evidence to suggest they represent some esoteric ritual in which only men profit. In short, the fundamental significance of the "cult" activities seems to be that they are a means by which the opposed, yet necessary relationships between sexually defined groups are given content in the domain of village activities. The "trumpet cult" exists both at the village and intervillage levels, since all men of the Upper Xingu may observe, and even participate in, the associated ceremonies performed in any one local group. Thus, men of the Upper Xingu are united, regardless of village affiliation, by their ability to participate in the cult.

SPATIAL DISTINCTIONS

Because of the presence of the *kuakutu*, the Kalapalo say that men are the "owners" (*oto*) of the *fugombo* or central plaza. This area is normally shunned by women, not only when the *kagutu* are being played, but during other ceremonies in which men are the major participants; women usually watch these events from the doorways of their homes.

Women avoid the *fugombo* on nonceremonial occasions as well. Whenever they must go outdoors, they are almost always running or walking clustered together in groups, so close as to be touching one another's bodies. On their way to the lake to bathe or to other houses to visit, women literally run across the public area of the village. In part this avoidance of the *fugombo* is due, as I have indicated, to the *kuakutu*. It is also related to the designation of the *fugombo* as an avowedly public region, where the self is displayed openly and exhibitionistic behavior is permitted.

Since Kalapalo women are supposed to be continually *ifutisunda* (in a state of shyness), their presence in the *fugombo* is antithetical to their culturally defined psychological state. Unlike women, men have no shame in walking about the plaza, and in fact display the opposite kind of behavior. While in the *fugombo*, men appropriately joke and make ridiculous exhibition of themselves, for they are normally expected to participate in public display without embarrassment.

SEXUAL CONTACT AND POLLUTION FROM BODY FLUIDS

The opposition between men and women is also symbolized by criteria more obviously associated with physiological differences. Most important in this respect is a set of beliefs concerning pollution. The Kalapalo believe that sickness can result from contact with fluids specifically associated with men and with women. They consider seminal fluid, the body substance most closely associated with men, dangerously polluting for both men and women, especially when ejaculated during sexual intercourse. For this reason, sexual contact itself is believed to be somewhat dangerous, weakening the body and causing illness if performed excessively. Whereas men are especially jeopardized by seminal fluid loss, women who engage in excessively promiscuous relations may become seriously ill by seminal substance accumulated from different men, which, remaining uncongealed inside the womb, becomes "rotten" (*ñekugu*).[4]

Blood, especially the female substance (which may be either menstrual tissue or that discharged after birth), is especially polluting to men, but it may also harm women if it remains inside their bodies, resulting in disorders the Kalapalo associate with childbirth and menstruation. Menstrual blood in particular is the object of an extremely elaborate set of precautions which are taken during the production and consumption of food.

The majority of menstrual prohibitions center around the notion that contact with menstrual blood is disgusting. This kind of pollution is particularly offensive to men, and the possibility, though remote, that such blood could become mixed with food is considered thoroughly revolting. Although Kalapalo men are preoccupied with this thought, menstrual blood is not considered especially *dangerous* and can only result in the weakening of men preparing for wrestling matches. Therefore, the prohibitions seem less concerned with preventing a serious calamity than with setting women apart from men within the household.

Because of this fear of menstrual pollution, a household's food supply is distributed in such a way as to minimize accidental contact with the polluting substance. Each household prepares almost daily a common stock of *telisiñi* and manioc bread for the use of unmarried men, those whose wives are menstruating, and small children. This food is kept on or near the central household platform and can be offered to visitors. In addition, each married woman is given a share of this common stock for her and her husband's exclusive use. Women are expected to restrict

---

[4] Seminal fluid donated by a single man during repeated sexual intercourse results in conception, it is believed.

themselves to this food. If it does become necessary for them to make use of the common stock left near the *ogo*, they must drink from a gourd dipper, rather than directly from the pot in which the *telisiñi* has been put, and must ask their husband or child to hand them a piece of the bread.

When a woman starts to menstruate, she must tell her husband and other women in her household, so that any communal food which has been prepared that day or left over from the day before will be thrown out.[5] All the manioc cakes, *kwigiku*, *intsene*, and *telisiñi*, including the men's share, are discarded and new food is prepared. During menstruation, in addition to these restrictions on processing and handling food, a woman is not allowed to draw water for household use, nor bathe while men are nearby. It is said that at one time women who were menstruating used special paths when going to bathe, so that men would avoid treading on their blood.

THE RITUAL OF CHILDBIRTH

As the "trumpet cult" rituals unite men in an exclusive social and intellectual set, regardless of their village or household affiliation, so the rituals of childbirth distinguish women as a special group. The public act of birth, during which all the women and girls present in a village are gathered together, forces a young person pregnant for the first time to join a community in which the most hidden secrets are revealed. The usual modesty of a Kalapalo woman, who consciously conceals her vulva at all times, becomes violently thwarted by her position during childbirth. As she lies straddled across her hammock, women facing her remark upon the progress of the birth, observing and commenting freely on the condition of her genitalia. At the same time, however, the new mother is given the utmost physical and psychological support by all the women of the village, whether they are her relatives or not.

A woman who is pregnant begins preparing for her child's birth several months in advance by making a new hammock. Tied above her old one, she will eventually use this for support during childbirth, and finally will sleep in it after her old one (upon which she has given birth) has been discarded. The new hammock is strung up near those of the future parents, and is an explicit symbol of an impending birth, being called *emukugu itigï*, "her child's hammock." During pregnancy no specific taboos fall upon either parent, but the woman is expected to crave "spicy" foods, especially wasp larvae, grasshoppers, and ants.

Childbirth takes place indoors, while the men of the mother's household wait outside in front of the *kuakutu*. First, the new hammock is placed above the mother's. Beneath her is a small pit dug into the house floor, to collect the fluids of birth as they drip through the hammock. An ingenious system is employed to aid the woman during labor, during which she is helped by experienced midwives. The woman half-lies in her old hammock, with her legs straddling it. Above her is

---

[5] Conveniently, these practices are less stringently followed during the rainy season when men do not wrestle and when food supplies are very low.

the new hammock which she grasps with both hands, and upon which she pulls to raise herself during labor. A woman at one side sits holding her around the chest, just under the breasts, and at the same time two others sit in such a way as to have their feet on top of those of the woman giving birth, while simultaneously they spread her knees with their hands. A fourth woman supports her head. In this way, force is exerted downwards by the midwives, so that the abdominal muscles receive most of the pressure and at the same time, the force of the mother pulling on the hammock to raise herself is prevented from dissipating outwards towards her limbs.

As the newborn child leaves the body, it is allowed to fall gently to the ground. The women at the mother's head and shoulders immediately pull her off the hammock and press at the abdomen to force the placenta out. Care is taken during birth to prevent the mother from pressing at her abdomen, which would cause the placenta to break. The child is ignored, and all attention is focused on removing the placenta. At this time, the mother is given a large quantity of one of several kinds of herbal infusions. After swallowing several quarts of the liquid, she forces it up to agitate the stomach and abdominal area, thus releasing any placental material which has remained inside her.[6]

Only after the placenta has been entirely removed does attention turn to the child. The umbilical cord is cut, the child washed, and the placenta and cord buried behind the house or underneath the mother's hammock. The mother and child now enter a period of seclusion during which the former continues to *tuw̨akita*, until "there is no blood in her stomach," a period of approximately one to three months. After this, she may or may not maintain a strict seclusion for up to a year, depending upon how many children she has already borne (see Chapter 6 for further details).

THE BOYS' EAR PIERCING RITUAL

Most Upper Xingu boys participate in an elaborate ritual during which their ears are pierced. This ritual, called *ipoñe* by the Kalapalo, is in one important respect very much like the *kagutu* "cult," for it establishes through exclusively male ceremonial activity a symbol by which men are differentiated from women.

The *ipoñe* is one of several rituals sponsored by village representatives (*anetaw*), the general features of which are described in Chapter 8. Here I will concentrate on a description of the sequence of events leading up to and including ear piercing itself.

The decision to hold an *ipoñe* is made by an *anetu* whose son has recently entered puberty seclusion, and is therefore of the proper age to have his ears pierced. The sponsor is assisted by non-*anetu* who have sons between the ages of six and nine; these boys are also participants in the ritual.[7] The difference in age between the young *anetu* and the rest of the group of boys is the central symbol by which the

---

[6] This practice is known as *tuw̨akita*, "watering."

[7] Some boys have their ears pierced shortly after leaving postpartum seclusion. They seem to be sons of men who are of relatively low status with respect to others in their own household group and who are unable or unwilling to take initiative in ceremonies (see Chapter 8).

former is made distinctive; several other symbols, which will be discussed shortly, also emphasize his *anetu* status.

Preparations for the *ipoñe* begin about two months before the event itself. Each day men and women of the village prepare their boys for the ordeal by singing and dancing with them and by applying an herbal infusion to their earlobes which is designed to prevent bleeding.[8] While these preliminary dances are held, the boys' fathers collect expensive ceramics with which to pay the ear piercers and the men who hold their sons during the ordeal. Two or three other village groups are asked to assist in the event. The *anetaw* from these groups who are also ear piercing specialists are requested to pierce the boys' ears, while younger men are assigned by the fathers to be "guardians" of their sons during the ritual. All of the men of the assistant groups help accumulate fish for distribution among themselves and the hosts, which is payment given by the fathers in return for the preliminary performances. Finally, a date is set for the *ipoñe*, and other village groups are invited to attend the events which immediately precede it. Only hosts and assistants actually attend the *ipoñe* itself, however.

On the first night, the members of each visiting group dance and sing around the boys as their fellow villagers have been doing for the past two months. This time, however, the boys are elaborately decorated with new cotton belts and shell collars, while the young *anetu* wears a yellow feather headdress. These objects seem heavy and cumbersome on the immature bodies of the initiates. Normally worn by adult men only, this awkward ornamentation seems to emphasize the ambivalent status of the boys. The mood, however, is one of excitement and joviality, as the visitors decorate themselves in costumes representing *itseke* clowns, and each group competes to sing the most beautifully—in Kalapalo terms, maintaining unison, rhythm and sonority.

On the second night, the eve of the *ipoñe*, the boys are undecorated, and only members of the host village perform the ear piercing songs. The solemnity of this event contrasts with the high spirits of the preceding night's dance. Now, *agifoñati* is applied in earnest, and the boys begin to look frightened. At dawn the singing ends, and the participants go to refresh themselves at the bathing place. In the Carib speaking villages, ear piercing then follows immediately; in other groups the ritual does not begin until shortly before noon.

Steps in the Ritual

1. The boys are seated on stools in front of the *kuakutu*. Before them are placed newly made mats (*tuafi*) normally used for storing feather ornaments. The "guardians" then proceed to cut the hair of the initiates, carefully placing the cuttings on the mats. The sponsoring *anetu* then collects the *tuafi* with the boys' hair inside and takes them to the forest surrounding the village, where he disposes of them.

2. On the sponsor's return, the fathers of the boys place portions of fish and

---

[8] It is interesting that this medicine, called *agifoñati* by the Kalapalo, is also used by women to *tuwakita* after childbirth, in order to release any bloody tissue which has been left in the womb. It is thus apparently associated with bleeding disorders in general.

Ipoñe. *Shamans (kneeling, facing boys) blow tobacco smoke on newly pierced ears at the end of the ear piercing ceremony. The* anetu *sponsor (man on right) proudly observes his son's apparent indifference to pain. Note the ear plugs and section of ear piercing stick in the mouth of the boy in foreground. (Mehinaku village)*

manioc bread before their sons, pointedly instructing them to share the food with the onlookers. After the initiates have distributed most of this, they are advised to eat some themselves, for henceforth they will be prohibited from eating fish for three months.

3. The boys are then instructed to go to the outskirts of the village and relieve themselves. They are cautioned not to stumble, lest their lives be shortened. This break in the ritual occurs "so they will not defecate during the ear piercing when they are very much afraid."

4. On their return, the boys are slowly led by their guardians to the sponsor's house. Shamans from the host group now begin to sing, and continue until the ear piercing itself. The group advances and retreats several times, until they finally reach the door of the sponsor's house. Here the boys are seated once more, facing the plaza, while a large cooking pot is brought from inside to provide soot for painting their bodies. The guardians then smear this soot in lines down the boys' arms and chest; the *anetu*'s son is also painted on his cheeks and temple.

5. After the cooking pot has been removed, a piece of plastic or other protective covering is placed on the ground in front of the boys. Then, the ceramics which their fathers will give to ear piercers and guardians (and which have been carefully concealed in the sponsor's house) are brought out. They are displayed for several minutes, then returned to the house.

6. The boys are once more led to their original seating place in front of the *kuakutu* for the climax of the ritual. The sponsor dons the ceremonial headdress worn by his son two nights before and, imitating the cry of the bird from which the dominant feathers of this headdress are taken (the oroupendola, an oriolelike bird), advances to his own house by hopping on one foot. There, from a hiding place high in the rafters he removes the ear piercing sticks. Carrying these in his hand, he hops back to the plaza.

7. The ear piercing sticks are distributed to the ear piercers by the sponsor. The specialists then sit in a circle in front of the boys, about two yards away, polishing the sticks and making certain the instruments have been properly made. Each stick is approximately five inches long and less than an inch in diameter. That used to pierce the *anetu*'s ears is of jaguar bone; the others are of wood. Each end is sharply pointed, while approximately one quarter of an inch from each tip is an indentation, made so that the ear piercer will be able to snap off a plug to be left in the boy's ear. While the sticks are being examined, the one held by the specialist who is to pierce the young *anetu*'s ears is rubbed by jaguar fur. Only *anetaw* are supposed to decorate themselves with jaguar fur; rubbing the ear piercing stick in this way thus seems to be a further emphasis of the boy's special status.

8. While the ear piercers are preparing their instruments, the guardians place themselves behind the boys, preparing to hold them during the operation. Each guardian sits behind a boy, who is clutched firmly under his arms while he crouches between the man's legs.

9. (See Figure 6) The preparation of the ear piercing sticks completed, the ear piercers line up facing the boys, each man holding a stick in his hand. The shamans increase the tempo and intensity of their chanting, until the sponsor gives a sign that the ear piercing should begin. The piercers rush suddenly at the boys. In less

Figure 6. Participants in ear piercing ritual (at stage just before piercing).

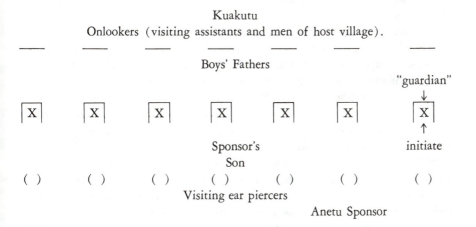

Kuakutu
Onlookers (visiting assistants and men of host village).

Boys' Fathers

"guardian"

Sponsor's
Son

initiate

Visiting ear piercers

Anetu Sponsor

than a minute, each man has jabbed the stick into both ears of his initiate, breaking off the prepared stubs and jamming the remaining center piece between the boy's clenched teeth to prevent him from crying. Almost immediately the ear piercers check one another's work to be sure it has been successful. The boys' fathers, who have been standing apprehensively behind their sons' guardians, now break into smiles. The host shamans then blow tobacco smoke on the boys' ears to ease the pain.

10. The boys are placed on the backs of their guardians, who carry them into the sponsor's house where a large seclusion chamber has been built. Here they remain isolated for the next three months. A wall of about eight feet is built of saplings and thatch, or of bamboo poles lashed together. A small opening leads from the seclusion chamber to the rest of the house. This kind of chamber is built not only for the ear piercing ritual, but for seclusion associated with widows and widowers, adolescents, and shamans.

11. For the first five days, the Kalapalo say, the boys in seclusion are not allowed to touch food or drink, nor may they leave their hammocks. After this initial fast, for the next month they may eat only wild fruits and *telisiñi*, together with manioc bread. This is a period of general fasting, during which flesh may not be eaten. From the second month on, they are allowed to eat anything except fish. At the end of the third month, they are sent off on a fishing expedition with their fathers and other adult men. On their return they are decorated and their adult names formally declared in public. From now on they are released from seclusion and permitted to return to their own housholds.

During ear piercing seclusion, the boys may not leave for any reason except to relieve themselves at night. Their mothers may not visit them, and only their fathers are allowed to present the food through an opening in the partition. Special attention is paid to the initiate's dreams, since these are thought to influence their futures. A boy who dreams of the song of the large toucan (*kafoko*) will become the manufacturer of the larger trumpets, and must be taken as an apprentice by the present *kagutu* manufacturer in his village. Similarly, one who dreams of the *fiji* (a smaller toucan) will make the smaller trumpets. Dreams of monsters are said to indicate a short life, and those who dream of arrows will be the victims of snake bite.

Two important symbols of adulthood are conferred upon the boys after ear piercing. The first, pierced ears, enables them in the future to wear toucan feather earrings, an important male ornament. The second is their acquisition of adult names. However, neither symbol implies that they have achieved adult *status*. Like the sons of low status men whose ears have been pierced almost at birth and who have been called by their adult names from infancy, the boys who have undergone *ipoñe* are still referred to as *itotokusïgï*, "little men" or "boys," rather than as *itoto*, "men." (The *anteu* in puberty seclusion is referred to by a term indicating his seclusion status.) They do not wear adult male ornaments because they have not yet acquired the skills to make them nor the wealth to purchase them. Furthermore, boys whose ears have been pierced do not have any ceremonial prerogatives over those of similar age but without pierced ears; both participate in ceremonies only as imitators of their elders, slightly more adept and no more significant than the tots who straggle behind them. Thus, *ipoñe* seems to be relatively insignificant as a *rite de passage*, for it does not involve a transition from one social status to another.

From the point of view of male–female oppositions, however, the *ipoñe* takes on special importance. During the early stages (1–8) of the ritual, women are allowed to watch from their doorways, but as the ear piercers line up before the initiates just before they pierce the boys' ears, the women are asked to enter their houses and shut the doors, for they are not permitted to see the initiates shed blood. Nor, after the *ipoñe* has ended, are they supposed to speak of the event which has been concealed from them, to speculate on whether the boys' ears have bled during the operation, or to see them during their seclusion. In connection with this, the prohibition on eating fish during the period of isolation should be remembered, for the ear piercing ceremony parallels in an interesting way the prohibitions surrounding women who are "bleeding." This is summarized in Table 3. In each instance, the shedder of blood is prevented from eating fish and from coming into contact with persons of the opposite sex.

Finally, as in the *kagutu* ceremonies, important social relationships are found in the context of sponsor–assistant complex. Here, the fathers of the boys are responsible for providing food payment to the persons who have assisted in the performance of the ceremony. The intervillage associations are equally significant, for the ceremony requires the active participation of several "foreign" groups in its most critical phases. This is a dominant feature of *anetu*-sponsored ceremonies, and will be therefore discussed at length in Chapter 8.

TABLE 3   SYMBOLS ASSOCIATED WITH "BLEEDING" RITUALS

Bleeding Ritual	Participants	Avoidances
a. Ear piercing	immature boys	women; fish
b. Menstruation	mature women	men; fish
c. Childbirth	mature women	men; fish

THE DEVELOPMENT OF SOCIAL AND ECONOMIC RESPONSIBILITY

From an early age, Kalapalo boys and girls are expected to be different both in their behavior and in the responsibilities ascribed to them. As soon as they are strong enough, girls are expected to help their mothers and older sisters with household and subsistence chores: drawing water, collecting firewood, making palm fiber string, spinning cotton, processing manioc and piqui, and caring for younger siblings. A girl is gradually taught the skills necessary for performing these and other tasks properly, so that she becomes economically important to the household a number of years before her first menstruation. By contrast, a boy is considered incapable of contributing to a household's welfare until he is able to cultivate a garden and to fish and hunt by himself away from the village. Although he is trained to shoot with bow and arrow, he spends most of his time in or very close to the village, except on those occasions when he is allowed to accompany his father on fishing trips. Only upon reaching puberty do boys begin to participate seriously in economic tasks.

PUBERTY SECLUSION

> Tomorrow let's go together to bathe.
> Tomorrow let's go together to bathe.
> Before dawn let's go together to bathe.
> My younger kinsman said to me.
> Tïfuniñu said to me, he did.
> The maned wolf's call I will imitate.
> The owl's call I will imitate.
> The maned wolf's call I will imitate.
> (women's song)

In order to "make them grow beautiful," the Kalapalo seclude their adolescents inside the communal houses for periods of several years. Puberty seclusion is characterized by isolation behind a barrier constructed inside the person's natal house, by which contact from all persons except parents, siblings, and shamans is normally precluded.

Persons who are secluded are supposed to be in a state of *ifutisu*, in the sense of retirement from public activity. Ideally, they must behave as if they did not exist, speaking in whispers only if necessary, refraining from appearing outside the barrier, and concealing themselves from the light of the sun and from eclipses (to prevent freckles). The period of seclusion is supposed to be a time of self-improvement, and thus adolescents are forced to submit to continual *fifitsa* (scraping with dogfish teeth) and *tuwąkita* for the purpose of making their bodies fat and strong. They also practice the manufacturing skills necessary in adulthood—such as, for a girl, hammock making, spinning cotton, and twining thread, and for a boy, making arrows, shell ornaments, and featherwork. Most of the time, however, the secluded adolescent grooms himself or gazes idly at the plaza through a hole in the thatch; especially after the first year, it can be a time of intense boredom only occasionally broken by a parent's insistence on teaching a particular craft. For this reason, two or even three young people of the same sex and from the same household may ask to live together in a single seclusion chamber.

A woman reminisced about puberty seclusion in the following way:

> After the seclusion wall was built by my father, my mother came to me with a great amount of cotton thread. She was making this cotton for me every day for a long time. She put this cotton around my ankles and my knees, very tightly, so that my legs swelled up. They were beautiful; they were very big. Then she took a scraper and scraped my legs. It was very painful, her scraping. I cried all the time. Every day she would come inside my seclusion chamber and scrape my legs, my arms, my buttocks. This is to make you beautiful, she said.

A girl in puberty seclusion, who is called *mazope*, must remain behind the barrier for three years, starting with her first menses. She may only exit publicly to dance during the *anetu*-sponsored ceremonies, after which she reenters. Thus a girl may normally be seen in public by her fellow villagers only three times during the course of her isolation. A boy (who is called *uŋalï*, "person being housed"), on the other hand, may remain in seclusion for as many as five or six years. However, his seclusion is broken frequently. In the first place, one of the important purposes of a boy's seclusion is to make him able to wrestle properly by building up his strength. He is therefore expected to engage in practice matches in his own village and is encouraged to travel to other villages when important ceremonies take place, so that he may wrestle on those occasions. Furthermore, a boy is expected to begin growing manioc, and must therefore exit at dusk to prepare his garden and plant the stalks. Finally, boys of puberty seclusion age are required to lead the men of their village group in certain kinds of ceremonial dances, and often leave their houses for this purpose. During puberty seclusion, therefore, a boy seriously begins his economic and social responsibilities, which during childhood were at best attenuated. In contrast, when a girl enters seclusion, she relinquishes her responsi-

Girls on their way to bathe with younger kinsmen.

bilities to the household and remains from a social and economic point of view entirely idle.

Male and female puberty seclusion differs in another way as well. A girl in seclusion is usually engaged to be married and is expected to receive her husband in order to be gradually initiated in sexual activities. However, she is considered not only of a proper age for sexual relations, but an especially beautiful person because of her light skin, corpulent body, and the presence of a definite waistline. The *mazope* is thus frequently visited by men other than her husband, whom she surreptitiously takes as lovers. These men must be unusually daring, for they can only enter the seclusion chamber at night, unseen by the girl's parents and husband, who sleep on the other side of the wall. A boy, in contrast to the *mazope*, is expected to be celibate during his seclusion, in keeping with the idea that sperm loss weakens the body. Thus a boy's parents attempt to keep him secluded and virgin as long as possible, in order that he become strong for wrestling. A boy finally is able to end his isolation by being seen more and more frequently in the plaza, and becoming the subject of scandalous liaisons with older women. Those men who are small and weak are pointed out as examples of recalcitrant adolescents who had sexual relations with too many women while they were still in puberty seclusion.

Puberty seclusion is in summary a different experience for young men and women. The former voluntarily begin the tasks associated with their social and economic responsibilities, yet are expected to refrain from sexual intercourse. The latter, in contrast, begin sexual experiences at the same time that they are temporarily released from economic responsibilities. Only upon exit from this long period of isolation do men and women, as married individuals, become fully adult members of their communities.

6 / The network of kinship and affinity

My mother didn't hold me in her arms when I was small.
She didn't feed me, she didn't give me her breast, the women say.

(*kwambï* song)

Upper Xingu society is marked by the absence of units defined in terms of a principle of descent, that is, a means by which individuals are classed together on the basis of their common relationship to an ancestor figure.[1] The composition of villages and household groups is, however, most directly influenced by relationships based on kinship and marriage ties. For this reason, it will be necessary to discuss in some detail how the Kalapalo define and differentiate these (and other) social ties, to specify what the obligations associated with them are, and to illustrate how they operate in the lives of individuals.

Almost all Kalapalo participate in an extensive system of kinship relationships, both within their own village and throughout the Upper Xingu Basin. These ties, together with those based upon marriage arrangements (affinal relationships), form a network which extends into every Upper Xingu village and which thus serves to unite individuals throughout the entire society.

THE RELATIONSHIP OF KINSHIP[2]

Kinship relationships are deemed the most important of all social ties by the Kalapalo. Considered permanent and unbreakable, they are expressed in terms of personal rights and obligations which persist throughout an individual's lifetime, and which exist even after death. The behavior kinsmen properly show one another is based upon *ifutisu*. In Chapter 2, I spoke of how the Kalapalo use this term to designate an ideal of "good" behavior (implying generosity, politeness, and a lack of public aggressiveness) for all who participate in Upper Xingu society. The term is also used in a more specific sense to refer to the ideal kinship relationship.

The importance of *ifutisu* as a model for behavior is that the Kalapalo speak of it in order to justify the formation of groups organized by kinsmen to perform

---

[1] This is a definition proposed by Schneider (1967).

[2] Much of this section has been taken from an article of mine concerned with the semantic analysis of Kalapalo kinship terminology (see Basso 1970).

74

specific activities, and appeal to *ifutisu* when they wish to obtain assistance from a specific person who happens to be a kinsman. Thus, on the basis of *ifutisu* they hold for one another, kinsmen can be expected to assist when called upon to participate in difficult tasks such as building a house, preparing and planting gardens, manufacturing a hammock, cooking food for ceremonial distribution, or making a new canoe. Kinsmen should also support one another verbally and should refrain from public criticism of each other. They are expected to mourn at funerals and to revenge a kinsman's death if it has been diagnosed as a witchcraft murder. Finally, *ifutisu* serves to justify requests for marriage partners. Thus, kinship for a Kalapalo is an all-pervasive bond which extends into virtually every area of his life: Religious, economic, political, and familial relationships are all deeply influenced by kinship. Although a person may have "friends" if he is without kinsmen, he is truly a social outcast.

The *Otomo* or Kindred Category

The Kalapalo speak of "kinsmen" in general by referring to the *otomo*. This is a category of persons who are considered related to a specific individual through ties based on two kinds of relationships: *filiation*, or the relationship of parent and child (see Schneider 1967), and *siblingship*, or the relationship of persons who share a filiative bond (common maternity or paternity, or both). Together, filiation and siblingship form a network of ties from which all individual kinship relationships can be worked out genealogically. A simple illustration can serve to demonstrate how this works.

Frequently I would ask an informant why he referred to a specific individual by a kinship term. The response was inevitably structured in the following way: "X's father was my father's brother, so I call X 'brother.'" The informant's answer contains what are to him the two significant features by which he defines his relationship to X: a tie of filiation (between X and his father) and a tie of siblingship (between X's father and informant's father). No matter how complex the association, the Kalapalo consistently use ties of siblingship and filiation as links in a chain justifying the relationship.

The Kalapalo *otomo* concept seems to conform to current anthropological use of the term *kindred*. A *kindred* is a category of persons defined in terms of some cognatic construct, that is, a principle of tracing relationships through either parent regardless of sex. Second, a kindred is usually defined as ego-centered: Persons classed in such a unit are considered related to a specific individual, not necessarily to one another (though some may be). In both respects, the Kalapalo *otomo* concept corresponds to the anthropologist's concept of the kindred.

Kalapalo Filiation

The Kalapalo distinguish maternal and paternal filiation by making use of different symbols in each case. These symbols are concepts which refer to what are, for the Kalapalo, crucial aspects of procreation. As symbols of filiation, they define the sexual relationship between parents as distinctive and different from other kinds of sexual relationships, for example, that between casual lovers (*intsoño ajo*).

The Kalapalo believe that conception occurs when repeated intercourse on the

LIBRARY
MOUNT ST. MARY'S
COLLEGE
EMMITSBURG, MARYLAND

part of a single man results in the accumulation of congealed seminal fluid inside a particular woman. A woman who has promiscuous intercourse with many men cannot become pregnant; rather, she is in danger of falling seriously ill. Similarly, a woman who only has sporadic intercourse with a single man cannot conceive, because she has not received enough seminal fluid.

A woman's children are sometimes referred to as *etijipïgï*, "her things which come out (of her)." This term refers to the symbol of filiation by which a woman is defined as "mother" (*isi*) of her "children" (*mukugu*), the fact of having given birth to them.

The symbol of paternal filiation—the relationship between a "father" (*isuwï*) and his "child" (*mukugu*)—is that particular aspect of sexual intercourse which the Kalapalo consider important in causing pregnancy. This is the repeated sexual act on the part of the man, corresponding with the idea that accumulated seminal fluid alone forms the embryo, later nourished by maternal substance. In short, paternity is determined by repeated sexual intercourse on the part of a particular man with a certain woman, whose maternity is defined by her having given birth to specific children.

Filiation can be established between parents who are *ajo*, "lovers," rather than legitimate spouses. There are several ways in which this putatively secret relationship becomes publicly recognized. First, a woman can declare formally who her lover is, thus demonstrating a positive conviction on her part. Second, women are publicly marked as *ajo* of a man upon his death. In this way, any children born to them during the period of mourning are considered the dead man's offspring, unless the woman declares otherwise.

When a married person dies, a sibling of the deceased cuts the hair of the surviving spouse. Following this ritual, the widow or widower enters strict seclusion for a year, upon the end of which he or she is free to remarry. If a widow in seclusion is found to be pregnant, the child is considered the offspring of her dead husband. In a similar fashion, several days after the widow enters seclusion, the man's lovers are publicly marked as possible bearers of his children by having their hair cut. The following is a description of one such incident.

On the day following Nakï's burial, his weeping siblings gather together in the house where their older sister Kaitsanaka lives, in order to begin the hair cutting ritual. Early that morning, Nakï's widow Ausa has had her hair completely shorn, and now lives hidden behind a seclusion barrier, seen only by her children and older brother. Kaitsanaka, an ugly, disheveled woman soon to die herself from an intestinal ailment that has for many years grossly distended her stomach, begins wailing: "My younger brother, my younger brother, he is no more." As she sits weeping, she is joined by two men. The older of these is Waiyepe, an aggressive man who has become notorious for his mistreatment of women during jealous fits. Waiyepe has been without a wife for years, and women rarely allow him to become their lover. He carries a pair of scissors which he beats against his thighs in time to his own wailing: "My older brother, my older brother." Nakï's youngest brother Epasa completes the trio. A shy boy only recently out of puberty seclusion, he appears the least controlled, and truly shocked by his brother's sudden death. In fact, his hair is cut closer to the scalp than that of any other mourner. Conspicuously absent from this group is Jagakagi, a married brother whose wife is a daughter of Apihu, one of the village leaders, and in whose house the couple lives. Jagakagi does not wish to participate in the hair cutting for fear of offending his dominant affine, whose kinswomen may in fact be involved. Indeed, the mood of the grieving siblings is one of subdued aggression, and the act of haircutting by Waiyepe will be abrupt and antagonistic.

As the three leave for the plaza, other of Nakï's kinsmen join in the wailing from their houses, until the village is filled with the sounds of mourning. Children follow the three siblings, curious to see the women's hair removed; adults remain at a distance, commenting on who will be asked to have her hair cut.

The trio first enter the house of Nakï's young fiancée, Akugi. She had been engaged to their brother for approximately six months, but is not yet in puberty seclusion. Her mother leads her forward to Waiyepe, who begins to shear off the child's hair, all the time embracing her and weeping. Kaitsaṇaka and Epasa sit by the doorway, wailing loudly. Akugi's mother, Nikumalu, begins to cry herself, recounting the events leading to her daughter's engagement, how she had given Nakï presents, and how, only a month before, he had first visited her daughter in their house. Finally, Waiyepe finishes the haircutting, and Akugi returns to her hammock without having spoken. The trio leave.

Nakï's siblings enter a second house, this time to cut the hair of his *ajo*, Agikuagï. Agikuagï has recently fled from her husband to marry another man, and the pair are discovered in her father's house sitting together in a hammock—too intimate a pose for such an occasion. Apparently Agikuagï had not had sexual relations with Nakï for some time, and she is reluctant to have her hair cut, but her father's wife and Waiyepe insist she go through with it. Now all the onlookers press into the doorway of the house, for they know the amount of hair removed is a sign of how strong her relationship was with the dead man. They also know that Waiyepe dislikes this woman, for she has repeatedly refused his advances while accepting those of his brothers. He clips her hair above her shoulders, indicating that the relationship was more than a casual affair. Agikuagï's husband has shown no emotion during this ritual. When it is ended, the couple turn their back on Nakï's brother and sister, and the latter leave.

For a third time, the three mourners seek out Nakï's *ajo*. As they walk into the next house, a woman is seen fleeing out the rear door, hurridly walking in the direction of the bathing area. This is Kuna, also said to be Nakï's lover. After waiting for a few minutes, their wails increasing in intensity all the while, Kuna's sister-in-law reminds them the woman was only *intsoño ajo*, "little lover," and that her relationship with Nakï was over some time before he died. Kaitsaṇaka urges the two men to leave, and the three walk out to the center of the plaza to the grave. Here they weep until sundown, when they return to their houses.

In this incident, two women, including a prepubsecent girl, Akugi, are publicly marked as being possible mothers of the dead man's children. The ritual of haircutting marks the possible sexual relationships which they had with the man in the past. The more hair removed, the stronger the relationship. After the haircutting, these women are required to remain secluded from public affairs, though they are able to leave their houses to perform necessary chores. If any have a child during the year of mourning, it is considered to have been fathered by the dead man. Finally, they must all be publicly washed during the end-of-mourning ritual.

To summarize, the parents of a child need not be married to be formally declared its mother and father. What is important is the necessity of knowing who the parents are, since this is crucial for establishing the child's *otomo* relationships.

For the Kalapalo, filiation is a permanent relationship which cannot be broken or changed. Adoption is entirely absent, and although fosterage (by which a person is raised by someone other than his real parents) is common, the fact that persons may act in a way identical to real parents does not make them such in the Kalapalo view.

Kalapalo Siblingship

The Kalapalo see the *otomo* as a network of kinship ties—more specifically, as a series of linked sibling sets referred to as *ifisuandaw*, from which all individual kinship relations may be (potentially at least) reckoned genealogically. These sibling sets are defined in terms of common filiation; that is, they consist of individuals who have common paternity or common maternity, or both. *Ifisuandaw* sets which are linked together because of shared filiation can be considered a "generation." Note that this use of the word "generation" differs from that based on a definition in terms of relative age differences.

CATEGORIES OF KINSMEN AND KINSHIP RELATIONSHIPS

> My brothers don't help me, they fight with me.
> My cousins don't help me, they fight with me.
> Then, when I go to the plaza, they fight with me, the women say.
> (*kwambï* song)

Kalapalo kinship categories can be conveniently ordered into five generational levels, each representing a series of successively ascended or descended sibling sets, linked to one another on the basis of shared filiative ties. At each of four generational levels (+2, +1, 0, −1) a cover term can be used to refer to all *otomo* members at that level.[3] The cover term thus names the most inclusive category within a hierarchy of terms referring to kinsmen of a specific generation (see Figure 7). At more specific levels within a generation, wherein kinsmen are more finely distinguished, categories may be ordered in relatively deep (many levels) or shallow (few levels) hierarchies.

1. Alternate Generations (+2; −2). At the second ascending generation, that to which grandparents belong, categories of kinsmen are distinguished on the basis of sex: *isawpïgï* (men) and *initsu* (women) are the terms for these classes of kin. The male term in plural form, *isawpuaw*, can be used to speak of all kinsmen as a set in this generation, regardless of sex. At the −2 generation, that of grandchildren, only one category is distinguished. This is called *ifijaw*.

2. Ego's Generation: The *ifisuandaw*. One difficulty in understanding Kalapalo kinship terminology is the frequency of polysemy, or the occurrence of several ascribed meanings to a single term. The term *ifisuandaw* is one of these. Following Greenberg (1966) we can regard it as the "unmarked category" in a set. This means that the term labels both a general category and a more specific one; in the second instance, it is contrasted with at least one other specific category labeled by a separate term. To simplify the explanation at this point, I will enumerate the

---

[3] At a fifth generational level, −2, only one category exists.

various meanings, summarized in Table 4; the letters in the text correspond to those used in this table.

a. I have already shown how the term *ifisuandaw* can be used to refer to the sibling set, which is the "nuclear unit" of the kindred structure. In this sense, it refers to persons who share a filiative relationship. With reference to a member of ego's *ifisuandaw* set, a person may be termed *ifisuagï ekugu*, or "true" *ifisuagï*, to distinguish him from other kinds of *ifisuandaw* (referred to as *ifisuandaw otohongo*, "other *ifisuandaw*").

b. At the most general level, *ifisuandaw* refers to all of ego's kinsmen at his own generational level. We can say the term used in this sense contrasts with all others in the *otomo* when generational differences are specified.

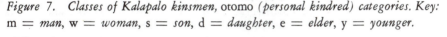

Figure 7. Classes of Kalapalo kinsmen, otomo *(personal kindred) categories. Key:* m = *man,* w = *woman,* s = *son,* d = *daughter,* e = *elder,* y = *younger.*

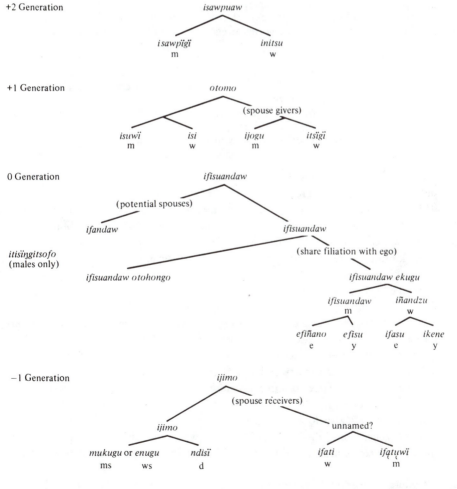

TABLE 4. SUMMARY OF IFISUANDAW DEFINITIONS

a. as "nuclear unit" of *otomo* (and referred to as *"ifisuandaw* set"), defined as persons with shared filiation; may appear as distinctive feature of categories at any generational level.

b. all kin of ego's generation.

c. all kin of ego's generation whose parents are same-sex *ifisuandaw* (by definition "a"); here, contrasted with *ifandaw*, who are "potential spouses."

d. for a male ego, all males of his *ifisuandaw* set, contrasted with all other male kin at 0 generation, who are called *itisïngitsofo*. These *ifisuandaw* may be distinguished from other members of category "c" by the auxiliary *ekugu*, meaning "real" or "strong."

c. *Ifisuandaw* can also refer to "nonmarriageable kinsmen" at ego's generation, in comparison with "marriageable kin," who are labeled *ifandaw* (*ifau*, singular). When this distinction is made, the speaker is referring to the potential for initiating or participating in an affinal relationship with ego (that is, "affinibility"). *Ifandaw* thus contrasts with *ifisuandaw* as "marriageable–unmarriageable" categories at ego's generation, but only when the notion of "affinibility" is made explicit. When kinsmen are being distinguished in terms of generational differences, *ifisuandaw*, in the sense of "kinsmen of ego's generation," is the only term available to the speaker. There are, however, more specific terms which distinguish *ifisuandaw* (in contrast to *ifandaw*) on the basis of sex and relative age.

d. A fourth use of the term *ifisuandaw* is to refer to males of a male ego's *ifisuandaw* set, that is, male siblings. Here, *ifisuandaw* is contrasted with (1) a category known as *itisïngitsofo*, which includes all other male kinsmen of ego's generation, and (2) the category *iñandzu*, or female siblings.

3. Adjacent Generations. At the +1 generation (that of ego's parents) same-sex siblings of ego's parents are distinguished from their opposite-sex siblings, resulting in four categories: *isi* (mother, mother's female siblings); *isuwï* (father, father's male siblings); *itsïgï* (*isuwï*'s female siblings); *ijogu* (*isi*'s male siblings). The latter two categories are defined by the Kalapalo as "potential affines"; that is, those kinsmen who can give spouses to ego—they are the parents of *ifandaw*, "potential spouses."

At the −1 generation (that of ego's children), offspring of ego's same-sex siblings are called by the same terms as ego's own children, *mukugu* or *enugu* for a male,[4] *ndisï* for a female). These categories are contrasted with those for offspring of ego's opposite-sex siblings, called *ifati* (female) and *ifatuwï* (male). The latter two categories are defined as "potential affines" of ego and his same-sex siblings, since they can marry children of those individuals.

In short, we are faced at three generational levels with a classificatory system which allows for two possible terminological sets. When speaking simply of kinds of "kinsmen," a Kalapalo will select terms which are primarily differentiated on the basis of generational distinctions. However, when referring to the potential for affinity between kinsmen, a Kalapalo will select from another set of terms. These

---

[4] According, respectively, to whether a man's son or woman's son is being referred to.

two principles of classification result in the possibility of applying separate labels to the same kinsmen.

Parent–Child Relationships

When a child is born, a seclusion wall is built around the parents' living space in order to conceal the child and mother from the rest of the household. Here they may remain for a period lasting as long as a year, the stringency of postpartem seclusion depending upon the number of children previously born to the woman. The seclusion wall is most carefully built, and the period of confinement most lengthy, after a woman gives birth for the first time. Seclusion upon the birth of second and third children is less strict, and finally is considered unnecessary for subsequent offspring.

Seclusion is primarily designed to benefit the newborn child, who the Kalapalo say is in danger of dying at any moment, "because it is weak." By concealing the child from the rest of the household group and from the outdoors, the parents are able to ensure its proper growth. Only when it is strong enough can it survive the dangers inherent in contacts with the outside world. Indeed, the child is regarded much as is any sick person, and aside from instances of curing when it shows symptoms of illness, is not the subject of special rituals other than seclusion itself.

Postpartum seclusion also is related to the mother's condition. The confinement of the mother after birth parallels in a more stringent fashion the retirement of women during their menstrual periods. Because "she is bleeding," the mother is enjoined not to eat "water creatures" (kaṇa) and subsists on what monkey meat her husband can provide, together with vegetable food. As mentioned in Chapter 2, the flesh of birds is prohibited to both parents because eating it is said to cause weakness and brittle bones in young children. In fact, the parents may not eat birds until the child has been weaned, which usually occurs when it is four years old.

To aid the quick flow of blood from her body and to make her strong again, the Kalapalo mother frequently practices tuwąkita with various kinds of herbal infusions. She refrains from bathing in public, preparing food, and walking about the house. In short, her behavior is but an extreme expression of menstrual taboos.

Although the father also sleeps inside the seclusion chamber, unlike the mother he is free to appear in public. The restrictions imposed upon him are few, and in the main are consequences of his having a sick relative (that is, his child). He does not paint himself when the other men of the village decorate before dancing, nor does he fish. The only explicitly paternal taboo is that he is enjoined from killing jaguars if his newborn child is a son. Even if one is encountered in the forest, it would endanger the boy's life for the father to make the kill.

The length of seclusion depends upon two variables. First, the Kalapalo mother must note the end of postpartum bleeding. She cannot resume her normal household routine if it has not ceased. Second, the progress of the child is assessed. When it appears to be growing and becoming strong (often marked by the length of its hair), seclusion should be ended. Because of the differing influence of each of these variables in specific cases, seclusion can last in individual cases for a period falling somewhere within the range of three months to a year.

When the seclusion wall is torn down, the parents usually present their child to a grandparent of the same sex, who cuts its hair.[5] From this moment, the child is referred to by a set of names, and having received an identity, it is treated like a true member of the village group. The mother and father appear with it in public places and take it into houses other than their own to show to its relatives. If it should die, it is buried in the center of the plaza, just as any other member of the group. In contrast, stillborns, infants who die shortly after birth, and those who succumb during seclusion are buried beneath the mother's hammock inside the house.

Until the age of weaning, a child spends virtually all its time close to its mother. Throughout the first four years, it is the only infant whom she must care for; if the mother becomes pregnant, she mechanically induces abortion by violent pressure and blows on the abdominal region. When a child is able to walk alone in the village without fear, and can be safely left in the care of older siblings, the mother usually becomes pregnant once more.

A parent is expected to be both nurturer and teacher to his children. The most important task of the parents, especially the mother, during the early years (that is, before puberty seclusion) is to provide food for their offspring. As a child grows, it is particularly important that it be fed whenever it asks for something to eat, not only to keep it strong but to prevent it from becoming dissatisfied with its parents. The Kalapalo believe a child is capable of suicidal revenge after it has been denied food. Children who are rejected in this way are said to wander off into the forest, thereby attracting jaguars who devour them.

Children are believed to inherit the proclivities of their parents, be these good or bad, because the parents are supposed to teach their offspring the things they themselves specialize in. Thus a man who is expert in trumpet playing tries to teach his son this skill; a woman who knows many stories and songs passes these on to her daughter. Similarly, a man whose father was considered a witch is himself likely to be suspected of having been taught these nefarious skills, and the acts of a person who is a notorious thief may cause others to remember his parent as having committed similar crimes.

In their role of teacher, parents are frequently demanding and often chastise their young for misbehavior. Children are expected to perform assigned tasks without showing laziness, and their relationship with their parents is therefore one which to a certain extent implies their inferiority and submission. Although beating children is considered a serious offense, and almost never occurs among the Kalapalo, parents are not adverse to inflicting punishment in equally, if not more painful ways. Accepted means of punishment are particularly severe instances of practices normally designed to insure the health or good looks of the subject, like scraping with dog fish teeth (fifitsa), and eyebrow or eyelash plucking. Many Kalapalo carry scars on their bodies from severe fifitsa by an angry parent.

---

[5] Trimming the hair, together with public bathing and subsequent decoration of the body with urucu, are ritual activities associated with a person's exit from seclusion of any kind, be it a function of childbirth, puberty, mourning, or ear piercing. This sort of haircutting contrasts with more drastic measures (described earlier) taken by close kinsmen and spouses of a deceased person, whose hair may be completely shorn.

As children become older, they are more and more subject to parental wishes. When they reach adolescence, they must enter puberty seclusion, during which time the parents repeatedly encourage them to *tuwakita* and *fifitsa*. A girl is often married to someone she dislikes, whereas a boy becomes interested in sexual relations, yet is forced to remain celibate for several years. Indeed, a boy's final exit from puberty seclusion (marked by his destruction of the seclusion wall) is an act deliberately contrary to parental wishes, which would keep him confined as long as possible.

When informed of other peoples who beat their children, the Kalapalo express revulsion, but this should not be taken as an indication of leniency in child rearing, for such an impression would be illusory and misleading. In fact, Kalapalo parents are extremely authoritarian, enforcing modes of conduct which are often unpleasant, exacting physical punishment, and making decisions which go against the opinions and wishes of their offspring, even (as with the selection of spouses) decisions bearing upon some of the most critical matters of their lives.

The Sibling Relationship

Individuals who share at least one parent have by far the warmest, most relaxed relationships of all in this society. Kalapalo brothers and sisters maintain ties which correspond in several important respects with our own Western ideas of friendship. Siblings of the same sex are free to use one another's material possessions and are companions in subsistence activities and ceremonial performances. Siblings of opposite sex defend one another when abused by spouses, and concern themselves with the welfare of one another's children, who are in fact potential spouses. When siblings live in different villages, they frequently visit one another, and as mature adults often attempt to live together in a single household, or at least in the same village. The consistently authoritarian relationship of parents toward their children is lacking among older siblings. Whereas parents often punish their children for wrongdoings, older siblings can at best quietly suggest to their juniors that different behavior be exhibited in the future. Finally, the warm ties between siblings are often the basis for marriage exchanges wherein one set of siblings marries another set. Often two men who are both "friends" (*ato*) and "potential affines" (*ifandaw*) marry each others' sisters; such a relationship, combining ties of friendship, siblingship, affinity, and kinship, is especially strong.

Filiation and Siblingship in Relation to Illness

> Your daughter prohibits, Amanufa, Amanufa.
> Your daughter prohibits, Amanufa, Amanufa.
> You can't eat sting ray, Amanufa, Amanufa.
> You can't eat painted catfish, Amanufa, Amanufa.
> Your daughter prohibits, Amanufa, Amanufa.
> (women's song)

The ties of filiation and siblingship are especially marked during a person's illness, when parents and siblings refrain from eating *kaŋa* in order to make him well again. Even when the victim lives at a distance, the relevant kinsmen are expected to observe this taboo. For example, on one occasion during August, when many of the village groups in the Upper Xingu were seeking turtle eggs on the sandbanks of larger streams, several Kalapalo men happened upon a group of Kuikuru camped along the Culuene. Most of the latter were suffering from eye infections, including a woman whose brother lived with the Kalapalo. When the men returned to Aifa, they immediately went to Enumï, the brother of this woman and told him of his sister's illness. Enumï then refused to eat fish or turtle eggs for about a week, until he felt certain his sister was not dangerously ill.

Relationships between Potential Affines

In a ceremony known as *fagagi* ("sariema," a bird living on the *cerrado*) the relationship of "opposition" between *ifandaw* is vividly expressed. At the beginning of the event, men grease themselves liberally with a mixture of piqui oil and soot to make their bodies slippery and therefore difficult to grasp. Then, brothers helping brothers, they attack their *ifandaw* in an informal, friendly skirmish, during which there are no winners or losers and no individual tests of strength. The struggle between sets of brothers defined in a structural opposition (as a consequence of their *ifandaw* classification) is a symbolic illustration of the future struggle between them, that is, when a marriage bond is established and after their potential affinity is fulfilled. Upon the occasion of a marriage which establishes two sets of *ifandaw* in an *ifametigi* ("brother-in-law") relationship, the previously equal relationships will become sharply skewed, so that those brothers who "give" a sister to a man in the other set are clearly superior in the amount of *ifutisu* due them. However, which group will give and which will receive is always unclear. Thus the contest can be thought of as a ritual enactment of the ambiguity of "strength" (or *ifutisu*) which exists in the *ifandaw* relationship.

The concept of *ifandaw* "opposition" is also expressed in the practice of referring to a dancer who performs opposite another as *ifaų*. Here, the term for a potential affine is used to symbolize a structurally opposed relationship that is a consequence of the dance pattern. Similarly, certain species of animals who are much alike in appearance, yet slightly different in their plumage, morphology, or habitat, are called *ifandaw*.

In contrast with *ifandaw*, who are defined and symbolized as opposed, the relationships between other kinds of potential affines (*itsïgï, ijogu; ifati, ifatųwï*) are not so marked. Before a marriage takes place, these relationships are not characterized by any special rules of behavior beyond what must be displayed as a consequence of normal *ifutisu* between kinsmen. However, Kalapalo behave quite differently towards their opposite-sex siblings' children (*ifati, ifatųwï*) than towards the offspring of their same-sex siblings (*mukugu, enugu, ndisï*).

To begin with, there is an attitude of protection shown towards the child, especially in opposition to the parent who is brother- or sister-in-law. This is especially true when the other parent, sibling to ego, is dead. In such a situation a Kalapalo takes great interest in his *ifati* or *ifatųwï*, and can be said to represent the deceased parent's *otomo*, who are of course included in the child's *otomo*. Furthermore, *itsïgï* and *ijogu* are more tolerant of their *ifati* and *ifatųwï* than of their same-sex siblings' children. Men in particular comment frequently upon the beauty or good behavior of their *ifati* and *ifatuwï*, even in the face of contradictory evidence. Thus, from an early age opposite-sex siblings' children are more leniently treated and regarded than are same-sex siblings' children.

There is, then, a clear contrast between the attitudes and relationships of parents and those of "spouse givers" (*itsïgï* and *ijogu*) in Kalapalo culture. While the former are in their teacher roles authoritarian figures who exercise considerable command over their offspring's initiative, the latter respond to their "spouse receivers" in a tolerant, nonauthoritarian manner.

Relationships between Persons of Alternate Generations

The relationship between grandparents and grandchildren is also one of warm affection, but not much else. Few Kalapalo today, except infants, have grandparents, and their association with them is at best based upon memories.

The elderly are never accorded special respect solely because of their age, and persons who are not their kinsmen often make cruel jokes in their presence about their appearance, weakness, and feeble attempts to participate in village ceremonies. Only kinsmen treat the aged with any respect, but even this attitude is not so much one of special deference for old age, as respect for a kinsman. The elderly hold no special positions in ritual, solely on the basis of their age, nor are the most aged necessarily those with the most ceremonial or esoteric knowledge.

Naming

The giving of names is closely associated with kinship relationships, specifically those between sets of siblings who are grandparents, parents, and children. Naming among the Kalapalo is particularly important because it signifies that a child has kinsmen.

Every Kalapalo has two sets of inherited names, one set given by each parent. A set contains at least one "child" name and one "adult" name, although usually several names of each type are contained in a single set. The names are given, or rather, are begun to be used when the infant and mother exit from postpartum seclusion. In fact, because the names are inherited, people often know in advance (even before their marriages) of a set of names which they can bestow on their offspring. These are the names of their parents and parents' siblings, which form a reserve available for potential use.

Each parent gives to the child the names belonging to his own parent, according to the appropriate sex.[6] For example, a son is called by a set of names inherited from one of his paternal grandfathers (which are used by his father and father's *otomo*) and by another set inherited from one of his maternal grandfathers (used by his mother and mother's *otomo*). This is an idealized description of the system, however, which is in fact considerably more complicated.

Parents' relationships with persons who bear the same names as those that may be given to their children influence which names are actually bestowed. A person who is forbidden because of affinal connection to utter a certain name refrains

[6] Children's names are not generally distinguished according to sex, whereas adult names are.

from giving that name to his child. Similarly, the names of the dead (except when they are bestowed) are not supposed to be uttered, so that a child may not receive the same name as someone who has recently died.

Often a parent remembers the complete set of names which were held by his father and mother, and these are then passed down to the grandchildren. Sometimes, however, certain names are forgotten, or else become the subject of those taboos discussed above and are therefore not bestowable. Frequently, for these reasons, the names of a single individual are divided among several offspring, or several members of a sibling set will have their names bestowed on a single person. In a similar way, names can be given from the grandparental sibling set to the set of grandchildren without an exact correspondence between donor and recipient. Thus, the ideal rule of name bestowal from grandparents to grandchild is often distorted.

When a person dies, his names are not used again until the next appropriate generation; a name is thus "used up" for the sibling set of the person who has died holding it. In some situations, a parent is unable to find available names for his child, and is forced to invent one. In one instance this occurred when Taguwaki had no available children's names for his son, because several of his offspring had died, thus making all of his own father's child names useless. The name he invented was "Meloa," to commemorate something a pilot had once said to him in Kanugijafiti. Kafundzu, the boy's mother, although technically able to use her husband's made-up name (since it was not one by which her father-in-law had been called), almost always referred to her son by her own father's name, and usually avoided the name Taguwaki had given their child. In this way, she followed the rules of affinal name avoidance in treating the invented name as if it were that of her father-in-law, and thereby stressed her son's ties to her own kinsmen.

As indicated above, naming practices and affinal name avoidance are part of the same system. As the names of each donor are forbidden to the opposite spouse, each will call the child by the names he has given it, and will never mention the others. Similarly, as I noted earlier, if any of the available names happen to be those of a person's affines, they are avoided as well. This is not so unusual, given the small number of names in the system as a whole. In fact, individuals who are in the position of receiving names from one of the same set of siblings often are found being referred to by the same name because others were already taken by older kinsmen. Not only is the total set of names small, they cross linguistic lines as well, so that it is not unusual to find persons with the same names living in villages where different languages are spoken. This phenomenon results from the extensive network of kinship relationships which includes every Upper Xingu village.

Normally a person is called by the names appropriate to his life status. The child names are used until he passes through a certain life crisis. For boys, this is the ritual of ear piercing, which may occur at various ages up to and including that of puberty seclusion. Girls are called by child names until they exit from puberty seclusion, but normally it is only their parents who use their adult names shortly thereafter. Only when a young woman has a child of her own do most people begin to use her adult name.

Although they are freely spoken in most cases, names are commonly substituted for by terms which specify relationships between individuals, for example, kinship terms, terms of friendship, the set of composite terms which specify more formal relationships, and those used to refer to affines. When such a term can be easily used to designate an individual, it is substituted for his name. A name, then, is used when a person wishes to imply he has no relationship with the referent, or when there is in fact no such relationship. Similarly, persons who call adults by child names are stressing the informality of the situation in which they are speaking, together with the fact that they lack *ifutisu* (that is, a kinship or affinal relationship) for the person named.

Kinship and Affinity

Of all the classes of kin which comprise the *otomo*, only *ifandaw* are explicitly designated marriageable in terms of ego's *ifisuandaw* set. Marriage and sexual relationships with other kinds of kin is prohibited. Although Kalapalo sometimes wish to marry *ifandaw* in specific instances, marriage with an *ifau* is not an ideal kind of marriage, but rather the only kind permissible in the context of *otomo* relations. Put more simply, only *ifandaw* of all kinsmen are marriageable, but nonkinsmen may also be married.

Although kinship ties often are necessary for an individual's active participation in specific village and household groups, they are not sufficient reason for these associations, with the consequence that kinsmen are usually found widely scattered. Some of the important influences on residence include sorcery accusations and relationships of affinity with persons of considerable prestige. In each instance, kinship relationships are effectively disregarded because of more immediately important influences upon an individual's choice of residence. As a result, it is not uncommon to find kinsmen living in different villages and even speaking mutually unintelligible languages. However, because they are kinsmen, they can establish and justify contact with one another, and thus can appropriately ask for spouses.

Although it may be desirable for a person to marry within his own village group (for example, to avoid an alliance with someone whose language he does not speak), the Kalapalo do not specify that he must do so, and many persons marry out of their natal villages. The presence of *ifandaw* of appropriate sex and age in other villages often preclude individuals from remaining at home, since first marriages are arranged by parents who take advantage of kinship obligations to obtain spouses for their children. "Potential affinity," then, is expressed in terms of specific categories of kin: *ifandaw,* who are "potential spouses"; *itsïgï* and *ijogu,* "potential spouse givers," and *ifati, ifatuwï,* "potential spouse receivers." However, it is not expressed in terms of units (either categories of kin or local groups) defined as exogamous or endogamous. Indeed, given these marriage principles, "endogamy" and "exogamy" are meaningless, and obscure the many possibilities open to a Kalapalo seeking a spouse.

MARRIAGE AND AFFINAL RELATIONSHIPS

Kalapalo marriage takes one of two forms. First or "arranged" marriages involve a girl engaged before puberty and an older man, who may already be married. This type of marriage is marked by the giving of bridewealth, which is payment made to the girl's parents and their siblings by the parents of the future husband. The other form of marriage, which involves people who are lovers, takes place after the death or divorce of a spouse. In such situations, personal preferences (often in the face of disapproval by kinsmen) take precedence, and the persons who marry are always adult.

The Kalapalo seek to establish "arranged" marriages on the basis of previous relationships of kinship or affinity. Indeed, the very fact of having such relationships with individuals who have offspring of the appropriate sex and age enable Kalapalo to make formal marriage requests, either for themselves or for their children. When nonkinsmen are available, they can also be sought out as spouses, but it is difficult for Kalapalo to find such persons who do not have obligations to their own relatives. Hence, the majority of "arranged" marriages are alliances between persons who have prior kinship and/or affinal connections.

Brother–Sister Exchange Marriage

The Kalapalo consider marriage between two brother–sister pairs ("brother–sister exchange marriage") a highly desirable practice, because the powerful sibling relationship can be continued in the same household throughout adulthood. Such marriages are not agreed upon at the same time, however, and are in a real sense fortuitous arrangements. This is because they usually depend upon the death or divorce of at least one prior spouse. The case illustrated in Figure 8 is typical of such a situation.

Ugaki was first married to a real brother of the wife of one of her *ifisuandaw*. Ugaki's relationship with this man lasted until his death, by which time they had had four children. After her husband's death, she remarried, this time to the younger brother of her own brother's wife. Kafutani had been Ugaki's *ajo* for some time during her widowhood, although he is considerably younger than she. The two couples, Ugaki and Kafutani, and Taguwaki and Kafundzu presently form the "core" of one of the larger households in Aifa.

To single out "brother–sister exchange" as a special kind of marriage arrangement is misleading, however. It is, in fact, one form of a general marriage practice in which a group of kinsmen (in Kalapalo kinship classification, *ifisuandaw*) are allied with a second such group through marriage.[7] Brother–sister exchange is indeed a stated ideal, an arrangement the Kalapalo consider particularly worthwhile, but it is only one of a number of means by which alliances between kinsmen are reinforced.

---

[7] Claude Lévi-Strauss (1969) calls levirate, sororate, and avuncular marriage practices "privileged unions," since they "presuppose other modes of marriage on to which they themselves are grafted" (p. 120). The same may be said for "brother–sister exchange."

In Aifa, the majority of marriages repeated previously contracted affinal alliances, though not necessarily of persons within the same generation, nor always with the exchange of persons of the same sex (for example, "sisters"). Examples of these various affinal exchanges are given below. In Figure 9, two brothers (a, b) married two sets of closely related women (1, 2; 3, 4), these sets being in a mother–daughter relationship. All these women had lived in the same household before marriage. In each case, the brothers contracted polygynous marriages with two sisters.

In the second example, seen in Figure 10, the elder sister of Tetekuegï had been married to one of a pair of brothers. Tetekuegï was later married to the daughter of the second brother, who was the elder of the pair. Thus a brother–sister exchange occurred together with a skewed generational alliance.

What these genealogical illustrations indicate is the significance of exchanges of kin repeated between two groups. This often occurs within a single generation, but can also take place for several consecutive generations. Thus, either through the exchange of spouses, or the multiple presentation of spouses from one set of kin to another, two groups of kinsmen are defined as temporarily allied through marriage. (The Kalapalo do not see themselves as exchanging women but rather

Figure 8. An example of brother–sister exchange marriage.

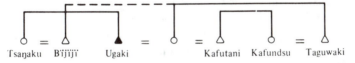

Tsaŋaku   Bïjïjï   Ugaki   Kafutani   Kafundsu   Taguwaki

Figure 9. Multiple marriage exchange between households.

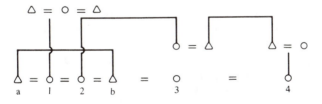

a   1   2   b   3   4

Figure 10. Multiple marriage exchange across generations.

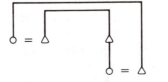

marriage partners of either sex). These groups, however, are related on the basis of specific and individual alliances only, rather than in terms of some generalized definition by which they are conceived as "spouse-exchangers" before the fact. Thus Kalapalo kin groups which give each other marriage partners are distinctively different from units or categories defined in terms of such exchange, such as is often the case with clans, lineages, and moieties.

The Marriage Arrangement

Negotiations between a girl's parents and those of the boy take place without fanfare, but only after considerable indication that each side is in agreement with the match. Because the participants are often kinsmen, their relationship of *ifutisu* does not permit them to deny the request, at least openly, and neutral parties are commonly sent to discreetly question the opposite side. The marriage proposal is made most often by the boy's parents to the relatives of the girl, not infrequently without the knowledge of the future spouses. After polite greetings, the proper opening remark is, *"aɲi endisï umukugu kai?"* ("is your daughter with my son?"), and if the match is agreeable, the answer is simply, *"ohsï"* ("it is permissible"). From the time the agreement is made, affinal attitudes are expected to be in effect between the future spouses, their spouse's siblings, and spouse's parents.

Two stories whose central figures are men presently living at Aifa illustrate the etiquette involved in these delicate marriage arrangements.

The main character in the first case is Enumï, a young man approximately 23 years old. Enumï's first wife, Upo, (his *ifaụ*) died just after she exited puberty seclusion, and as Enumï was still very young and frustrated by his inability to take revenge upon the person who was accused of murdering her by witchcraft, he left the Kalapalo village to work with some Brazilians in a settlement outside the Park.

Upon his return from the Brazilian settlement, Enumï became engaged to Upo's younger sister, Kaitsuka. Enumï refused to marry this woman, however, because Kaitsuka had on several occasions refused his seductive advances during her puberty seclusion. On the day of the marriage, when Kaitsuka went to Enumï's house to remove his hammock (as is customary), he fled out the back door, leaving her crying in the doorway. His kinsmen, including his mother's sister, who had raised him after his mother's death, had continued with the arrangements for their marriage even though he repeatedly asked her to end the alliance. Kaitsuka subsequently married a brother of Enumï, but divorced him several months later, and eventually settled down with a nonkinsman.

One of Enumï's many *ajo* was the divorced daughter of a man (Afinitse) in the Yawalipiti village, whom he classed as *ijogu*. This man frequently would invite Enumï to his village when they met at the Post, and would instruct his daughter (Enumï's *ifaụ*) to prepare special meals when the young man visited. Soon it became evident that Afinitse wished the two to marry. Finally he openly asked Enumï to marry his daughter and repeated this request several times when Enumï hesitated to give an answer. Each time, Enumï was extremely embarrassed, replying that the proper person to speak with was his mother, Ugaki. However, he himself said nothing to his kinswoman. Finally, the would-be father-in-law became angry and began to talk about Enumï's refusal and lack of *ifutisu*. Ugaki eventually found out through gossip of the situation and berated Enumï for not telling her of his *ijogu's* request. Enumï himself pointed out to me that the impropriety of his kinsman's making the marriage proposal directly was the reason for his not continuing his *ajo* relationship with the girl, but he also implied that he did not wish to accept a woman who had been previously divorced several times by men who had found her promiscuous.

Eventually, an arrangement was made by Ugaki for Enumï to marry the young daughter of one of her *ifisuandaw*. This request was made completely without Enumï's knowledge (perhaps because of his previous experiences). One day, talking with another kinsman, he joked about his future father-in-law, mentioning the man's name. Waiyepe reprimanded him, saying that he was speaking of his father-in-law, for whom he should have great respect. Although Enumï was at the time annoyed with Ugaki for not telling him about the engagement, he is now pleased with it, because it has been five years since he has had a wife.

The second case is that of a man K., perhaps nearly 30 years old. K. had been divorced at least twice, and was engaged when I met him to a prepubescent girl in the Mïgiyapei village. On several occasions, after he had formally established residence in his father-in-law's village, K. returned to Aifa, where he would stay for a week or more. Finally it came out that his relationship with his father-in-law was not going well. According to K., despite his willingness to work, he was always accused of laziness, of not providing the father-in-law's household with sufficient fish and firewood. After several months of this, the marriage arrangement was cancelled but the reasons given to the son-in-law did not coincide with those which came up during village gossip. Many people in Aifa said the girl had in fact refused to marry K. because he was old and ugly. Her father was said to have used the excuse of K.'s alleged laziness to get rid of him.

Categories of Affines

Persons who become affines (*ago*), be they kinsmen or not, are classified according to a system which distinguishes three specific kinds of relationships. Affines of adjacent generations—that is, spouse's parents and offspring's spouses—are classed as *ifotisofo*, a term which seems to mean "the one for whom there is continual *ifutisu*." *Ifotisofo* are always in a strong *ifutisu* relationship, unable to mention each other's names and avoiding one another's presence whenever possible. Siblings of one's spouse are differentiated according to sex; *itsahene* refers to same-sex siblings of ego's spouse, and *ifametigï* to opposite-sex siblings of ego's spouse. *Itsahene* have the most relaxed relationship of all affines, for they are permitted to call one another by name, to joke freely, and to have sexual relations or marry. *Ifametigï* do not mention one another's names, and are more ambiguous in their day-to-day relationships, for they are often opposed by siblings whom they are obligated to defend. (See Basso 1973 for a more detailed discussion of *ifametigï* relationships). None of the three terms which mark affinal categories are ever uttered within hearing of affines of the speaker. The terms seem to be confined to contexts where the need arises to specify an affinal relationship to an ignorant listener. The most common instances of the use of these terms are (1) in myths, where the relationship rather than individual or personal identity is important (and protagonists are often unnamed), and (2) in explanations of the details of proper affinal behavior. These situations are commonly those in which adults are speaking, children listening. Hence terms labeling affinal categories are rarely heard spoken by the latter.

The special use of affinal terminology is based upon the intensely respectful relationship known as *ifutisu ekugu* which affines are expected to display towards one another. This relationship is marked by elaborate expressions of respect, including repeated gift exchange, the free offering of material and nonmaterial assistance, name and (sometimes) physical avoidance, and the prohibition on using affinal terminology within hearing of affines. One might say that the more openly a person uses such a term in public speech, the less *ifutisu ekugu* he can be judged to hold toward a listener who is his affine.

Relationships between *Ifotisofo*

When a man becomes engaged for the first time to a girl who has not yet reached puberty, he begins to perform a series of services for her household, especially directed at aiding her parents and siblings. These duties or "bride service" mark the newly created affinal relationship. The Kalapalo do not consider "bride service" as payment, but say the groom performs certain tasks for his affines because he has "great respect" (*ifutisu ekugu*) for them.

Upon learning of his engagement, the future husband formally presents to his parents-in-law a gift of finely cut and tied firewood, or fish of a particularly delicious species which he has caught the same day. This gift publicly marks the new relationship between them, and from this time on, special terms designating their engaged status are used to refer to the future spouses. Affinal classification has already been in effect, however, from the time the arrangements have been made.

Normally avoiding the house of his parents-in-law, the future son-in-law is expected to continue giving them presents of firewood and fish, especially when the men of his future bride's household are away on a special trip and are unable to provide the women with the same. Then, he is considered responsible for the well-being of his female affines. In addition to the continuous presentation of fish and firewood, special gifts—combs, manioc processing slats, and dresses[8]—are periodically made by the groom for his future wife and mother-in-law. In return, they present the groom from time to time with newly spun cotton thread and well prepared food, such as freshly made manioc bread and well flavored fish porridge. Sometime during the engagement, the mother-in-law, aided by her kinswomen, makes an especially fine hammock for her daughter's future husband.

Before the marriage itself takes place, the son-in-law must assist his in-laws with any arduous tasks they organize. During the season of manioc planting, for example, the son-in-law must help both his father-in-law and brothers-in-law with their new gardens. He is also expected to plant a field of his own and to help men of his

---

[8] It is customary for Kalapalo men to sew women's dresses; the future bridegroom receives cloth from his mother-in-law to make a dress for his fiancée. Because it is necessary for the man sewing a dress to fit the woman who will wear it, the groom's dressmaking provides the engaged couple with an opportunity to become familiar with each other. Because of the prohibition on intimacy between them, a son-in-law does not make dresses for his mother-in-

own household group if they request his labor. In exchange for his work in the fields, the son-in-law often receives an especially valuable present from his father-in-law, but this is usually presented by a brother-in-law acting as intermediary.

Men who have few kinsmen or none who control a household group in the village they are affiliated with, move permanently to the villages of their fathers-in-law, often well before the marriage ceremony itself. When such a move is considered permanent, the son-in-law plants a particularly large manioc garden. After the harvest his affines assist him in preparing an enormous quantity of manioc flour. When the work is completed, the son-in-law invites the men of his former village to come receive the flour. In a group, and fully decorated with urucu and feather ornaments, they carry the manioc back to their own village, where the son-in-law, who has returned with them, supervises its distribution to each household. The act signifies the fact that he has, in the words of one woman, "made a field in his father-in-law's village and will not return."

Ifotisofo are required to avoid each other's names and physical presence. A son-in-law is especially careful to avoid passing near his in-law's house, and they in turn tend to keep out of his way, especially if he is in a position where he is unable to move. For example, during a long trip, I was traveling in the canoe of Bïjïjï and his eldest wife, Kofoṇo, while Bïjïjï's son-in-law, Enumï, was helping to paddle a second canoe with Bïjïjï's young unmarried son. In this second canoe were Enumï's fiancée, and her mother, Bïjïjï's younger wife Tsaṇaku. The two canoes kept at great distances from each other most of the day, but when by chance they did pass—for example, in the early morning as the group set out from the previous night's camp—the father-in-law avoided speaking with his son-in-law, though there was conversation between him and everyone else. Enumï, in turn, did not hesitate to speak with his brother-in-law and me, though he avoided looking at or speaking to Bïjïjï.

Newly married spouses who live in the households of their parents-in-law must conform to a number of restrictive rules that delineate their subordinate affinal relationship. They are required to rise in the morning before everyone else and to sit quietly by their hammocks, facing away from their dominant affines, though the latter may sleep right next to them. At night, in-married spouses must not lie down before the rest of the group have apparently fallen asleep. During the day, they must not walk in front of their parents-in-law, engage them in eye contact, nor initiate conversation in their presence. When spoken to, the new household member must reply in a soft voice, indicating in these (as in other) circumstances that he or she is in a state of *ifutisunda*. These restrictions on behavior often lead the newly married spouse to seek relief in the house of his own parents or among friends and lovers. Thus, it is not uncommon to see a number of young men and women visiting together in a single household where they can relax unencumbered by affinal taboos.

Although men and women who must live with their parents-in-law are severely restricted in expressing their individuality before their affines, they are treated with great respect and consideration. For example, they are given larger quantities of food and served before most other residents of the household (the exceptions are the father-in-law and visitors). Inadvertent infringements of the avoidance rules are ignored, although this ignoring is much like that in our own polite society. The guilty person is extremely embarrassed and looks about to see if anyone has noticed, but no one seems to care, as if they wish to lessen his shame.

A young woman who has married into a household has a much more relaxed relationship with her mother-in-law than does an in-married son-in-law with his father-in-law. This is due to the continual contact between female affines during subsistence activities, particularly during the processing of manioc. As this is an occasion for considerable gossiping, the daughter-in-law who can provide information is encouraged to speak before her affines, though she continues to do so in a subdued voice and avoids joking with her mother-in-law.

A man's mother-in-law, in her position of chief preparer and distributor of food, often comes into contact with the son-in-law, and therefore has a certain amount of opportunity to quietly assess his needs. She seems to be more actively concerned with his welfare than anyone else in the household, and is particularly interested that her daughter treat him properly. The most extreme avoidance between *ifotisofo* takes place between a father-in-law and daughter-in-law. Because avoidance rules and lack of common tasks decrease opportunities for contact between them to the near-vanishing point, there is almost no communication ever between these two relatives.

The *ifutisu ekugu* relationship between *ifotisofo* remains strong even with increased age and familiarity. Although persons who have been *ifotisofo* for many years speak freely to one another, even engaging each other in ordinary conversation and joking, they are said to still have *ifutisu*. One young man, speaking of a relative who had been married at least eight years said, "Yahila, he has been with his father-in-law Bïjïji for a long time. There are three daughters already, but still Yahila has *ifutisu ekugu*." And Bïjïji himself, a man of approximately 45 years of age, with two elderly wives and a position of considerable prestige and influence in the village, still refused to utter the names of his fathers-in-law who were long deceased.

Relationships between *Ifametigï*

There is considerable evidence to suggest that brother-in-law/sister-in-law relationships can produce considerable tension. The seat of this tension lies in the strong bonds between siblings, including the desire to live together in the same village or households and the repugnance at seeing one's siblings abused by their spouses.

Unlike *ifotisofo* relationships, which in many respects are passive and characterized by little direct interaction because of avoidance rules, *ifametigï* must often participate together in subsistence and other tasks where they have to cooperate. In many Kalapalo myths, the *ifametigï* relationship is depicted as extremely disruptive, resulting in divorce, death, and transformation. One set of myths about a woman who performs miraculous acts illustrates the tension between *ifametigï* very nicely. Each story in the quartet begins with a stereotyped conversation, indicating that the woman is newly married and lives in her husband's village. She is thus a subservient affine. The following four separate situations then develop:

(a) It is during the dry season, and there is no fruit to eat. The woman's affines have been drinking manioc soup, of which they are beginning to tire. A sister-in-law says, "I want to drink piqui drink [intsene]," and the new wife answers, "I will bring you piqui drink." "But there is no fruit yet," the itsahene [husband's brother] answers. Then the woman went to get intsene. She cut a branch from the piqui tree and poured out the drink directly from it into a large pot. This was brought back to her affines, who drank it with much satisfaction. Every day the woman went out to get intsene. Finally, her ifametigï said, "I am tired of drinking piqui drink, make me some telisiñï [manioc drink]. The piqui doesn't taste good anymore." "Now I am ashamed, I am going away," the woman said.

(b) The woman's affines were eating boiled fish without salt [agafï]. Her ifametigï complained about this, so the woman went outside and urinated into a small pot. This she placed on the fire. She boiled the mixture, and then added it to the fish, which she gave to her affines. Every day, the new wife prepared the fish with urine, which her affines ate unknowingly, and thought very good. Then her itsahene saw her urinating into the pot. He told her sister-in-law. "Kïtsï! Don't eat this fish, my ifametigï has put urine in it," said the sister-in-law. The wife heard this and said, "Now I am ashamed, I will leave here."

(c) When the new wife and her husband went to bathe, the fish in the stream were killed as if with fish poison. Every time the woman entered the water, this would happen. Delighted, the people took the fish and ate them. For a long time, they lived on the fish the woman killed, and huge grills were made in all the houses. Finally the bathing area became choked with rotten fish, and the fetid smell kept people away, so that they could not draw water. Then the woman's sister-in-law said, "This is not a bathing area any more, she has killed too many fish. It is disgusting." The woman heard, and left the village.

(d) The woman took cotton, urucu, charcoal, and burity palm fiber [items normally used in hammock making], and burned them together in a pot. Then she took the ashes and rolled them into little balls, which she placed in her nostrils. From her nose she pulled out newly made hammocks of the type made with very closely twined cotton threads. She made one for her husband and one for each of his kinsmen. Then her sister-in-law said, "What kind of hammocks are these? They aren't made like real hammocks." The woman heard, and said she must leave.

The four miraculous acts of the new wife involve the manufacture of things which normally can only be produced through prolonged, difficult labor. The woman's affines are at first delighted with her gifts, but as the items are all in some way excessive, they soon object to them. The woman becomes ashamed because of the criticism of her sister-in-law and leaves both her husband and her affines. The husband, it will be noted, who is the person originally responsible for the relationship between the two antagonists, never appears in the stories.

The following myth tells about the ifametigï relationship from a man's point of view.

Origin of the Rainbow   Two men in an ifametigï relationship, together with the woman who has caused this relationship [the sister of one, the wife of the other] go to the forest to collect honey. The bees' nest is in a large hole near the top of a tall tree, and the younger brother-in-law climbs up to reach it, while his two companions wait below with a large pot into which he throws pieces of the honey comb. Suddenly, the woman suggests they leave the man up in the tree, and the couple returns to their village. A tree toad comes to the rescue of the man in the tree and invites him to visit his home in the forest. There he tells the man how he can take revenge upon his disloyal relatives. The tree toad gives him two pieces of urucu. One is large and beautifully prepared, and he is instructed to give this to the couple who have deserted him. The other is small and dried up from age, but this he is cautioned to keep for himself.

The *ifametigi* returns to his village, where he confronts the guilty couple. He tells them he has found two pieces of urucu, and offers one to them. Greedily they choose the larger, newer one, leaving him the old piece. The three then begin to paint themselves, but as they do, the two who have deserted their relative begin to rise in the air until they ultimately become the rainbow and its reflection.

In this myth, it is not specifically important which *ifametigi* (sister's husband or wife's brother) goes into the tree and which one stays on the ground, nor is the listener told what the specific relationship of the woman is to either man. In any case, the couple on the ground has offended the man in the tree by abandoning him; furthermore, they display the reverse of generosity (that is, greed) by asking for the beautiful piece of urucu. In return, they become transformed into a kind of *itseke*, namely the rainbow. Without wishing to enter into an analysis of the other symbols within the myth (the high/low opposition, the importance of honey, and so forth), it will suffice here to say that, considered from a moral point of view, the myth graphically illustrates the opposite of proper (that is, *ifutisu*) behavior and in addition shows the potential for disruption inherent in a relationship in which a woman's loyalties are divided between her husband and brother.

Although they illustrate extreme forms of *ifametigi* conflict, these myths reflect normal tensions, as the following cases illustrate.

The relationship between Taguwaki and Kafutani, who lived together married to each other's sisters, was normally peaceful, and one of mutual cooperation. The only source of strain was the sisters themselves, for each brother felt it necessary to protect his sibling in the face of her husband's jealousy. Taguwaki, the older man, would occasionally disappear for a day or two, and finally it became obvious that he was visiting his *ajo* in the Mïgiyapei village. At first, Taguwaki's wife, Kafundzu, pretended to ignore these trips, but during one of his absences she took down her hammock and moved into her mother's house, taking her young son with her. When Taguwaki returned to Aifa, he was forced to ask Kafutani, his sister's husband (and wife's brother), to convince the woman to return. Kafutani believed his sister had acted properly, and was unwilling to intercede. A crisis was averted when Kafundzu returned voluntarily to her husband, having been persuaded to do so by her mother. Although Kafutani privately took the role of his sister's protector, his participation in the brother–sister exchange marriage prevented him from publicly criticizing his brother-in-law.

Enumï believed his sister's husband X. was a witch, for X. was believed to have killed several people in his own village, and had only escaped death by fleeing to a distant group. One morning, Enumï was informed that his brother-in-law was planning a visit to Aifa together with Enumï's sister. Although Enumï was delighted to be able to see his sister and her son again, he did not welcome the presence of a notorious witch in his household. However, when X. arrived, Enumï was forced to extend his hospitality to the older man, and could only vent his anger by leaving in the evening to chop wood, even though a large supply was already present in the house. After X. left Aifa Enumï continually remarked about his brother-in-law's brutality toward his sister, who had complained of being beaten for her numerous love affairs. Although it was clear to Enumï that his sister wanted to be divorced and was deliberately provoking her husband, he felt she was acting properly and that X. was unjustified in beating her.

Brothers-in-law who have previously established *ato* relationships and who are also kinsmen seem to be able to avoid hostility and maintain affectionate, mutually supportive contacts with one another. One example at Aifa was the relationship of Enumï and another of his brothers-in-law, Kusi (Bïjïjï's son). These men were both *ifandaw* and *ato* before Enumï became engaged to Kusi's sister. On those occasions when Bïjïjï was present, Enumï and Kusi maintained a formal relationship and called one another "brother-in-law." However, when they were alone or in informal situations, they spoke of one another as "friend." Enumï wanted his sister to divorce X. so that she could marry Kusi, which would have enabled the two couples to live together in a single household. Bïjïjï claimed that his son was too young to marry anyone, thus avoiding the issue. In fact, Kalapalo believe a witch will revenge himself on a divorced wife by killing any men who marry her.

Itsahene

Because *itsahene* are considered potential spouses, their relationship is considerably more relaxed and unambiguous than that of *ifametigï*. Often, *itsahene* are lovers, for they are considered appropriate sex partners. *Itsahene* marriage is believed to be particularly acceptable because it reinforces a prior relationship between the two groups of kinsmen who have already exchanged spouses.

The Marriage Ceremony

I would like now to turn to the Kalapalo marriage ceremony and to the significance of the marital tie for the participant groups of kinsmen.

An Upper Xingu wedding commonly takes place in conjunction with a ceremony associated with village representatives, such as *egitsu* (see Chapter 8), during which a number of Upper Xingu village groups are present. The event is thus a supremely public affair, establishing the new couple's relationship with and within, a particular village group. After the major ceremony itself has ended, the *mazope*, who has participated in the dancing, is led to the center of the plaza where she is seated on a mat or woman's seat made from split bamboo. Facing her is the groom. First, payment in the form of shell belts, shell necklaces, and toucan feather headdresses is given by the groom's parents and their siblings to the bride's parents and their siblings. Each person is supposed to receive one item. After payment has been made, the groom cuts the bangs of the girl, which have been allowed to grow over her face during seclusion. This marks the end of her confinement. She then goes into the house where he has been living and removes his hammock, retying it above her own in her father's house, thereby symbolizing the establishment of a new nuclear family within the communal household.

Although the Kalapalo refer to the bridewealth presented to the woman's kinsmen as "payment" (*fipïgï*), it is not necessary for legitimizing a marriage. Payment is rarely given to more than one or two persons related to the bride, and in some cases is not given at all. Such an accumulation of wealth is indeed hard to produce in a society where hoarding is looked upon with extreme disfavor. Furthermore, payment for the bride is supposed to be the product of the groom's labor rather than donations collected from kinsmen, although men try to buy the valuables in anticipation of the ceremony. During arguments a woman may criticize her husband for not having paid for her, and will thereby claim he is not really her husband. However, the Kalapalo say that such women are as equally married as those who have been paid for. Finally, payment for the bride should only be made during the wedding ceremony, and if it cannot be collected in time for this event, it apparently is never presented to the girl's parents. Nor should it be given to a girl's parents if she is no longer *mazope*. An incident in Aifa illustrates this clearly.

During her puberty seclusion, a young Kuikuru woman's engagement to a Kalapalo man was abruptly broken off by her father, ostensibly because the young man's estranged wife was about to return to him. The father-in-law claimed he did not want his daughter to be involved in a polygynous union. Several months later, after the daughter had been released from puberty seclusion, another Kalapalo man traveled to the Kuikuru for the purpose of obtaining the young woman for himself. He had the right to make this request, since his older sister was married to the girl's father's brother. After two months' bride-service, during which the young aspirant helped the Kuikuru man plant a manioc garden, the couple returned to Aifa. Shortly thereafter, the father-in-law appeared to claim his daughter once more, on the pretext that the husband was unsuitable. Again, the Kalapalo man returned to the Kuikuru village to ask for his wife. Before he left Aifa, however, he declared that he would present the older man with a shell belt he had just finished making. This statement provoked considerable consternation among his mother and sister, who reminded him that because the Kuikuru woman was no longer *mazope*, her father was not entitled to payment for her. When the couple once again returned to live in Aifa, the husband was chastized for having given bride wealth, but the father-in-law was the subject of even harsher words for having taken it.

Bridewealth itself is a symbol of the transfer of certain rights to the woman and her children to a special category of kinsmen, the *ifisuandaw* set of the groom. After marriage, these men have definite rights to her person, consider her children their kinsmen, and therefore must treat those children the way kinsmen should. Payment, then, marks but does not determine this transfer of rights.

Widow Remarriage

> When you leave seclusion, when you stop crying,
> When I stop crying, when I leave seclusion,
> Let's paint together, let's go outside together.
> We'll walk around together.
>
> (*kwambï* song)

The sequence of events connected with a widow's remarriage (*ifombïgï*) serve to stress the significance of the presentation of bridewealth during the marriage ceremony, and of the formal marriage arrangement itself.

When a woman exits from mourning seclusion, she is taken before the *kuakutu* by the man who originally cut her hair at the start of the period of her isolation. Surrounded by all the women of the village, she is washed and painted by those who are not themselves kin of the deceased. A female sibling of her dead husband also undergoes this ritual. The women paint the two sisters-in-law, cut their bangs, and place new belts around their waists. After this ritual is completed, a young and as yet unmarried man, also unrelated to the deceased, is asked to paint the widow's forehead.

This ceremony marks the release of the widow from mourning behaviour imposed by the dead man's kinsmen, especially his male siblings. Her obligations to the deceased are thus ended, though his brothers may extend a second marriage proposal to her parents. The significance of the forehead painting by an unrelated and unmarried young man is that other persons may also ask for her hand in marriage.

The successful suitor of a widow must ask her deceased husband's brothers for permission to marry her, because, as a consequence of the bridewealth originally paid to her parents by the dead man, these brothers have residual rights to her person. If the widow is still young and under the influence of her parents, she is often given to another brother in marriage, but if she is an adult and no longer associated with her natal household, she usually selects her new spouse without interference from her kin. Therefore, the brothers of a dead man can only expect to be allowed to make the first formal offer for his widow's hand, but are not assured that it will be accepted.

When the suitor goes before the brothers-in-law of his future wife, they are expected to agree to his request for permission to marry her. Upon the birth of their first child, the new husband must give expensive presents—such as large ceramic vessels and shell ornaments—to each of the brothers. This payment (sometimes made several years after the actual birth of a child) releases the woman from her obligations to the deceased's sibling set, and marks the fact that rights to her person and to children she will bear in the future are now established with her husband and his sibling set.

Divorce and Remarriage of *Ajo*

Divorces can occur at any time after the marriage arrangement has been settled, even before the marriage ceremony has taken place, that is, during the engagement period. However, because the severance of a marriage agreement conflicts with the ideals of *ifutisu* and *ifusitu ekugu* governing kinship and affinal relationships, the seriousness of breaking an engagement is very great. In three cases I observed, no contact was ever again made between the offender (that is, the side initiating the divorce) and the offended party, a difficult thing to achieve in a society which stresses formal visiting and amicable relations between all, even alleged enemies. Thus, a person wishing to disengage himself from an unwanted future spouse must initiate strong forms of protest in order to force his kinsmen to withdraw support for the alliance. The following story illustrates how repeated efforts must be made to convince one's kin and one's spouse of the desire for a divorce.

Kajagi and her husband Kamïlei, a couple about 23 years of age, had been married for more than six years. During this time, Kajagi had had two children, both of whom had died before their first year. It was said she had "drunk something" to prevent more children from being born after her second child died.

The couple lived in Kajagi's father's house, in which there also lived a bachelor who was Kajagi's *ajo*. This man, however, was only one of many lovers, for Kajagi was somewhat notorious for her continual faithlessness towards Kamïlei. However, Kamïlei was known to have only one lover, a divorced woman in Mïgiyapei, and was a man who could not manage to make himself personally attractive to other Kalapalo, perhaps because his father had been accused of sorcery by the Waura. He was often referred to, despite his long residence with the Kalapalo, as "that Waura." Kamïlei had no *ato* relationships and never took the initiative when the young men joked or danced together in the plaza.

One day, Kajagi disappeared from Aifa with Kofi, one of her bachelor *ajo*. She returned that evening, but refused to go to her husband. Instead, she hid in her lover's house, in the compartment of another young man who was soon to exit puberty seclusion. In the morning an older woman in the household persuaded her to return to Kamïlei, but Kajagi maintained her dislike of her husband and her desire to leave him.

Because Kamïlei was living in his father-in-law's house, he was often compelled to leave the village to fish and frequently returned with a large catch indicative of his skill and perseverence. Kajagi inevitably took advantage of her husband's absences to meet her lovers, especially Kanawa, the bachelor in her own household, who, it transpired, was seeking to marry her.

Kajagi could not flee to another household or village with Kanawa, because he was obliged to remain with his only kinsmen (who happened to live in her father's household). Thus, she was again forced to make quite explicit her desire to divorce Kamïlei. Throughout the week following her excursion with her *ajo*, Kamïlei repeatedly complained of his wife's refusal to cook the fish he brought her. Finally, one afternoon he returned from fishing to find Kajagi lying with Kanawa in her own hammock in full view of several household members. Kamïlei began to beat his wife with a piece of firewood, but realizing her father was present, left off and ran out of the house. For the next few days Kamïlei lived in another household, some of whose members were distant kinsmen. He eventually left to marry his *ajo* in Mïgiyapei. Kajagi had finally succeeded in divorcing him. She immediately began acting as Kanawa's wife, cooking the fish he brought and processing the manioc in his fields. Kanawa in turn assisted her father during the building of his new house, and in other ways performed the tasks associated with bride service.

Effects of Depopulation on Marriage Practices

According to genealogies, most older men in the past had at least two wives, and it was not uncommon for some to have had three. The situation today is quite different. In Aifa there were only two cases of polygyny among the people who were still living. In the Upper Xingu villages as a whole, not more than eight or nine polygynous marriages existed.

One case of polyandry exists, among the Waura, which the Kalapalo consider amusing but not a matter for any considerable comment. This marriage, which has lasted for many years, includes a woman and two men who had been her lovers. As one Kalapalo woman said, "At first there was much fighting, everyone was yelling, but then they began to like it because there is always fish in that house." What she meant was that each man, obligated to provide food to his wife, at the same time fed her other husband, since the woman always shared with the husband who had not gone fishing that day. Thus, everyone was well provided for. Although this situation is unique, it is interesting that the system allows for such flexibility.[9]

Both polygyny and polyandry in the Upper Xingu seem to be two specific consequences of the general rules associated with marriage arrangements. The first is usually the result of formal alliances between two groups of kinsmen, since most of the plural marriages are between a man and several successively married *mazope*. The second situation, however, clearly resulted from the *ajo* relationships which the Waura woman had contracted with two men. Her unusual arrangement really is a consequence of the nature of second marriages, which are based on the personal choices of adults and their lovers.

The lower incidence of polygyny and the unusual situation in the Waura village can be explained by depopulation. Earlier in this section, I noted the "arranged" marriage relationship is characterized by age differences between husband and wife. This age difference is a function of puberty seclusion practices, in which girls are secluded at their first menses for about three seasonal cycles, and boys less stringently so but for a longer period of time, starting at a somewhat later age. In the case of two young persons marrying on exit from seclusion, the husband is typically at least five years older than his wife. During 1966–1968, there was some indication of a generational skewing because of increased age discrepancies between spouses. Women married early (as before) on exit from seclusion, but men had to wait longer because there were few available women. This was the result of an epidemic of measles which took place in 1954.

During this epidemic, a great many adults died in proportion to the total population, and thus very few children were born in that and subsequent years. This resulted in a lack of available women of ages 12–14 during 1966–1968. In the Kalapalo village, with a population of roughly 110 persons, there were no girls in puberty seclusion, and only at the end of my stay did two, about 10 years old, start to menstruate. In comparison, there were 19 young men between the approximate ages of 18 and 28 who had no wives. These men were young children or adolescents during the measles epidemic; women in their own age group had been married for several years. Normally, the men too would have been married, or at least engaged to a secluded girl. Although members of three defunct village groups were living with the Kalapalo, they could hardly provide spouses themselves. Of the four engaged men, three were engaged to young girls

---

[9] Although this case occurred in another village, the Kalapalo seemed to find it an acceptable arrangement and not a peculiarity of the Waura.

in other villages, whom they classed *ifandaw*. A number of the unengaged men repeatedly made trips to other village groups visiting kinsmen who might provide them with wives, and trying to persuade *ajo* to leave their husbands. One man, divorced several times in the past and long unmarried, went so far as to travel to the Suyá, a distant and culturally distinct group whose women are normally not married by the Upper Xingu villagers. In short, unmarried men were, in various ways, establishing or reinforcing relationships outside their village group with the aim of acquiring wives.

"SPOUSE," "LOVER," "FRIEND"

> Dear uncle, dear uncle, dear uncle,
> Dear uncle, dear uncle, dear uncle.
> Just now your son had intercourse with Aṇapeija.
> Your son had intercourse with Baggy Breasts.
>
> (women's song)

In Chapter 5, symbols signifying the opposition between men and women were discussed. As we saw, this distinction is made explicit not only in terms of physiological differences, but in the context of village and household activity as well.

Based on this fundamental cultural opposition, there are at least two specific kinds of activities jointly engaged in by men and women which the Kalapalo consider important. These are sexual intercourse and subsistence activities resulting in an economic division of labor. Together, these two activities serve to define special categories of male–female relationships, namely those of "spouse" (*iṇiso*) and "lover" (*ajo*).

Spouses and lovers are primarily defined as persons who are engaged in sexual relationships. Sexual relationships between men and women are especially important because they determine parenthood, which in turn, we saw, figures prominently as a means of establishing kinship ties. As I noted earlier, "parents" are not necessarily "spouses," and some Kalapalo trace kinship ties through fruitful lover relationships rather than through legitimate marriages.

The relationship of "spouse" is distinguished from that of "lover," however, on the basis of special mutually supportive subsistence activities which a husband and wife are expected to undertake publicly. The fact that a man and woman participate together in subsistence tasks and repeatedly and openly share food is the mark of a Kalapalo marriage.

One important symbol of a newly established marriage is the creation of a manioc garden by a man for a particular woman, who is responsible for harvesting it and who has exclusive rights to it. A wife, in turn, processes the manioc and corn from her husband's gardens and prepares several kinds of food from these cultigens. While he is away fishing for her, she is expected to make manioc soup and bread in anticipation of his success, for the ideal Kalapalo meal unites the fruits of the manioc harvest (which is women's labor) with the fish and game caught by men. Such is the importance of this mutual subsistence endeavor as a symbol of marriage, that a woman wishing to divorce her husband must indicate this by repeatedly refusing to prepare food for him with the manioc he has planted or with the fish he has caught. We saw this in the case of Kajagi's divorce from Kamïlei.

To summarize, the relationship of spouse is defined in terms of sexual intercourse and subsistence activities designed for mutual benefit. The sexual aspect, however, is a defining criterion not only of this relationship but of that between lovers as well.

Ajo relationships are almost universal in the Upper Xingu and among the Kalapalo in particular, for nearly every adult appears to have at least one extramarital sex partner. Many individuals have over ten lovers, both in their own village and scattered throughout the Upper Xingu, though most of these ties are necessarily attenuated because of the social and geographical distances involved. In contrast with the spouse relationship, however, that between lovers is putatively secret. Although everyone in a village seems to know the *ajo* of their fellow residents, it is rare for a Kalapalo to confess his own lovers or those of his spouse (see Carneiro 1956–1958). Whereas spouses may engage in sexual joking relatively openly, lovers usually take precautions against being discovered together. From time to time, lovers in the same village present one another with food in imitation of the spouse relationship; the man usually gives part of his fish catch to the woman, who reciprocates with hot manioc soup or fermented piqui. Similarly, lovers exchange presents of the sort spouses make for one another. A woman spins cotton thread for her lover, who then makes some of it into a palm splint comb for her. However, all these activities are always performed in secret, for the *ajo* relationship is one which is almost never proclaimed publicly, in fear of a jealous spouse's anger. Normally the Kalapalo make use of siblings and friends as intermediaries, through whom messages are sent to their lovers.

Although the presence of sexual intercourse is a defining criterion of the *ajo* relationship, persons who form these ties do not seem to be entirely motivated by a desire for sexual pleasure. Such feelings, though perhaps important in individual cases, seem to be relatively insignificant in the long run, and a poor explanation for why married individuals (as well as those without spouses) contract them. Although some *ajo* relationships seem to be true "love affairs," many more are very casual relationships between individuals from different villages who barely know one another. The fact that a Kalapalo has lovers, and specific persons as lovers, seems to be more important by comparison.

The motive for contracting *ajo* relationships is often an obviously retaliatory one. For example, some men attempt to seduce their wife's lover's own wife; an older woman, noticing her husband's interest in a younger sister, will encourage young men to proposition her. Newly married women, just released from puberty seclusion, seem to take revenge on unwanted husbands to whom they have been married against their wishes. In fact, the younger the couple, the more *ajo* relationships are had by both husband and wife. As Tsaŋaku laughingly told me, on the very day of her daughter's engagement to a man almost ten years her senior, "At first, they don't like one another; they have many lovers. Then, they have sexual intercourse again and again until they have a child. Then, they begin to like one another."

Ajo at the village level are most frequently persons who call themselves *ifau* or *itsahene*; that is, potential sex partners who are either kinsmen or affines. However, any person who is not a kinsman living in the same household is considered fair game. Although kinsmen who are not classed *ifau* or *itsahene* are not supposed to have sexual relations, persons who are classed in other kinship categories often do become lovers, and in fact may marry if they are socially distant kinsmen. (For example, Kafutani and Ugaki were classified as grandson–grandmother to each other, but became lovers and eventually married without having to face community disapproval). To turn down a proposition for sexual relations is sometimes taken as a serious insult by the offended party. It is the antithesis of generous behavior, and one of my informants suggested that it was suggestive of not giving someone food when he asked for it.[10] Such rejections may have consequences when the person insulted is later asked for assistance. Kalapalo frequently appeal to a distant kinship relationship if the asker is not desireable as a sex partner, in order to avoid an *ajo* relationship suggested to them.

Lovers who live in different villages are more frequently nonkinsmen, but are at any rate determined by the friends a man has in the host village and into which houses these friends have access. For example, on one occasion the Kalapalo were visited by a young, newly married Kuikuru couple. The woman was regarded throughout the Upper Xingu as particularly beautiful, and many Kalapalo men talked about how they would visit her when her husband was occupied outside the household which he was visiting. While the husband was conducted to the bathing area by his Kalapalo friends, and then to the trumpet house, his wife's prospective lovers entered this house one by one, at first shyly standing by the doorway, then sitting in her hammock. In less than two hours, she had been visited by eleven Kalapalo, with whom she had intercourse. However, these were only men who normally had access to the house in which she was staying, being either kinsmen or friends of persons in the household group. Men who were avoiding this house because of affinal relationships or disputes with members of the group waited until the woman went to bathe before attempting a seduction. Her husband, knowing full well that his wife was entertaining *ajo* during his absence, pretended to ignore it. However, to the delight of some of his wife's seducers, he managed to visit one of his local *ajo* inside her house, while her husband was playing the trumpets in the plaza at night.

In many respects, the *ajo* relationship corresponds with the relationship between *ato* or friends, who are persons of the same sex. *Ato* relationships are typical of men roughly from puberty seclusion age on. Perhaps because they do not travel much, are expected to behave in an unaggressive manner when visiting other houses, and do not visit one another as much as men, women appear to have many fewer *ato* than men, and it was not uncommon for women to have no friend relationships at all. In contrast, a man usually has at least one person in his home village whom he calls "friend" and one in almost every other village in the Upper Xingu. Although they are often kinsmen, they are always persons who otherwise would be socially

---

[10] In fact, the word for sexual intercourse, *itikuta*, is the same as that used to refer to the concept "to eat something sweet."

distant, either because they are allied with different political factions or because they are presently living in different villages.

Men living in the same village who are friends continually spend time with one another, acting as partners during games, on trips to collect raw materials and to the Pôsto Leonardo, and during practice wrestling matches. *Ato* also play important roles as intermediaries with each other's *ajo*, who are often their own sisters.

Ato who live in different villages, however, seem much less friendly, and like lovers from different village groups, may hardly know one another because of the infrequency of their contact. Sometimes they are even unable to communicate verbally because of language differences. Most often these intervillage ties are established during an extended visit of one partner and his kin to the village of the other partner. Usually this has taken place when both were young, and may have lived together in puberty seclusion. Then, because of the need in a strange village to associate oneself closely with one's kinsmen, the two young men participated together in many common tasks, and established some measure of familiarity. As they grew older and began to live in different villages, they became more distant socially, but retain the *ato* relationships by exchanging presents whenever they meet. During intervillage ceremonies, the gestures which mark friendship between men, including embracing and hand holding, are commonly seen as individuals publicly proclaim their *ato* ties (see Basso 1973 for further details).

Ato wrestle one another frequently during the formal bouts between men of different village groups. Their expressions of amiability in these situations contrast sharply with the hostility evident between men who are not *ato*, but who must wrestle one another during the general combat in which all participate. Men who are not *ato* and who consider themselves relatively equal in strength and experience tend to throw one another violently, but *ato* who win a match only signal this by touching their friend's shoulder to the ground in a token gesture. During these intervillage ceremonies, *ato* walk around together visiting their hosts' houses, wherein they receive presents and food. Similarly, *ato* from different villages often call upon one another for material assistance when traveling, especially when they have run short of food. For example, returning from a trip to the Waura village for a major ceremony, several Kalapalo men found themselves running short of manioc bread. As they were passing close to the Yawalipiti village, they urged one of their group to enter that village and find his *ato*, hoping the latter could be persuaded to give them all food for the rest of the journey.

Both *ato* and *ajo* relationships are marked by generosity and good humor; friends and lovers are both expected to assist one another informally and to exchange presents. However, these relationships are dependent upon the frequency of personal contacts, are based to a great extent upon personal choice, and can be quickly broken if offense is given by one of the partners. Thus, men who have been accused of sorcery tend to have fewer friends than others. In all these respects both friends and lovers differ from kinsmen, who are held to be in a permanent and unchosen relationship which cannot be broken. The relationship of solidarity which is expected between kinsmen is based on the norm of *ifutisu*, rather than the emotional feeling between them.

The *Iniso–Ajo* "Continuum"

Although the Kalapalo are quite able to determine which individuals are lovers and which are spouses, they also classify persons as "little" or "strong" spouse, and "little " or "strong" lover, according to how active the former are in sharing food and engaging in sexual relationships, how secretly the latter maintain their affair, and how often they have sexual relations. A person who is obviously not interested in his or her spouse and has many *ajo*, or a person who is visited often by lovers is called "little spouse" (*intsoño iniso*). A very casual lover is a "little lover" (*intsoño ajo*). In this way, the Kalapalo actually see the spouse and *ajo* relationships as two poles at either end of a continuum of relationships which may be more or less true to one or the other ideal type. Thus, many *ajo* relationships become spouse relationships by relatively subtle trends in the behavior of the persons concerned. Divorces begin to turn into new marriages as lovers more frequently engage in sexual relations and as they engage jointly and publicly in subsistence activities. Divorce is only completed, however, when a woman removes her hammock from beneath that of her husband and changes residence, or when a husband leaves his wife. Remarriage, as I noted, is symbolized by the woman harvesting and processing the manioc of another man with whom she has sexual relations, or by the man openly providing food to another woman.

7 / Specialists and authorities

PRESTIGE AND INFLUENCE

Although the Kalapalo do not concretely define or name a position of authority, there are several individuals living at Aifa whose actions indeed designate them true village leaders. In contrast with the majority of villagers, these persons seem to consistently influence the decisions and control the initiative of a large number of individuals, and thus to implement power. Most commonly, a leader's authority is exerted solely among a group of his own relatives, and only under special (usually ceremonial) circumstances, over the members of Aifa as a whole. Because the relatives over whom a leader has power need not necessarily be members of his own household, his influence is not confined to a single group of that kind, and thus he can be properly called a "village leader" rather than simply a "household leader."

Kalapalo leaders are able to exert their influence because they have acquired considerable prestige. This prestige in turn results from their continual exemplification of communal values expressed in the ideal of *ifutisu* behavior, especially generosity. Unlike most of the people living at Aifa, these men are able to display ideal behavior because of a lucky combination of two interrelated determinants: (1) their having a large number of subservient relatives who are willing to support them materially and verbally, and (2) their accumulation of special statuses (*ifi*, or "ceremonial specialist"; *oto*, or "ceremonial sponsor"; *fuati* or "shaman"; and *anetu* or "village representative") covered in Chapter 8. By performing the services connected with these positions, or more exactly, by actively holding several offices, a continuous flow of wealth to and from these persons takes place. With this wealth, relationships of kinship and affinity can be epitomized in the ideal, for generosity can be dramatically and continually displayed. Furthermore, new social ties, such as affinal relationships based on plural marriages, informal short-term trading partnerships, and clientships, can be made with nonrelatives or those who are socially distant, for wealth can be used to pay for new wives, to trade for scarce commodities, and to pay for being taught an esoteric skill. Thus, Kalapalo leaders are persons who are continually expanding and reinforcing social ties, and in so doing, actively demonstrating their ability to influence a large number of individuals.

Control over Relatives

As noted in Chapter 6, a Kalapalo speaks of his obligations to another person by speaking of the *ifutisu* he feels for him. This relationship is almost always founded in ties of kinship or affinity, which, as described earlier, consist in long-term, if not permanent, expressions of material assistance and public support. Although the Kalapalo define kinship and affinal roles in the abstract as mutually supportive, stressing unqualified assistance whenever needed, most relationships between individual relatives are somewhat weighted in favor of one or the other. Thus, a son- or daughter-in-law who lives with affines is expected to act subserviently in their presence and to provide assistance without being asked to do so. An unmarried sibling is obligated to freely assist a married one. Offspring live under the continual authority of their parents. Relationships can also become skewed when relatives are scattered in different villages. Kinsmen who live far away cannot be expected to maintain their *ifutisu* obligations in the same way as kinsmen living in the same village do; to a lesser extent this is true of persons living in different households within a single village. Similarly, kinsmen or affines who are also friends or lovers are more apt to lend assistance if they live in the same village, than the same kinds of relatives who do not have such relationships.

As a result of inegalitarian kinship and affinal ties, certain men and women find themselves surrounded by "satellites," relatives who are in relationships of comparatively greater *ifutisu* and who therefore feel constrained to lend assistance when called upon. In contrast, these same men and women find they have few relatives who can make demands upon them. On the other hand, most Kalapalo, regardless of the number of relatives they may have, find themselves continually obligated to these persons to such an extent that they make few decisions on their own. Kalapalo leaders are thus men and women who are truly able to express their individualism, for they can uncompromisingly determine their own actions. By contrast, and in opposition, most of the villagers live from day to day under the authority of their powerful relatives.

Leaders of large household groups have the authority to direct the subsistence activities of a relatively large number of adults, as well as less mature relatives. Thus, the potential for food production in these groups is higher than in others. Such household leaders who can also rely on the assistance of individual members of other groups are in a position to initiate major projects involving the labor of the entire village, for only by calling upon the many kinsmen and affines who are obligated to them can they provide the enormous food payments which must be distributed during those occasions.

Such a project is the shoring up of a rickety house structure with cross-braces, in order to forestall its inevitable collapse. One such endeavor (initiated by Taguwaki) began with his selection of two large trees in the forest beyond his manioc gardens. These were cut down, stripped of their bark and branches, and carried to a site at the edge of the cultivated zone, where they were set on a rack to dry for about a week. This preliminary work was done by all the men who lived in the house needing repair, together with two of Taguwaki's subservient affines who lived with his

Apihu (left, facing) raises the main post of his future residence, assisted by sub-ordinate relatives and another anetu *(left, back to camera). Included in the group are the leader's two brothers, his son, a son-in-law, and two brothers-in-law.*

brother Apihu, whose daughters those men had married. After the preparation of the braces was completed, the logs had to be carried from the forest to the village, and for this the entire adult male population of Aifa was mobilized. Each log was quickly carried along the trail which ran from the forest to Taguwaki's house by groups of about six men, who took turns with one another. Finally, there was the delicate task of raising the braces into place, during which a large group of men supported them as they were inserted by Taguwaki's brother-in-law, Kafutani, underneath the ceiling beams. Apihu and Taguwaki's sister Ugaki gave directions during this procedure. Although Taguwaki organized the project, in accordance with Kalapalo custom, during the final stages (involving the public activity of the village as a whole) he only stood by and did not play an active role.

In initiating the project Taguwaki counted on the help not only of his fellow male household members, but nearly all the men of the village in order to be able to complete the task of repairing his house. To be able to pay all these assistants, he had to have sufficient relatives who were willing to prepare a quantity of food great enough to share with the men of the village as a whole. Even though in many similar instances not everyone who lives in the village actually participates, the sponsor of the project is obligated to distribute food to all.

When it becomes evident that large food payment will have to be made in the near future, the household group and individual subservient relatives of the leader begin gathering the necessary raw materials. Only those materials which can be accumulated in very large quantities are used; these include (according to the season of the year) fish, manioc, piqui, and corn. For several weeks, or even over the course of a number of months, the leader's relatives concentrate on processing these subsistence items. Men leave for long fishing trips, often lasting two weeks, during which they accumulate ten or more carrying baskets of fish, enough to feed everyone for at least a week. An expedition may be made to the piqui groves at Kanugijafitï where several hundred pounds of fruit are processed and preserved under water until the time for distribution. The women continually process manioc, in order to provide flour for *telisiñï* and *kine*, with which the fish are to be distributed. In short, a food distribution given to the members of the village in return for their labor involves the intense cooperation of a relatively large number of persons, both men and women, over an extended period of time.

CEREMONIAL SPONSORSHIP

In order to justify the major activity a leader wishes to have the villagers undertake for him, he must be able to sponsor a ceremony in which everyone participates. Technically, the food which is distributed is payment for the ceremony's performance rather than for the work itself. A ceremony given under such circumstances can be considered a marker, then, of the relationship between the individual sponsor and the group of villagers as a whole.

Before Taguwaki initiated the house repair project described in the previous section, he was obligated to call for the performance of some ceremony which he sponsored. To this end he asked that *tafaku* ("bow"), a series of dances involving brilliantly decorated pairs of men and women, be performed by the residents of Aifa. The performance took place each day for over a week before the men of the village began assisting him in repairing his house. While the dancing and singing went on, Taguwaki's wife Kafundzu and his sister Ugaki prepared enormous quantities of manioc bread and piqui soup, assisted by their subservient female relatives from several other household groups. The piqui had been gathered several months before under the supervision of Ugaki's son Tufulei, who had traveled to Kanugijafitï for that purpose. The day after the last *tafaku* dance had taken place, Taguwaki began distributing large vessels of piqui drink, placing them in a line before the *kuakutu*, and inviting each man to carry one back to his family. When all the containers had been returned to him, the food distribution was officially ended.

The majority of ceremonies performed by the Kalapalo have little ideological significance beyond their association with specific sponsors. The performances are extremely stereotyped and repetitious, and almost invariably the songs associated with them are unintelligible to the singers, being most often in languages other

Assisted by two anetaw, *Kafukwigi (in raincoat) distributes green corn to the men of Aifa in return for their performance of a ceremony he sponsors.*

than Carib. Finally, there is little, if any, manipulation of ritual symbols, and the performances often offer no excitement after the first or second day, until the final climactic event marking the last day of the ceremony.

Most ceremonies the Kalapalo perform (as the three associated with *anetaw* which are discussed in Chapter 8) are found among all the other village groups of the Upper Xingu. A few are specifically associated with a single village: the spear throwing ceremony, *ifagaka*, is said to have been introduced by the Trumai; the women's *yamurikuma* is said to "belong" to the Waura; the *žakwikatï, ndufei,* and *fugei oto*, to the Mehinaku; the *kwambï*, to the Carib villages. Whatever local significance these ceremonies may have had when they were introduced into the Upper Xingu (or still have within particular "donor" groups) has been super- seded by their present significance as markers of conspicuous communal activity performed by a village group for the benefit of an individual sponsor.

Ceremonial sponsorship may be conferred upon a Kalapalo in several ways. Certain sponsorships are associated with *anetu* status, including those of the *ifagaka, ipoñe,* and *egitsu.* More commonly, sponsorship is conferred upon a person who, during severe illness, becomes associated in some way with a particular ceremony. After an individual has been cured of a severe illness by the performance of a particular ceremony (see below), he is then considered the ceremony's *oto.*

Similarly, if during illness the patient dreams of the performance of a particular ceremony, or even of some item (such as a mask or instrument) associated with it, he must sponsor that ceremony when he becomes well.

For approximately a year after the successful cure, the new *oto* prepares for the first performance under his sponsorship. Trips are organized to collect food to be distributed after the performance, and specialists (*ifi*) are instructed to manufacture new paraphernalia for the dancers. Finally, after these preparations have been completed, the *oto* calls for the performance in a formal speech indicating the day previously agreed upon by the rest of the villagers who have been assisting him. From the Kalapalo point of view, the *oto* status is one primarily involving a set of obligations, not rights. The *oto* is only a channel through which ceremonial performances are properly initiated, enacted and paid for, not on the basis of coercion, but according to the needs and desires of the village group itself.

The initial performance of a ceremony under new sponsorship does not coincide with some communal effort for the *oto*'s benefit. Rather, it takes the form of a commemoration of the victim's cure. Only after this first performance can the *oto* declare his need for communal labor and specify a project with which the villagers are to help. However, only those persons with the ability to mobilize relatives for assistance in procuring essential food payments are able to take advantage of this privilege. Because an *oto* must count on the members of his household group (at the very least) to assist him in the collection of food payment, persons who have very little control over their relatives rarely hold this office. Despite the supposedly uncontrollable origin of *oto* status, only men and women (or their spouses and immature children) with relatively large numbers of subservient relatives hold it.

The importance of ceremonial food distribution is manifested in the distribution of cornfields. Only five men in Aifa grew corn during 1966–1968, although it is the most important subsistence item during January. The rest of the village depended upon these men to distribute their harvest in order to survive. Equally significant are the quantities of piqui collected by similar kinds of sponsors, most notably those responsible for *anetu* ceremonies (see Chapter 8). Although everyone collects some piqui during the harvest, only *oto* of these ceremonies accumulate large quantities, for they must give eventual payment to assistants and performers over a long period of time.

THE ACQUISITION OF *IFI* STATUS

From the time a young person is confined in puberty seclusion, he is continually instructed in ceremonial lore, and listens to myths recited for his benefit in order to be able to memorize their contents. Usually parents and other members of his *otomo* who live in the same household participate in this instruction, often at his explicit request. Thus, the pubescent girl or boy who has knowledgeable kinsmen is in a position to accumulate a considerable amount of specialized knowledge over the years. In contrast, those who have been raised by persons without such knowledge can only learn by contracting client relationships with specialists, but they must be prepared to continually pay their teachers during the course of study. For this reason, the client relationship is most often contracted by persons well beyond seclusion age.

Men and women who are recognized as especially learned, who are known to be able to remember the contents of lengthy ceremonial songs, who can manufacture ceremonial paraphernalia, and who know the details of rarely performed ceremonies, are known as *ifi*, "makers." *Ifi* are responsible for the performance of those ceremonies in which they specialize. Usually there are from two to four *ifi* for every one of the thirty or more ceremonies known to the Kalapalo.

Most Kalapalo men and women hold at least one *ifi* position, and there are some who have managed to become *ifi* of several ceremonies. Those persons who are specialists in ceremonies which are performed frequently (such as *kagutu*, described in Chapter 3) or which mark a major event (such as those commemorating dead chiefs and the *ipoñe*, the boys' ear piercing ceremony) have more serious responsibilities, and the status of *ifi* of such ceremonies carries more prestige than do those of lesser events.

The *ifi* are primarily responsible for seeing that the ceremony in question is properly performed; this involves their own participation, but they are expected to urge their fellow villagers to participate as well. Furthermore, *ifi* are supposed to train new specialists by willingly entering into client relationships upon request. In return for all these services, they are periodically paid by the *oto* with eagle feathers, parrot tail feathers, well-made arrows, beads, and ceramics.

Often *ifi* participate officially in ceremonies held in villages other than their own. If they are visiting kinsmen when "their" ceremony is being held, they are frequently asked by the local specialist to join the performance. Similarly, *ifi* are sometimes asked by persons of villages other than their own to teach them the particular ceremony in which they specialize. Usually this takes place during an *ifi*'s extended visit to the client's village. For these reasons, persons of considerable experience become renowned not only in their own villages, but throughout the Upper Xingu as well.

Although *ifi* status can bring prestige to an individual, it is a relatively common practice for adults to become specialists in one or more ceremonies, and thus the position is relatively unimportant with respect to the acquisition of political power. For young men and women it is just a beginning, the first step towards social success.

FUATI: SHAMANISTIC CURERS AND DIVINERS

Men who have met the conditions for establishing their own households—that is, who have a number of subservient relatives willing to live with them—and who are able to sponsor ceremonies which permit the village group to assist them in this endeavor often become shamans. The Kalapalo call these men *fuati*. Only one man in each household group is *fuati*, and he is always a member of the core, if not the actual household leader. Men who become shamans while living in a household where one is already present inevitably move to a house of their own shortly thereafter. It seems then, that a person does not actually begin his training for the position until he is certain of being able to lead a group of his own. In short, *fuati* are men who have previously accumulated a number of *oto* and *ifi* statuses, and who have therefore already acquired considerable prestige.

The powers of *fuati* mark them as extraordinary men, for they are able to control nonhuman forces, especially those connected with monsters. Through their ability to influence *itseke* and to confront them without fear of dying, *fuati* are able not only to cure minor illnesses, but to recapture the souls of severely ill persons and to divine the cause of a calamity.

The Kalapalo say a man begins to sense his calling to the position of shaman when he continually finds himself dreaming of monsters and dead persons, and seeing these beings in visions. Normally such visions presage a sudden death, but the future *fuati* does not become ill. As the dreams and visions increase in intensity, he requests an experienced shaman to teach him the secrets of control. A clientship tie is thus established which continues for some time. The initiate first enters seclusion, during which time he is taught how to smoke tobacco, how to extract darts which caused illness, how to lure monsters by singing, and how to induce trances for the purpose of divination. When the experienced shaman has become convinced his pupil has mastered these skills, the latter is asked to treat his first patient. Because skill in curing is supposed to come with practice, younger shamans are considered less capable than their elders, and the first attempt is not always well performed. Indeed, some men never achieve success, and are rarely asked to treat people who are seriously ill. It is in fact up to the shaman himself to prove his worth, and the man who is not successful is commonly the subject of ridicule.

Shamans of great repute are often asked to cure in villages other than their own, especially if some person is seriously ill and does not respond to the efforts of the local *fuati*. Under such circumstances, it is considered perfectly acceptable to ask for the assistance of men from other villages who are thought to be especially adept. However, only men who have been shamans for many years or who are known for their dramatic ability to cure difficult cases are asked to help in this way.

Curing Rituals

Curing rituals are the only explicitly manipulative ceremonies found among the Kalapalo, for they are regarded as specifically designed for the achievement of definite goals, and make use of material and nonmaterial items as "tools" for achieving these goals. The power in the *fuati*'s hand which allows him to draw out *kwifi*, his use of tobacco smoke, rattles, songs, and *kejite* leaves, the procedures he follows, and the participants themselves are all seen as intimately involved in a conscious relationship which seeks to produce a specific result—the restoration to health of the victim. These aspects make curing rituals unique among the Kalapalo, if not the entire Upper Xingu.

The Kalapalo believe that illness and pain are caused by *kwifi* which have been "shot" (*tuelu*) into the body by monsters, or by witches (known as *kwifi oto*, "masters of darts"). Although the Kalapalo are fortunate to live in a relatively healthy environment, throughout the year people are wounded by stingrays, bitten by cayman, stung by tocandira ants, accidently shot with arrows, and suffer from malarial fevers and toothaches. Women wish to avoid complications during child-birth, to have skin rashes caused by snake monsters or jealous wives healed, and to have their children cured of fevers. In order to treat these illnesses and to relieve the pain associated with them, it is necessary to have the *kwifi* causing them removed. For this purpose the victim or his kinsmen must hire *fuati*.

A minor case is first treated by a shaman who lives in the victim's household (usually a kinsman of the victim) or by an outsider who has the reputation for successfully curing that ailment; for example, one Kalapalo shaman is known for his ability to ease the pains of childbirth, and most women ask for his services as they start labor. If further treatments are necessary, shamans from outside the household group are called in one by one.

The curing itself is, in these instances, performed under extremely informal circumstances. When the shaman enters the victim's residence, he is greeted by the members of the household and given a stool on which to sit while he works on the patient. He begins by lighting a cigar and blowing tobacco smoke over the body of the victim, while passing his hands over the afflicted part in order to attract *kwifi* to the skin's surface. He sucks violently against the patient, in order to receive the darts in his mouth. These appear in the shape of fish scales, bits of bone, bark and string, or other tiny objects. When a *kwifi* is found, it is quickly thrust outside the house through the thatch, with the words, "go away, go away, go away." During the entire procedure the victim is often talking with his curer, sometimes even joking about the event which caused his misfortune. Although a spouse or parent of the victim may stand nearby watching the ritual, most members of the household group continue with whatever they happened to be doing before the *fuati* entered.

When a person becomes seriously ill, and curing by individual shamans has failed, it is assumed that the victim's shadow has been captured by *itseke*. The sick person's kinsmen then request a communal curing ritual, involving all the shamans who live in the village. Known as *itseke ili*, "calling the monster," the purpose of this ritual is to entice a monster into returning the victim's shadow.

At the beginning of the ritual, the house is emptied of all residents except the patient, who is left lying in his hammock, under which has been built a small fire. Then one shaman, usually the eldest or most experienced, leaves his own house, whistling to the others to come join him. After all the *fuati* are inside, doors are placed over the front and rear openings, and holes in the thatch are covered. The patient and *fuati* are thus left in complete darkness, save for the fire. The shamans then light cigars from this fire and begin to smoke. Gourd rattles are shaken and their handles rolled along the houseframe as the men begin to sing to attract *itseke*. Sometimes one of the *fuati*, assisted by the tobacco, enters a trance and is able to make contact with the monster who has stolen the victim's soul; or he may see a dead person who predicts whether the victim will die or not. Upon seeing such a being, the shaman's reaction is to run shrieking from the house and around the plaza, seemingly out of control. After a few minutes, the shock wears off and he is able to tell the others of what he has seen. More often, however, *itseke ili* ends quietly, after about half an hour of singing. The house is then reopened, and the members of the victim's group enter once more, to wait for signs of a successful cure.

If a shaman has divined that a particular monster has caused the illness, or if the victim dreams of a specific monster, then a group of *fuati* travel to where it is believed to live, again hoping to persuade it to release the captured shadow.[1] One particularly dramatic shadow recapture was witnessed by me in August, 1967.

The Kalapalo were camped beside the Culuene River near a swamp from which plants were being gathered to prepare salt. Kofoŋo, the elderly wife of Bïjïjï, became feverish. At first, no one seemed concerned, since most Kalapalo suffer from malarial attacks which subside after a day or two. Several days went by, however, and she did not become well. Much weakened by the sickness, she was unable to leave her hammock to gather the swamp plants with her cowife, and spent the days wrapped in my heavy blanket, shivering over a fire. From time to time, Bïjïjï attempted to cure her by blowing tobacco smoke over her body and sucking violently to draw the *kwifi* out. This standard shamanistic cure failed repeatedly, until Bïjïjï felt certain that his wife had been "shot" with a dart sent by *itseke*. After a week passed, the salt plant gathering was completed, and Bïjïjï's family returned to Aifa, where it was hoped the village shamans could persuade the *itseke* to allow Kofoŋo to become well again.

I remained behind at the river camp with several other families, who had not yet completed their salt plant gathering. Several days after Bïjïjï had left, Taguwaki and Kafukwigi, two of the more experienced shamans of Aifa, arrived. Because of a dream she had had during an attack of the fever, these shamans diagnosed Kofoŋo's illness as caused by *itseke* who lived in the Culuene, called Tifagikuegï, "monstrous stingray," who had stolen her shadow one morning as she drew water from the river. The aim of the shamans' visit was to recapture Kofoŋo's shadow by confronting Tifagikuegï in person.

First, the two *fuati* cleared a small area about three yards from the river bank, where they built a fire and began smoking cigars. In each hand they clutched *kejite* leaves. As they smoked, the men sang to the monster in order to draw it to the side of the bank. Without warning, they leaped up, ran to the edge of the steep bank, and plunged into the water, diving deep beneath the surface. After a few seconds Kafukwigi appeared, shrieking unnaturally, followed by Taguwaki, who did the same. Several of the young men who had watched from the edge dove in to rescue the two shamans, for they were in danger of drowning if they had seen *itseke*. Kafukwigi and Taguwaki were pulled up the bank and made to sit by the fire until they had revived. After approximately ten minutes, the *fuati* announced they had seen Tifagikuegï, who had given them Kofoŋo's shadow. Taguwaki clutched this in the *kejite* leaves which he still held in one hand. Shortly after, with these leaves carefully wrapped in a neat package, the two shamans departed for Aifa. There, they returned the shadow to her owner, who recovered in three days.

When the old woman was able to resume her normal life, she declared that she must soon sponsor a ceremony called *žakwikatï*, for in her dream she had seen Tifagikuegï dressed in the mask of that ceremony. Thus, Kofoŋo became the new

---

[1] Certain landmarks—trees, areas of a river, regions of a particularly deep forest, and so forth—are supposed to be the homes of particular monsters. While passing by these places, one is expected to be silent in order not to attract the creatures.

žakwikatï oto. The following spring, *ifï* began preparing costumes for a performance that was to take place in May.

Another kind of curing ritual involves the performance of secular ceremonies of the sort discussed in the beginning of this chapter. Such ceremonies as *kagutu*, *yamurikuma*, *afasa*, and others which are usually performed for the sake of justifying labor for their sponsor's benefit are, in circumstances of curing, presented in attenuated form without the participants decorating themselves fully. The singers, led by *ifï*, begin the ceremony in the center of the village, then walk, still singing and dancing, to the victim's house, where they continue the performance around his hammock. The communal effort by the entire village group is supposed to assist in a cure.

For example, Agifuti's son Agimeti, seriously ill with meningitis, resisted all attempts at curing by the shamans of Aifa. Agifuti had even asked several men from Mïgiyapei (where he had many relatives) to come to Aifa and help his son, but they too were unsuccessful. After more than two weeks of repeated *itseke ilï* and continuous vigil around Agimeti's hammock by the shamans, who hoped the monster responsible for the illness would suddenly appear with the stolen shadow of the sick boy, Agifuti requested the performance of women's songs, which he hoped would result in a cure. The women gathered together in the plaza the next morning and formed a line by linking arms tightly with one another. They began singing, and still linked together, walked quickly to Agifuti's house. Entering the front door, they stood around the hammock of the sick boy, continuing the song. After three more verses were finished, the shamans guarding Agimeti indicated that the ceremony had been sufficiently performed, and the women left. Later that day, Agifuti's wife Aṇasagu gave manioc soup and strings of beads as payment to Kofoṇo, Tsaṇaku, and Ugaki, the *oto* and *ifï* of women's singing.

Several days after the performance of women's singing, the boy showed no improvement. This time, Agifuti asked that a men's ceremony called *afasa* be performed. Normally, this ceremony involves the manufacture of elaborate burity palm fiber costumes, but on this occasion it was performed by men painted minimally with urucu. *Afasa* began with the Kalapalo men walking from the formal entrance path of the village to the plaza. Taguwaki, the ceremony's sponsor, led the group, followed by Waiyepei and Fagatu, who were *afasa ifï*. Behind these men came the two individuals in Aifa who are repeatedly accused of witchcraft; by participating actively in a curing ritual, they wished to demonstrate their innocence to Agifuti. As with the women's singing, the ceremony was initially performed in the plaza, then the men sang around Agimeti's hammock. Finally, they returned in a single file to the plaza, where they finished the songs associated with *afasa*. The *afasa oto* and *ifï* were immediately given parrot tail feathers by Agifuti. He had called for the performances in vain, however, for the boy died several weeks later at the Post, where he had finally been taken as a last resort.

Because there is always hope that a particular ritual will cure the victim or entice a monster to give up a stolen shadow, some kind of curing takes place up to the moment of death. Which particular rituals are resorted to by the victim's kinsmen throughout the course of his illness depends in part, of course, upon the seriousness of the ailment, but also to a great extent upon his relatives' abilities to pay for them. Because the large communal ceremonies are the most expensive, they appear to be performed for curing purposes relatively infrequently and kinsmen of seriously ill persons rely more heavily upon the skill of shamans.

Divination

A less frequent practice of shamans is divination. Persons who suffer severe calamities, such as the sudden death of a kinsman, a house destroyed by lightning, or the theft of some treasured object, may ask a particularly prominent *fuati* to divine the agent of the misfortune. The shaman enters a trance by gulping large quantities of tobacco smoke during the course of smoking several cigars. Then, while in the trance, and in a manner similar to the trances of shamans who are *itseke ili*, he experiences visions of monsters and of dead individuals, who tell him the names of witches and thieves. *Fuati* who can successfully divine the future course of events are especially admired.

The Use of Curing Payment

A shaman is well paid for his services. The most valuable items in a person's possession are given away in payment, and during a protracted illness, the wealth of kinsmen (both of the victim's household group and other households) is displayed on or near the hammock of the sick person. Beads and shell ornaments are twined on the hammock cords, while ammunition, feathers, cloth, arrows, and other possessions are piled neatly beneath the victim. These items represent contributions from his relatives for payment to the shamans after curing takes place.

Curing payment has the effect of making shamans the wealthiest persons in the community. This wealth is in itself a source of prestige for a number of reasons. First, having a quantity of material possessions enables shamans to participate more actively and frequently in the *uluki* or trade ceremony (see Chapter 8) than less wealthy men, and to acquire items which are infrequently made or owned, for example canoes, bamboo platforms for drying manioc, and jaguar claw necklaces. Second, the accumulation of "payment wealth" such as beads and eagle feathers result in shamans' conspicuous decorative display. Because men in particular are concerned with the accumulation of wealth in the form of body decoration (feather earrings and arm bands, shell collars and belts, beaded belts and necklaces, feather headdresses, urucu, and piqui oil), the shaman often effectively competes in this way.

The social and ideological pressures to distribute any accumulation of wealth exist for shamans as for all Kalapalo. As household head or core member, a shaman must encourage his fellows to participate in the *uluki* by presenting his own wealth as incentive at the outset of trading in his own house. Trade ceremony participation is only one way in which wealth is transferred, however. The shaman often diverts his curing payment to other individuals by calling for the performance of ceremonies which he sponsors (and thus paying the *ifi* for their service as well), or for the manufacture of special equipment needed to carry out certain tasks (for example, canoes for long fishing trips, manioc drying racks, or elaborate weirs made from woody vines and used for important fishing ventures). The use of continuously acquired wealth involves him in a long-term series of relationships marked by the transference of payment. These relationships include that of *oto–ifi*, but also new affinal relationships resulting from the acquisition of second and third wives, and informal short-term trading relationships with men in other villages. Like the ceremonial statuses of *oto* and *ifi*, that of *fuati* is a means of acquiring or increasing prestige which is founded on the ability to share wealth and to engage in beneficial service to the community. Both are defined by the Kalapalo as *ifutisu* behavior, and thus a prestigeful person is known as a "good" (*atutu*) person.

FACTIONS

It is convenient to refer to the persons upon whom a leader may depend for support during disputes as a "faction." Although all of the prominent persons in a village have subservient relatives who assist them, only some of these relatives are consistently opposed in what political anthropologists refer to as "conflict groups."[2] The opposition of Kalapalo factions as "conflict groups" is manifested in verbal disputes, or more exactly (because there are rarely direct confrontations) in verbal statements and in physical avoidance.

One of the most common sources of conflict between factions is their leaders' claim to *anetu* status (see Chapter 8). When a faction is led by an irregular claimant (not all are), they maintain support for him by continually justifying his position through the tracing of genealogical connection to a dead *anetu ekugu* (legitimate *anetu*) and by denigrating the claims of other irregular claimants (*intsoño anetu*). An example of this kind of conflict in Aifa is the intense rivalry between two men of relatively the same age who are both *intsoño anetaw*.

The conflict between these men probably began around the time when pressure was put upon the Kalapalo to move their village closer to the Post. By the end of the measle epidemic in 1954, there was only one surviving adult *anetu ekugu*. The two present rivals, Apihų and Bïjïjï, were able to fill a vacuum left by the death of other *anetaw*, for they were among the very few survivors who could claim any kind of *anetu* status at all, and were thus able to hold office. Several years later the one *anetu ekugu* holding office died, leaving Apihų and Bïjïjï the senior Kalapalo representatives. Shortly thereafter, the boundaries of the Park were formed. As several villages (including Kanugijafïtï) lay outside these boundaries, they became vulnerable to probable conflicts with members of the expanding Brazilian frontier society, and thus the administrators urged them to move further north. The Kuikuru, who lived near the Kalapalo, were one of the first to move, and they began to pressure the Kalapalo to do the same by telling of bombs which would fall on those who remained outside the Park. Uncertain whether this was true, Apihų and Bïjïjï began to dispute the desirability of a move. Because Apihų's father was Mehinaku, he was limited in his ability to harvest certain resources in the territory around Kanugijafïtï. Thus he was more willing to establish a new village. Bïjïjï, on the other hand, had extensive rights to the resources of the old village and felt strongly that the group should remain. Although the Park administrators had

[2] See Beals and Siegel 1967; Nicholas 1965.

promised the Kalapalo metal tools, cotton, beads, and other presents if they made the move, Bïjïjï was skeptical (with good reason, it turned out), and could not see why such bribes had influenced other groups to leave their traditional territories. However, the pressure continued, especially from the Kuikuru who continually repeated stories of bombs and soldiers who would come and kill anyone not in the Park. The administrators themselves selected a site, once occupied by the Kamaiura, on which the Kalapalo could settle. Finally, Bïjïjï agreed that Apihu should travel to the new site to see if it was suitable. Accompanied by his own male relatives and Bïjïjï's brother, Apihu made the trip. He returned with a satisfactory report. Thus, reluctantly, the Kalapalo moved their village site. When they arrived at the site, they realized that the territory of the new village would not be as bountiful as that of the old one. The main advantage was an abundance of fish in the nearby lake and in the Culuene River, which was much closer than it was to Kanugijafïtï. However, there were no land snails, nor were there extensive groves of piqui trees, for the previous Kamaiura occupation had been very brief. Thus, ties with the old territory remained strong. Today, during the piqui season, Bïjïjï leads his relatives to Kanugijafïtï, where they harvest piqui, wild pineapple, and mangabeira fruit, plant cotton and arrow cane, and gather the shells of land snails with which they manufacture belts and necklaces. Apihu's group, however, is forced either to remain at Aifa, where there is very little piqui and no land snails, or else to travel to the Post, where they must compete with members of other villages for the fruit of the few trees there. Resenting the fact that he has moved to Aifa "for nothing," Bïjïjï continually makes remarks about Apihu's affiliation with the Mehinaku, how he is therefore not really a Kalapalo and thus should not act as village representative. On those occasions when Apihu sponsors ceremonies, Bïjïjï remains inside his house and does not participate with the other men. The two men bathe in different places and sit far from one another in front of the *kuakutu*. The only thing which prevents these two from seriously dividing the village is an extensive network of affinal relationships between their two factions. Even though Bïjïjï and Apihu are personally unfriendly, individual members of their supporting groups have intermarried and maintain close ties (see pp. 122–123).

Prominent persons who find themselves accused of witchcraft, especially those who are subject to disparaging remarks because of their past association with other village groups (which they or their parents fled as a result of witchcraft accusations against them), often are the focus of factional disputes. Under these circumstances, it is common for a faction leader to speak of his desire to leave the group and to form a new village elsewhere. These threats (which, as far as I could determine, have been actually carried out only once during the past fifty years) are a statement of the importance of the leader's faction in village life. In order to form a new local group, he must have the support of a large number of persons who have agreed to live together, apart from relatives in their original village to whom they also may have obligations.

Aside from these two kinds of disputes—that is, those focusing on *anetu* status and on witchcraft accusations—the members of a faction are not actively involved in significant conflict from day to day. All groups of relatives support their leaders by following their initiative on trips and during ceremonies which they sponsor, by expressing solidarity through mutual assistance, and by forming groups which make witchcraft accusations and which occasionally take revenge for witchcraft murders. As I will describe in a later section, factions are vehicles for witchcraft accusations, but are not opposed by these accusations. Not infrequently, factions otherwise in conflict are agreed as to who is a witch.

A MAN OF PRESTIGE AND INFLUENCE

Three men living in Aifa were prominent individuals, persons who had managed to accumulate a considerable number of statuses and who could thus demonstrate more power than anyone else. Having already briefly considered Apihu and Bijiji, the two senior *anetaw*, let us now turn to the position of Taguwaki, who in many respects was a mediator between these two opposing faction leaders. This was due to his extensive kin ties with the former and his affinal relationships with the latter.

Taguwaki, a man of approximately 35 years of age, was one of several siblings (including the *anetu* Apihu) whose father had fled the Mehinaku village upon being accused of witchcraft. The father was married to several women, one of whom was a Kalapalo *anetu*, and he took refuge among his wife's relatives. Thus, Taguwaki (like Apihu) grew up among the Kalapalo and eventually married several women of that group, by whom he had a number of children. One sister, Ugaki, had married a Kalapalo *anetu ekugu*, leaving him five children, including the youngest *anetu* presently holding office. Two other sisters also married Kalapalo men, by whom they had offspring. Thus the children of the Mehinaku man had established themselves very solidly in the community. Although they still have relatives among the Mehinaku, they do not care to return permanently to that group for fear of being accused of witchcraft themselves.

An examination of the membership of Taguwaki's household, which is the largest in Aifa, illustrates the complex and varying relationships between this leader and the rest of the group, over whom he exercises considerable control (see Figure 5a, p. 50).

As I have had occasion to note earlier, Taguwaki and his older sister Ugaki are presently married to a pair of siblings, Kafundzu and Kafutani. Although Kafundzu considers Bijiji's wife Tsanaku her mother, she and Taguwaki live apart from Bijiji's own large household. Both Kafundzu and Taguwaki have been married previously, and are middle-aged by Kalapalo standards. The "brother–sister" exchange marriage of Ugaki and Kafutani also provides justification for the separate household. A younger unmarried brother of Kafundzu and Kafutani also lives here, while an older married sister lives with her husband, a member of the Kuikuru village with a household of his own.

Taguwaki and Ugaki have reared several children who were born to two of their other siblings. One member of this group, Enumï, expressed his reason for living with them in the following way:

My mother died when I was small, so my father was the only one who raised my sister and me. Then, when the measles came, lots of Kalapalo were dying, everyone was mourning all the time. We were very weak, and couldn't dig the graves. Then two *kagaifa* came and dug a big hole, and put the ones who had died in it. My father slept in his hammock strung over mine. It seems that he died during the night when I was sleeping underneath him. I didn't know anything; I was feverish. In the morning when I woke up, other people told me he was dead. After he was buried, my mother's brother, Taguwaki, came and asked me if I wanted to come live in his house. Then I said, "yes," I agreed to live with him.

This same man spoke of another young person who lives with Taguwaki and Ugaki in the following way:

You see that Kofi lives with Ugaki and not his real mother (Ugaki's sister). After Kofi's father died when the measles came, his mother married a Kuikuru man who didn't like him. That man said over and over that Kofi was lazy and that he didn't want him in his house. It seems he didn't like Kofi's father either, when he was alive. Then Kofi came to live with Ugaki at Kanugijafitï. Kofi calls Taguwaki "awa" [my *ijogu*].

This boy Kofi's other brother, Waiyepe, whose mother had died during the epidemic, also lives in the household. As I noted earlier, Waiyepe (who is about 27 years old) is unmarried. He says, "My Kamaiura wife always went with other men, so I beat her very hard and left them. Then I went to the Kuikuru to get a wife, but again she didn't like me, only those Kuikuru *ajo*. I don't like a wife to do this, so I beat her and went away. Now I live with my brother-in-law and my sister. It's good because they always have fish to eat." Waiyepe considers Kafundzu and Kafutani his *ifisuandaw*, and thus refers to Taguwaki as his brother-in-law. Because he has "given" Taguwaki a wife, he is in a favorable position with respect to the entire household, for whom he need not continually perform subsistence obligations, but from whom he always receives food. For example, Waiyepe very rarely harvests manioc, and is an unlucky fisherman, perhaps because of the fact that he makes little effort to develop his skill. However, he is always the first to appear at mealtimes, especially when Ugaki (whom he considers a "mother" because of a connection between his grandmother and Ugaki's mother) is preparing the food. The complexity of relationships between Waiyepe and Taguwaki's group, and lack of close ties elsewhere serve to justify his presence in Taguwaki's household.

Ugaki's two unmarried sons, her married *anetu* son Tufulei, and her daughter and son-in-law complete the adult members of this group. Tufulei's wife Ambo continually urges him to move to the newly built house of her mother, and mother's husband, but Tufulei's position as an active village representative encourages him to live with relatives who are continually obligated to him, namely, his unmarried brothers and his brother-in-law. These men are willing to assist him during ceremonies which he must sponsor as *anetu*. In his mother-in-law's group, there are none who are obligated to him in this way, and he himself would be constrained to obey the wishes of his wife's mother, Afualu, and her husband, Sagama, who is himself a prominent person and *anetu*.

Ugaki's son-in-law, as an in-marrying spouse, is perhaps the most subservient of all the members of this household. Though married for a number of years, he remains with Taguwaki and Ugaki because his other few relatives are also in-marrying spouses, scattered in several villages throughout the Upper Xingu.

The size of Taguwaki's and Ugaki's household is in part the result of fortuitous circumstances; namely, (1) the measles epidemic, which left many children orphans and which forced survivors of several households to live together, and (2) the circumstances of fate which caused certain of their affines to have few relatives of their own. Indeed, the brother–sister exchange arrangement took place only after the death of previous spouses of three of the parties involved. However, relatively recent additions to the group, especially Waiyepe and the daughter and son-in-law of Ugaki, demonstrate the ability of this "core" to draw in relatives previously living elsewhere, and possibly under obligations to other persons. In 1968, only Enumï, engaged to the daughter of another village leader (Bïjïjï), was expected to leave Taguwaki's household.

In addition to his household group, Taguwaki has established a complicated network of relationships in nearly all the households of Aifa. Most important are his kinship ties with his brother Apihụ's household, and the affines who have married sisters, daughters and sons of this older brother. Second are the kinship and affinal relationships he has with persons in Bïjïjï's group. Taguwaki considers himself Bïjïjï's *ifisuagï*; also, his sister Ugaki's first husband was the brother of two of Bïjïjï's wives. On the other hand, Taguwaki is also the son-in-law of one of the latter (Tsaŋaku), having married her daughter Kafundsu. Thus, a large segment of Taguwaki's household is linked through kinship and affinity to Bïjïjï's group; some of these same persons have close ties with Apihụ's group. Taguwaki's large household therefore presently stands as a link between the two rival factions of Apihụ and Bïjïjï. In conflict situations it is opposed to the other groups only minimally, since the relationships which tie it to both rival *anetaw*'s factions prevent entire positive siding with one over the other. This is especially true with respect to witchcraft accusations. Taguwaki's group in the main accuses two members of Bïjïjï's faction; in return, a nonresident affine of Apihụ's faction is accused by Bïjïjï's group, but also by Taguwaki's group. Taguwaki frequently threatens to leave Aifa, especially when those men whom he has accused of witchcraft abuse him for being a Mehinaku. He has from time to time planted corn, arrow cane, and cotton near a small lake south of Aifa, using the land for larger quantities of crops than could be grown at Aifa, and thus has laid claim to the territory. It is to this site that he wishes to move with his household group, though nothing definite has come of it, perhaps because of his complex relationships with Bïjïjï and Apihụ.

Taguwaki performed services associated with a larger number of statuses. As might be expected, he was the household shaman, and often was asked to cure and divine not only within Aifa, but by persons living in other villages. Although he was not *anetu*, he was a prominent figure during many intervillage ceremonies, for he was a champion wrestler and spear thrower. Furthermore, he was *ifï* of at least ten ceremonies, including those associated with the *egitsu*, *ipoñe*, and *ifagaka*. Within the village he was *oto* of at least five ceremonies. As *kagutu ifï*, he was one of the few men who knew how to make *kagutu* and other ceremonial flutes, and was a particularly fine performer of lengthy songs associated with the *ndufei*.

As a result of all these positions, Taguwaki was one of the wealthiest persons in the village; he owned a canoe, a manioc drying rack, a hardwood bow, several guns, feathers to make at least two large headdresses, two shell collars, two shell belts, two toucan feather headdresses, several large ceramics, and many items of lesser value which are not commonly owned in great quantity. Furthermore, he was an active participant in the *uluki*, and was never criticized for his stinginess. Although he counted on the continual support of his household membership, he never was critical of them, always lent out equipment, made presents of minor objects, and in general exemplified the ideals of generosity and pacificity.

Prestige and Influence: Summary

The Kalapalo distinguish a number of special statuses, each associated with specific duties or obligations to perform services, and with the privilege of receiving payment or other rewards for those services. Thus the *anetaw* are village patrons, men and women who act as representatives and mediators between household and village groups. *Oto* are sponsors of ceremonies, who are obligated to pay for the performances, but who may often ask for village labor in return for their sponsorship. *Ifi* are ceremonial specialists, men and women who are responsible for a ceremonial performance and who must perpetuate ceremonial knowledge by teaching others. In return they receive payment for these services. *Fuati* are curers and diviners, persons with unusual skills; in return for their services they receive considerable payment. In general, all these statuses are specialist positions, which involve services to the community.

This conscious model does not take into consideration the possibility of status "accumulation," nor the cumulative effect of this accumulation in terms of the acquisition of power. The Kalapalo do not speak of any one of these statuses in terms of leadership or the ability to control the initiative of others. However, in reality leaders are those few persons who have managed to acquire a great many statuses and who thus stand apart from the rest of the community as powerful individuals.

WITCHCRAFT

Among the residents of the Upper Xingu Basin, one of the most common subjects of gossip is witchcraft accusations. Any untoward event personally affecting an individual in some adverse way is liable to be attributed to a witch, and though individuals are not always accused as witches, the practice of witchcraft is itself always of interest as a topic of conversation. Details of particular witchcraft cases are described with considerable relish, especially by those directly affected. Nonetheless, there are many occasions (even disastrous ones, such as a sudden death) which are not attributed to witchcraft, but which become associated with some other, equally probable cause. The problem examined in this section is how witchcraft accusations come to be made among the Kalapalo, and under what circumstances. As will become apparent, this problem is intimately connected with the relationships between factions, village leaders, and subordinate kinsmen.

Although people are commonly labeled witches, the Kalapalo justify their accusations by reference to secondhand decisions. Almost invariably, they resort to accusations made in the past by others—either by their own kinsmen or by persons who were somehow associated with the accused. Such statements as the following serve as justifications for naming a witch: "He killed X.'s sister, people say." "He killed many people in Y. village." "The people of Y. village say he killed so-and-so." "Just before he died, X.'s father asked X. who had 'shot him,' and X. said Y.'s name." References to observable or inducible behavior do not enter into specific accusations. In other words, personal attributes are not considered when making verbal judgments about who is a witch.

Furthermore, when a diagnosis of witchcraft is made, there is no necessary con-comitant accusation. On occasion, the calamity is attributed to an unnamed or unknown person or persons. Then, the interest in witchcraft seems to rest with the victim's ailment.

There are, it is true, a few criteria which, for the Kalapalo, justify suspicions of witchcraft. These are variables which are recognized as "indicators of possibility," but are not sufficient reasons for a diagnosis or accusation of witchcraft. When in-dividuals are named as responsible for specific misfortunes, it is necessary to examine the historical background to the specific relationships between accuser, victim, and accused, as well as the assessment of possibility made by the Kalapalo. In short, the criteria which are important for explaining witchcraft accusations and diagnoses appear almost exclusively in the area of nonexplicit behavioral phenomena, rather than explicit diagnostic features in a native model. Among the Kalapalo such features are relatively unimportant, often appearing *post hoc*, and seem at best to serve as criteria for narrowing the field of possibilities. Put another way, it is combinations of situational criteria that seem to influence witchcraft accusations, rather than the assessment of specific individual relationships.

Becoming a *Kwifi Oto*, or Witch

It is doubtful that anyone actually practices witchcraft among the Kalapalo, but a fairly elaborate technology is known to most people, and techniques of witchcraft are freely discussed, at least by those persons who have yet to be accused.

In general, a witch's practice focuses on the manufacture and use of *kwifi*, or "darts," invisible projectiles which are shot into victims, twirled in the hand, or otherwise manipulated at a distance. Hence the term for witch, *kwifi oto*, "master of the darts."

Any severe or congenital misfortune can be attributed to witchcraft, and different kinds of *kwifi* are said to be made in order to effect them. A death or severe illness can be caused by darts shot into a victim through the house thatch. Some *kwifi* are said to be wound with the victim's hair (though curiously, haircutting, in fact grooming in general, is not marked among the Kalapalo by elaborate precautions). A strong wind can be sent for the purpose of destroying a house, caused by *kwifi* whirled vigorously by the witch. A manioc blight, affecting only one man's garden, is said to be the result of *kwifi* made from manioc plants secretly removed from that garden. Even an uncomfortable excess of mosquitoes in the house is attributed to malicious manipulations of a witch. The greatest number of witchcraft-related incidents, however, are those involving serious illness and death. The witch is therefore considered a truly dangerous individual, not simply a malicious person.

In keeping with the Kalapalo observation that offspring are taught the skills of their parents, witches are said to learn at an early age how to inflict misfortune. During puberty seclusion, the traditional period of intense parental instruction, a witch is said to expose his son's hands to medicines and fire, thereby enabling him to manufacture and shoot *kwifi* effectively. The filiative relationship is therefore an important criterion for determining a person's possible identity as a witch, though it is not, to repeat, a sufficient criterion for accusation.

Witches are associated with the maned wolf, called *isogoko*, a nocturnal carnivore whose cries are believed to presage a death somewhere in the Upper Xingu. Although considered potentially malevolent in its own right, the Kalapalo believe that any particular maned wolf may in fact be a witch who has transformed himself in order to travel to distant villages at night. A witch may also make use of various kinds of monsters, with which he travels about after dark. In short, the witch's power includes control over nonnatural powers of transformation, by which he transcends the ordinary human association with *itseke*, or potentially malevolent beings. Since *itseke* may cause illness and death by their own *kwifi*, by capturing a seriously ill person's shadow or by merely confronting a person traveling alone, the relationships between witches and *itseke* are doubly dangerous.

Motivations for Witchcraft

A witch's motives are only explicitly recognized in certain situations when he is said to revenge himself upon an individual who has offended him in some way. In such cases, the witch has already been identified, and a specific conflict can be cited between witch and victim. Conflicts of this sort usually occur between persons belonging to two different village groups, or when the kinsmen of the victim who make the accusation are of a group different from the accused. These conflicts seem to occur most often between husband and wife. Two cases, where specific revenge motives were cited, serve to illustrate this type of accusation.

Case 1   M., the youngest of three cowives, wished to leave her husband, a notorious witch, because he repeatedly abused her for taking lovers. Although she wanted to return to her natal village, she showed great reluctance to do so, since she was certain her husband would bewitch her if she left him.

Case 2   T., a woman whose husband was previously accused of witchcraft by members of his own village group (the Mehinaku), wished to remarry, but had difficulty despite her youth and good looks in persuading any one of her many lovers to take her as a wife. Finally a young Waura, just out of puberty seclusion, married her. Within two months, he was dead. His kinsmen, as well as the unfortunate T., attributed this catastrophe to her former husband.

A second configuration of witchcraft accusations leave the witch's motive unknown and unrelated to actual social situations. These kinds of accusations seem to most frequently occur among persons living in the same village. The following cases serve to illustrate this configuration.

Case 3   B. attributed to witchcraft an unusually violent wind which threatened his newly finished house, but claimed he had always spoken well to everyone and therefore had offended no one. He thought the witch might have acted "just because he is an angry (*itsotu*) person."

Case 4   The swollen stomachs, associated illnesses, and eventual deaths of six senior women in a certain village were attributed by their kinsmen to X., a woman who had fed them all fish "without reason" on a single occasion. There was considerable puzzlement about X.'s wishing to give them food, since some of the victims had had little social contact with her prior to the incident, and were neither her kinsmen nor her affines. The survivors could not say why she would have wanted to harm them.

Case 5   The senior *anetu* of Kanugijafitï suddenly died after being given a small handgun by a European visitor. His death was attributed to a young man in his village group who was said to have become angry because he had not been given the gun himself. Since the man who died was a legitimate village representative, it was thought proper that he should have received the gift, given by the European in return for the village's hospitality, and the Kalapalo could not understand why anyone should become jealous for that reason.

By far the greatest number of cases withhold judgments about the witch's motives. This may be attributed to the fact that in the Kalapalo view, revenge as a motive implies a prior fault or offense of the victim. Since most Kalapalo who accuse others of witchcraft are kinsmen of victims or are themselves victims, they cannot attribute wrongdoing as a cause. This is because persons who are kinsmen are not supposed to criticize one another, and must consistently support each other during conflicts. Thus, witchcraft remains to a significant extent an inexplicable fact of human existence. A witch is seen as an individual whose hostile acts are unjustified and therefore intolerable. They demand, when serious and frequent enough, his execution.

Defining a Case as One of Witchcraft

Defining a severe illness or a death as caused by witchcraft appears to involve the assessment and manipulation of social, epidemiological, and historical variables by kinsmen of the victim. Calling a man or woman a *kwifi oto* is a matter of such seriousness as to place the accuser himself in a potentially dangerous position. Because an eventual counterattack can be made, the Kalapalo make diagnoses of witchcraft much more frequently than direct accusations against individuals. For these reasons, many cases of death end with a witchcraft diagnosis only, less frequently with an accusation, and only very rarely with the execution of an individual witch in revenge for the murder. Often, a diagnosis of "shadow capture" by *itseke* accounts for such disasters. Between 1961 and 1968, a total of 17 persons died at Aifa. Of these, 11 deaths were positively attributed to witchcraft, and three to *itseke*. These attributions appeared to be made by various factional groups, not simply kinsmen of the deceased, and were apparently consensual conclusions. However, only two individuals were executed as responsible parties, and of these, only one was a member of the Kalapalo village group.

The only prerequisite for diagnosis of witchcraft concerns the course the sickness takes. Witchcraft-induced illness is believed incurable, unless the witch releases the victim voluntarily. During periods of high fever or intense pain, Kalapalo sometimes call out to the witch whom they believe is causing their illness, asking him to withdraw the *kwifi* which he has shot into their bodies.

The illness must be either a very prolonged and disfiguring one, or one whose onset comes quickly and with an abrupt but agonizing death. These two types of sickness are almost invariably attributed to witchcraft, especially when repeated attempts at shamanistic curing have failed. Where shamans do cure successfully, symptoms are most often thought to be caused by *itseke*.

There are occasions where illness resulting in death is also attributed to *itseke*. Such a diagnosis seems rare and limited to situations where witchcraft seems inappropriate as a diagnosis. An accusation against *itseke*, who cannot be the subject of reprisals or ostracism, can be considered a means by which kinsmen of the deceased avoid coming into conflict with their fellow villagers. The *itseke*-caused death diagnosis satisfies the requirements of explaining a curious death without compromising the survivors in a factional conflict which they would be incapable of handling or which would expose themselves to witchcraft accusations in the future.

Itseke are frequently thought to cause minor illness, such as skin diseases in young children, and can be directly useful to a witch by stealing his victim's shadow when he has become weak from the witch's *kwifi*. Thus, *itseke* are possible, even probable, agents of a person's illness at any time, and their designation as such in a specific case is therefore entirely legitimate and acceptable as a substitute for a witchcraft diagnosis.

The circumstances surrounding Nakï's death provide interesting material on a dramatic and sudden death which resulted in an *itseke* diagnosis. Nakï was the son of a man executed for witchcraft, but he himself was never accused. Nakï, like his father, was considered *anetu*, but (some say because of his father's execution) had never held office. His elder brother had left the Upper Xingu to work for the Brazilians when their father died. Two younger brothers, also living in Aifa, were personally retiring, without many *ato* or *ajo*, and with no *ifï* statuses. Although Nakï was popular with the men of Aifa (he had acquired considerable status by being *kagutu oto* and a somewhat notorious lover), he was not identified with either of the two central factions of Apihu and Bïjïjï; perhaps this added to his popularity. When Nakï died, no accusation of witchcraft was made, nor was witchcraft even mentioned as a reason for the illness while he was still alive. It was entirely attributed to *itseke* visions Nakï had before his death (see p. 22), although these visions were only mentioned after he died. Whether Nakï actually saw, or claimed to have seen, *itseke* is irrelevant. Circulation of this explanation for his death enabled the group at large to find a correct solution to the problem of how this ostensibly healthy man could have succumbed so quickly. His weak group of kinsmen were without a considerable number of supporters and, closely related to a man who was himself executed, they could hardly make an accusation of witchcraft themselves. However, two men from the Kuikuru village, who considered themselves "fathers" of the dead man, felt free to make a diagnosis of witchcraft, for they had no social contact with the people of Aifa, yet were prominent members of their own group and thus had some support for their statements.

Accusations of Witchcraft against Individuals

Each Upper Xingu village contains men who are consistently thought of as witches, being accused by members of factions to which they are not related and by persons in other villages to whom they are not related. An accusation is always denied by a close kinsman of the accused, but sometimes socially distant relatives (especially those living in other village groups) may concede that the person accused is in fact a witch. Once a man has been accused by members of a faction, he is likely to be repeatedly accused by them when a person affiliated with the faction dies.

Accusations made against the deceased's parents or other of his close kinsmen (especially older *ifisuandaw*) by someone else's older relative often result in a repeated accusation in the next generation. As a result, historical feuds sometimes occur, going back at least three generations, and involving lineal descendants of men accused of witchcraft many years in the past. This is partially due to the belief that a father transmits his witchcraft knowledge to his sons, but also seems to be motivated by revenge. In one case for example, F.'s father accused T.'s father of witchcraft. In return, T. accused F. of the death of his first wife. F., his kinsman B., and other members of B.'s faction attributed T.'s wife's death to an outsider, X. However, X. was presently married to T.'s sister. Although T. agreed X. was a witch, because they were brother-in-law, T. did not accuse him of that particular death.

Again, consistent with beliefs concerning the inheritance of witchcraft techniques from parent to child, a man whose father was accused of witchcraft in one village might be accused by members of his own village group or by the descendants of his father's accusers. Kalapalo frequently justify their accusations by stating that a witch's father had been accused by the members of his own village, the implication being that those persons, of all people, should have known who the witches were in their midst. For example, when I asked several persons why Agifuti had publicly accused a certain Kalapalo man of witchcraft in connection with his son's death, they replied that Agifuti's son, when interrogated by his father, had made the accusation. Such questioning of the victim is made of course by the very persons who feel sure witchcraft is involved, and they may suspect individuals as well. However, as in other cases of explicit accusation, what is important is the fact that kinsmen publicly declare a person guilty. If they have no support in the village, they must leave for another where they have relatives who agree with their judgment. After making his accusation, Agifuti in fact was forced to do this, and now lives in Mïgiyapei.

Flight from Witchcraft Accusations

While collecting genealogies I was struck by the number of persons who had fled from one village to another in order to escape witchcraft accusations and threats of execution. Once a man has fled to a village because of fear of execution, his relatives (kinsmen or affines) are expected to shelter him. If his relatives are faction members he may then be sufficiently protected, for a man who can count on the support of powerful persons (or those intimately connected with the latter) can make it more difficult for other members of the host village to support his accusers. However, although accused witches can take refuge with their relatives and thereby live for many years without fear of being killed, they are never entirely free from accusations against them, particularly by members of their old group. For this reason, there is a pattern of intervillage accusation which results not so much from local group hostility but from the practice of seeking asylum. The following cases illustrate this kind of situation.

Case 1   The story of Taguwaki's father was described by a younger kinsman in the following way: They all fled because the Mehinaku were about to kill Taguwaki's father. They left late at night, when everyone was sleeping, carrying only a small pot with a little fire in it to light the path. They came to Kanugijafïtï because that's where Taguwaki's father's brothers-in-law lived. The Mehinaku wouldn't kill him there. Even today, Taguwaki won't return to live with the Mehinaku; they say he is a witch like his father.

Case 2   You know X., he lives with the Kuikuru now. A long time ago he fled his own village, when the Wagifïtï people killed his father because he shot so many people with *kwifi*. Then X. lived with the people at Kanugijafïtï. They were afraid of him and gave him three women; that's how he married his wives. The Kalapalo said he killed a woman there, and his mother killed some women to whom she gave bad fish. Then X. became afraid again and went to the Kuikuru. It doesn't seem that he killed anyone there, but it was a Kuikuru who told the Mïgiyapei *anetu* that X. was the one who made his wife sick. N. [a Wagifïtï man] said he was sleeping when his "father" X. came to talk to him at Mïgiyapei. X. told N. he had come from the Kuikuru like a maned wolf, that's how he came so quickly from so far away, and at night when people are afraid to meet monsters in the forest. They talked a while, then X. went away. The next day, A.'s wife got sick, and K. [a shaman] said he found *kwifi* in her body. Then they all knew X. was the one who shot her.

Case 3   The members of Bïjïjï's faction made a trip to the Post, where they met Kanatu, a Yawalipiti man. Upon their return to Aifa, Tsanaku came to Ugaki and Taguwaki, saying she had heard from Kanatu that Y. was telling people that Taguwaki, Apihu, and Tufulei [the latter was *ifatuwï*, or brother's son to Tsanaku] were all witches. Y. was accused directly of several deaths by the members of Bïjïjï's faction, and although Taguwaki's and Apihu's factions strongly believed Y. to be a witch, they never had accused him. These factions contained many of Y.'s affines who were in a relationship of *ifutisu ekugu* with him. In addition, they were afraid that he would make his wives sick if their kinsmen threatened him. Bïjïjï's faction desired Y.'s death, but the other group could not condone it. Therefore, when Bïjïjï's group spread the story that Y. had called his affines witches, it was something of a shock to those relatives, who expressed considerable indignation. Tufulei, especially, was upset by Y.'s alleged accusations, for he had never before been publicly accused of witchcraft. Although both Taguwaki and Apihu had been previously accused by their own father's group, the Mehinaku [see Case 1], they had apparently never been directly confronted with the possibility that Y. thought so. In the midst of the resulting furor, Y. himself appeared unexpectedly, having apparently made plans to visit his affines—plans that had been known all along by Bïjïjï's group. Whether the story was spread by them in the knowledge that Y. was coming to Aifa, and with the hope that he be ill-received by Taguwaki and Apihu, or whether Tsanaku really believed Y. had spoken against his affines, the reception he met with in the Kalapalo village was surprisingly cordial. The very men he had allegedly accused greeted him with some warmth, invited him to play the *kagutu* [he was a specialist well known for his skill], and gossiped with him about other accused witches during his stay.

Men who are accused of being witches consciously attempt to increase their social contacts with the accusers or their relatives, and thereby to establish situations in which the display of fundamental social ideals (generosity and pacificity) are particularly appropriate or necessary. The reputed witch who consistently participates in village affairs and who even initiates them in the role of ceremonial sponsor or specialist hopes to become less noticeable as an antisocial person. His association with unjustified aggression (as an accused witch) is potentially weakened (at least temporarily) when he takes an active and beneficial role in society. One important means of doing this is to become sponsor or specialist of ceremonies which can be used in curing very sick persons. Then, the accused witches are in a position to demonstrate most clearly their positive attitude toward a victim. Assisting prominently in an attempted cure as they lead the singers during such a ritual, these men actively show their desire for the victim's recovery. However, once a person is accused, the chances are he will be accused again, somewhere, by somebody.

Revenge Magic

The Kalapalo consider the most reprehensible witchcraft murder to be that of a young person in puberty seclusion. When the death of such a person is attributed to witchcraft, and a powerful faction is able to publicly name the murderer, the response should be the execution of more than one person in revenge. In such a case, the murderer himself, together with adult male members of his household, are the targets of the enraged kinsmen of the victim. Ideally, the Kalapalo say, five persons should be executed in revenge for the death of a secluded boy or girl.

It sometimes happens, however, that the victim's relatives do not constitute a powerful faction who can gather support for such severe action. In such a case, the appropriate step to take is to consult a person known as *kifi oto*, "master of the revenge charm." This person is a shaman who has learned the art of manufacturing and controlling the power of the *kifi*, a large vessel in which parts of the victim's body are kept boiling in order to magically induce the death of his murderer.

During their mourning of the victim, the kinsmen wishing to consult a *kifi oto* cut pieces of skin from the deceased's palms and soles, or remove his little finger joints. These are brought to the shaman's house, where the aggrieved kinsmen request that a *kifi* be made. Having agreed to do so, the *kifi oto* builds himself a seclusion wall, behind which he must live for the duration of the charm's use. In the seclusion area he builds a large fire, over which he places a large cooking vessel filled with water containing the parts of the victim's body given him by the kinsmen. This must be kept constantly boiling until the murderer dies. As a consequence, the *kifi oto* live in an atmosphere of intense heat, which normal individuals cannot endure. The Kalapalo believe the *kwifi oto* ("the witch") experiences great pain from the heat of the fire, and at night leaves the village to run in the forest, where he is able to scream in agony undisturbed. Toward the end, his body begins to shed sparks, and young children who step on them develop sores on their feet. Only after the murderer has been killed by the charm may the shaman put out the fire and return to a normal existence.

8 / Relationships between groups: the role of village representative

In every village of Upper Xingu society, there are certain men and women who have inherited a special status. These persons, whom the Kalapalo call *anetaw* (*anetu*, singular) have often been designated "chiefs" or "headmen" by persons acquainted with the area, who have implied prerogatives of leadership and political authority by their use of these terms. Such appellations are unfortunately misleading, for the person who is *anetu* is primarily designated by his ascribed duties as village *representative*. Though we can call *anetaw* "chiefs," it should come as no surprise to find that they are not necessarily village *leaders* and are frequently without any political influence whatsoever. In fact, as Gertrude Dole (1966) has shown, the opposite can often occur; some *anetaw* are pointedly ignored when they try to initiate action.[1]

The Kalapalo conceive of their *anetaw* as village "patrons" or "sponsors" (*etu oto*), men and women whose presence justifies the actual existence of the social unit. As patrons, *anetaw* represent their group in situations where it confronts other villages, especially during ceremonial events. Within the village itself, *anetaw* serve to mediate between households whose autonomy normally prevents individual members from freely interacting. In general, *anetaw* are persons whose physical presence and actions during intergroup events sanctions those events and makes them legitimate.

Furthermore, as representatives of their villages, *anetaw* are supposed to personify the *ifutisu* ideals of generosity and pacificity. By organizing the distribution of ceremonial food payment or of gifts presented to the village at large by an outsider, by calling for the accumulation of gifts to be given visitors on formal occasions, and by acting as hosts during intervillage ceremonies, they exemplify the former ideal. By controlling the aggressiveness of members of their village groups during intervillage athletic events, by mediating between potentially hostile groups within the village, and by continually assisting one another in major activities (such as house building) regardless of their own personal feelings, they exemplify the latter ideal. In this manner, considerable prestige is derived from actively holding *anetu* office, for activities associated with that office exemplify the most

---

[1] The problem is one of polysemy, because the term *anetu* can be used in more than one way, that is, it can refer to more than one concept. In this book, the word "chief" is restricted to mean an exclusive leader or head of a category of beings; such leaders are also called *anetu* by the Kalapalo (as in *itolo anetu*, "chief of the birds," a reference to the king vulture).

fundamental principles of proper social behavior. If the person who is village representative is in addition the bearer of a number of other important statuses, his position of true village leader is assured. However, representative status does not in itself imply leadership, as I will show below.

INHERITANCE OF *ANETU* STATUS AND SUCCESSION TO OFFICE

All children of an *anetu* (male or female) inherit their parents' title, but only the eldest of a set of siblings inherits the right to hold office when his parent of the same sex dies. Thus, a male *anetu* is ideally the eldest surviving male child of a male *anetu* (his father) and a female *anetu* the eldest surviving female child of a female *anetu* (her mother).

Often, however, a representative dies without children of the appropriate sex to inherit his position, that is, his right to hold office. If this happens to a female *anetu*, no one inherits her position, but when a male *anetu* dies without sons, another person usually claims this right. Most often the claimant is the eldest son of the dead representative's younger brother, but sometimes a man whose mother was *anetu* claims the position. Whether or not these persons make claims to *anetu* office depends upon what their relationships are with men who are already holding this office. A person who is a subordinate affine to the latter will not press his claims, nor will a man actively seek to hold office if there are several other *anetu* active in the village. However, if an epidemic or other disastrous event leaves no surviving adults who can legitimately hold office, these "irregular" *anetu* are accepted in order to fill the vacant positions. These persons are usually leaders in their own right before acquiring *anetu* office.

The Kalapalo distinguish between "legitimate" and "irregular" inheritors of *anetu* status by calling the former *anetu ekugu*, "real" or "great amount" *anetu*, and the latter *intsoño anetu*, "little amount" *anetu*. The former are men who have inherited their status directly from their father (himself *anetu ekugu*), whereas the latter are individuals who claim their status on the basis of other ties. Of all the representatives in a village who hold office, the eldest is considered the head *anetu*, and he is the man with the most frequent obligations to act as village representative in ceremonial situations; he is also expected to harangue the villagers at dawn, urging them to rise from their hammocks and perform the work of the day. When a head *anetu* dies and his son begins to hold office, the latter does not become the new head *anetu*, for this position falls to the oldest surviving active representative.

In Aifa (as in all other Upper Xingu villages) live a number of *anetaw* of both types. Seven men held *anetu* status among the Kalapalo during 1966–1968.

1. The senior *anetu*, Apihu, is considered *intsoño anetu* because he bases his claim on his mother's status; she was a Kalapalo representative. His father held no claims to *anetu* status at all. Apihu's main rival, Bïjïjï, claims that Apihu is a Mehinaku man (because he was born in that village) and thus not a Kalapalo at all, let alone a Kalapalo *anetu*. Except for Bïjïjï and his household, however, Apihu was accepted as head *anetu* by all the residents of Aifa. However, Apihu very rarely made speeches in the early morning, which an unambiguous leader of the entire group would do.

2. Bïjïjï, who was only slightly younger than Apihu, was also considered *intsoño anetu*, because his claim was based on his father's brother's position. The latter had died without male children to succeed him, so Bïjïjï was able to claim the status for his own.

3. A third irregular claimant was Yafula. Although Yafula's father had been *anetu*, the latter's claims were themselves apparently based on an irregular inheritance, and thus the son was known as *intsoño anetu*.

4. The only *anetu ekugu* to hold office in Aifa was Tufulei, a man of about twenty-six years of age. Because of his youth, Tufulei was still inexperienced and in the process of learning *anetu* speeches, gestures, and other formal behavior characteristic of the representative role. Tufulei was recognized by all to have the clearest, most legitimate *anetu* status, having succeeded both a father and grandfather who were *anetu ekugu*.

In addition to these four, who actively held office, there were others, all *anetu ekugu*, who never acted as village representatives.

5. Nakï was a man who had never held *anetu* office, but whose legitimate status was recognized by the fact that upon his death in 1967, he was treated to all the elaborate burial and commemorative rituals which are accorded an *anetu*. Nakï's father had been executed for witchcraft when Nakï was still young, and the boy's eldest brother, who would have inherited his father's position, as a result had left the Upper Xingu Basin permanently to work for Brazilians. Nakï also refused to inherit his father's representative role, apparently in his reluctance to identify himself with witchcraft, a skill thought to be handed down from father to son. In this he was completely successful.

6. Kafutani was a young man whom everyone recognized as *anetu ekugu*, yet he too never held office. His explanation was quite explicit: he did not wish to embarrass his older brothers-in-law, Apihu and Bïjïjï, to whom he was subordinate as a "wife receiver." By actively holding office, he would be flaunting his legitimate status in the face of their *intsoño anetu* designation.

7. Finally, Sagama was a man who held legitimate claims to the *anetu* position in another village group, the Jagamï, who disbanded and scattered in various Carib speaking villages after several epidemics and invasions by hostile tribes had severely depopulated them. Although Sagama could not act as a representative of his own village group, he was recognized as an *anetu* and therefore was allowed to act as such during the intravillage trade game which is normally conducted by persons holding *anetu* status. However, when the Kalapalo came into contact with other village groups, Sagama never took this representative role.

Only three women held *anetu* status in Aifa, and all three from time to time participated in activities which indicated they held office. Like male *anetu*, these women seemed to be ranked according to age, so that Tsaŋaku, the eldest of the three, appeared the most active. Women are not apparently distinguished, like men, according to the means by which they have inherited *anetu* status, and thus were unquestionably "legitimate."

ACTIVITIES OF *ANETAW* IN THE VILLAGE

In the context of village affairs, male and female *anetaw* act as mediators between disparate household groups which are normally autonomous. The presence of an *anetu*, or his initial sponsorship of some activity, justifies the participation in that activity of household groups which are not necessarily related through kinship or affinal ties.

Insofar as women are assigned fewer roles during the course of public affairs, (and are expected to be shy and retiring on those occasions) female *anetaw* are much less active than male *anetaw*. Furthermore, because there are no female *intsoño anetaw*, there are fewer female representatives found in the village group. These two factors cause female *anetaw* to be considerably less noticeable in the life of the village than male *anetaw*. Their main activities are (1) leading the women's intravillage *uluki* (see p. 136), (2) distributing food payment to women, and (3) supervising the preparation of food for distribution to visitors during an intervillage ceremony. Female *anetaw* are treated at death in the same elaborate manner as male *anetaw*, but apparently never appear publicly as formal representatives of their village groups during intervillage ceremonies, as do men.

On occasions when large quantities of food must be presented to the village group (for example, when a ceremonial sponsor distributes payment for the performance of a ceremony), it is the *anetaw*'s responsibility to see that it is distributed equitably. Although the sponsor formally makes the distribution, he is supervised and often assisted by two or three male and female representatives who make sure every person or household receives a portion.

As village patrons, male representatives are also responsible for maintaining public areas, including the central plaza, the formal entrance path, the path leading to the lake, and the main bathing area. When it is necessary to build a new bridge over the creek which crosses the *tagiñu*, the Kalapalo representatives invite the men of Aifa to assist in its construction. Similarly, village representatives are responsible for keeping the plaza clean of debris, and before a visit from another village group they organize the men to weed and sweep this area.

Public declarations of *anetaw*, especially the senior man, and their "official" participation in a communal effort are only the result of a prior agreement made by the adult members of the village group as a whole. Major decisions regarding the village are not made by the senior *anetu* alone, nor even by a "council" composed of all the holders of *anetu* office. Decisions are made informally by all the adult men and women. In order to assess public opinion, the head *anetu* makes it a practice of questioning persons within their own houses or in front of the *kuakutu* where the men assemble to gossip in the afternoon. This is especially important when a decision must be made concerning a major ceremony, moving the village site, or ending a mourning period. After judging public sentiment, the head *anetu* formally declares what is to be done by means of a ritual speech making use of language differing in rhythm from common discourse, and containing words not used in ordinary speech. Although it is not often understood by the non-*anetaw*, this formal speech serves to publicly mark the fact that a decision has been made, a decision on the part of the majority to participate in a certain event together. The *anetu*'s speech thus stands as a symbol of the unity of the village for some common cause.

The ceremonial trading event (called *uluki*), which takes place between members of a single village or between two village groups as a whole, is another situation in which *anetaw* act in their special roles of group mediators and representatives.

Only men participate in the intervillage *uluki*. When the ceremony is held by members of the same settlement, it is always organized among persons of the same sex, women trading with women, men trading with men. Among the Kalapalo, the men's *uluki* occurs much more frequently than does that of the women. Kalapalo men say this is because women are shyer than men, and are therefore more reluctant to appear in houses other than their own. (In fact, women do seem to organize *uluki* only when most of the men are outside the village—this in order to avoid their teasing as they walk about the plaza.) However, Kalapalo women say they do not trade as often as men because they are poorer and have fewer things to trade. During women's *uluki*, one notices an air of stinginess not felt in the men's group. Women are more reluctant to trade simply for the sake of trading, since they own relatively few personal items, and most of these are either not easily replaced or are treasured gifts from lovers. Despite these differences, both women's *uluki* and men's *uluki* procede according to the same rules, each group being led by an *anetu* of the appropriate sex.

An intravillage *uluki* is initiated by an *anetu* acting upon the request of friends or relatives who want to participate in such an event. Beginning in his own house, the *anetu* invites other men to present items of material wealth which they wish to trade. When all the men of the *anetu*'s household have finished trading, they move on to the next house and then continue clockwise around the village circle until the last household, to the left of the *anetu*'s own, has been visited. The group picks up new members as it travels around the village, and often these new participants ask to have the *uluki* continue around a second time, in order to enjoy possible trade benefits in houses which have been visited before they joined in. Consequently, some houses are visited two or three times in a single *uluki*, often to the consternation of occupants who have previously given all they wished to trade.

When the *uluki* group enters a house, the head of the household is expected to call to the rest of the men in his group. Taking turns, the men of the household then come forward to the cleared area in front of the door which opens onto the plaza, and throw down before the assembled visitors objects they wish to trade. As each man presents something, the *anetu* asks him what it is that he wants in return: "*tükaitsuma?*" ("what is with it?"), and the man can give a specific answer or say, "*Ko, iñalu funumufeke*" ("I don't know"). If one of the men in the group (he cannot be a fellow household member) wants the object offered, he picks it up and leaves for his own house, returning with what has been requested, or if nothing has been specified by the owner, any object he believes a worthy exchange. Usually, however, the owner of the original item receives something of slightly less value. An *uluki* participant is expected to accept what is given him regardless of whether it is a fair exchange or not, and he is especially criticized if he complains about it. Although men and women trade for the sake of obtaining specific items which might otherwise be unavailable to them because of their inability to coerce the owner into giving it up, the *uluki* seems to be performed more for the sake of trading itself. It is therefore at one level a "game," in that it is enjoyed for its own sake, but it clearly has a deeper significance. The system allows the members of a particular village to visit houses they might otherwise be unable to enter, and to see the possessions of other members of the village, in particular those belonging to persons with whom they are not on relaxed, intimate terms. Thus, there are very few secrets of wealth in the Kalapalo village. The *uluki* forces men and women to behave according to the ideal of generosity by enjoining them to freely exchange possessions and to accept things which they do not want.

As the following story illustrates, however, the *uluki* is often used by individuals to obtain specific items which they cannot acquire from their own kinsmen. The speaker is a man describing his puberty seclusion.

> I had to sleep on an old hammock. It was very torn, and every night I would fall through it to the ground. Sometimes, I couldn't sleep at all, and I would cry at night because I couldn't sleep. My mother was dead, and my sister was too small to make hammocks. She didn't know how to do it at that time, she was just able to spin cotton. I felt very sad because there was no woman my father could ask to make me a hammock. Then my father gave me a short length of shell disks, a piece of a belt. "Take this," he said. "When you can buy more shells, you can make a good belt for yourself and you can wear it." I told him I didn't want it. I said, "When the *uluki* comes, ask someone for a hammock, and give this as payment." He did ask for a hammock during *uluki*, and gave the owner the shells. Then I had a good hammock and was able to sleep well.

The *anetu* who organizes an *uluki* is expected to join in actively, and in so doing to set an example for recalcitrant members of his own and other households. He should show enjoyment in trading for its own sake, without thought of gain and solely for the purpose of exhibiting his generous impulses. Through adherence to an ideal of behavior whose enactment confers prestige, the *uluki anetu* is treated with respect and admiration during a successful event of this kind which he or she sponsors.

Children's *Uluki*

From an early age, children, particularly boys, are encouraged to express the ideals of friendliness, generosity, and subordination of their individual interests to the will of the group. One of the most striking ways this is taught is through the children's *uluki*. This kind of trade ceremony is also one means by which a young person who is of *anetu* status learns to understand the prerogatives and duties associated with that position.

During the children's *uluki*, one of the adult male *anetaw* of the village, perhaps the grandfather or father of a young *anetu*, conducts the group of boys from house to house, counseling the future village representative in his role of *uluki* leader. The older man only instructs his younger kinsmen; the other participants are onlookers, and learn mainly through observing their adult counterparts during the adult men's *uluki*.

Household *Uluki*

Finally, *uluki* often is held by the members of a single household group. Here again, the result is a partial redistribution of wealth, motivated by the desires of individual members to obtain specific items they could otherwise not obtain from the owners. In this kind of *uluki*, the barriers between affines and between dominant and subordinate kin are temporarily broken, for any player can legitimately ask for an object from any other player.

In a later section of this chapter, I will discuss the most spectacular *uluki* of all, that which takes place between members of two or more village groups. It will suffice to say here that the intervillage *uluki*, like that which takes place among members of the same village group, is under the formal sponsorship of *anetaw*.

In summary, the formal activities within the village of men and women who hold *anetu* office are those which concern the entire village group and which unite the autonomous households into a community. Such activities can be said to involve mediation between these households, in order that members of such groups can work together for some common goal regardless of the individual relationships (or lack of them) between their members.

Other *anetaw* activities are those focusing upon intervillage relationships, and it is under these circumstances that *anetaw* serve as representatives of their village groups.

Anetaw and Intervillage Ceremony

The most important symbols of *anetaw* status are those relating to the performance of several major ceremonies whose enactment depends upon the participation of a number of village groups. These ceremonies are of two types. On the one hand are performances of the *uluki* or intervillage trade ceremony, during which two village groups are opposed as competitors in a ritual exchange of wealth between individuals. On the other hand are ceremonies which commemorate individual *anetaw* who have died, and which are sponsored by kinsmen of those dead *anetaw* who are themselves village representatives. Although there are other occasions when individuals from different villages come together (such as for the purpose of mourning or for major curing rituals), only these two kinds of events involve village groups acting as such.

ANETAW CEREMONIES

The Kalapalo participate in three major ceremonies sponsored by *anetaw* or their kinsmen. The *egitsu* is a ceremony which commemorates a recently dead *anetu*. It is sponsored by the dead person's siblings. The *ipoñe*, or ear piercing ritual, has been described in Chapter 5. It is usually held in conjunction with the *egitsu*, after the ceremonies associated with the latter have been performed. Finally, the *ifagaka*, or spear throwing contest, is sponsored by an *anetu* in commemoration of his father, the latter having been dead for several years.

All these events (several of which occur each year) have major features in common. First, each involves the participation of men from a number of (often all) village groups; women are most often onlookers, or at best, participate only in the dancing. Usually, the men of two or three guest groups are asked to assist the hosts in preparing enormous quantities of food which are later distributed among themselves. This assistantship role should later be reciprocated by the hosts when their guests sponsor a similar ceremony. A second feature held in common is the nature of the assigned roles of the village representatives. The visiting *anetaw* are in general not actively involved in the activities of the final climactic event, but are passive onlookers who must sit quietly throughout most of the day on stools placed at the edge of the plaza. Third, the guests are formally invited by the sponsor. The invitation is presented by messengers who are paid by him to travel to the various local groups which are to come to the ceremony. The Kalapalo refer to these men as *tiñi*, "those who go to ask."

The *Tiñi*

Because the groups invited to *anetaw* ceremonies often speak languages unintelligible to their hosts, both *tiñi* and guests make use of several nonverbal symbols which convey information about the ceremony. First, the number of messengers who arrive at a village indicates the nature of the ceremony; for the *egitsu* and *ipoñe*, two men are sent to each village, whereas in the case of *ifagaka*, three men are sent. Second, the messengers enter the village by the formal entrance path and, painted only with charcoal, wear no ornaments. They carry no possessions. Thus, they are recognized as *tiñi* and are not mistaken for ordinary vistitors.

When messengers arrive in a village, the head *anetu* makes a short speech indicating to his fellow residents that he is about to accept (or reject) the invitation. Like other speeches made by *anetaw*, this one is almost unintelligible to most people, but the significance is clear. Public opinion has already determined whether the village will go to the ceremony or not.[2]

The senior village representative then walks to the center of the plaza, to where the messengers have been seated on stools, and here waits for other *anetaw* who intend to travel to the ceremony. After they have all gathered together, the group of men standing before the *tiñi* attempt to determine the content of their message. If the languages they speak are unintelligible, they may call to some individual living in the village who can speak it; this person then acts as a translator and conveys a verbal message. Often, however, the *anetaw* must rely upon their knowledge of a very few Portuguese words. Most important, however, they depend upon commonly accepted gestures which serve as symbols of critical information for all the Upper Xingu groups.

Messengers indicate the number of days until the ceremony is to begin by counting on their fingers, then showing the appropriate number. A day is indicated by sweeping the arm over one's head to show the path of the sun across the sky. When these few facts are conveyed, one of the representatives who had already decided to attend the ceremony as a representative, kneels before the messengers and removes their bark ankle wrappings to indicate his village's acceptance of their invitation. He keeps these wrappings for himself, and may also be given what few ornaments the messengers are wearing. When this ritual is completed, the messengers usually leave to return to their own village as quickly as possible.

The man who has untied the ankle wrappings is one of three *anetaw* who have decided to act as village representatives. If other *anetaw* attend, they participate in

---

[2] If a village is in mourning, it does not participate in these intervillage ceremonies, but if the mourning period can be decently shortened to allow the group to travel and decorate themselves, they will do so upon the consent of the deceased's kinsmen.

the ceremony like the rest of the men in their village group. If there are many *anetaw* in the village, they take turns as representatives; the decision is an individual one, and depends to a significant extent on the person's good or bad relationships with the host sponsor, as well as the amount of movable wealth he controls at the time, for *anetaw* are expected to exchange expensive presents with one another at (or after) the ceremony.

The *Egitsu*

The activities associated with the *egitsu* begin with the death of an *anetu* (whether the deceased held office or not, and regardless of whether he or she had attained adult status.) In several important respects, the burial itself differs from that of non-*anetu*. First, all the surviving male village representatives dig the grave, whereas non-*anetaw* (and then, only two) dig the grave for persons who are not village representatives. Second, the grave is constructed differently. *Anetaw* are buried in a tunnel-shaped grave, formed by digging two separate shafts which are joined together at the bottom. The hammock in which the representative's body is wrapped is slung between poles placed at each end of the tunnel. The body is thus left in an extended position. Non-*anetaw* are buried in a single pit, and thus usually end up in a flexed position, as the corpse is bent to fit into the small space. There is, however, no difference in the nature of items which enter the grave. Third, before carrying the body to the grave, the *anetaw* walk with it around the outside of the deceased's house, "as he used to walk when he was alive."

After the washing ceremony which releases the village from mourning, a series of rituals begin which have little meaning for the Kalapalo beyond the fact that they are "for the *egitsu*." Their chief significance seems to lie in the fact that they are performed by the villagers under the sponsorship of the deceased's kinsmen, who must pay for them.

The first ritual is a distribution of fire made by the senior *anetu*. A small fire is built in the plaza, from which the *anetu*, hopping on one foot, carries a burning brand to each house, where new cooking fires are built. This marks the beginning of the *aougufi*, a set of songs performed by two specialists before a line of dancing men. The *aougufi* is performed every day until the *egitsu* itself.[3] The *aougufi* is said to have been invented by a mythical woman whose son had married a snake monster. In order to entice her son back from the *itseke*'s village, the woman invented the ceremony. Although this is mythological justification for the *aougufi*, it does not explain the form of the dance nor the meaning of the songs, which are unintelligible to the singers.

Several months after this ceremony begins, a mock imitation of it takes place at night. Men who are not specialists raucously imitate the singers, while others dance wildly about the plaza waving burning branches. These firebrands are supposed to represent fire that groups who have been invited to the *egitsu* steal as they enter the host village on the eve of the ceremony.

About the same time the *aougufi* is sung, *ataŋa* flutes begin to be played each day, the men of different households taking turns fulfilling this duty. The *ataŋa*

---

[3] This reflects the custom of practicing an *anetu* ceremony several months before its most critical performance.

Figure 11. Tafite *design.*

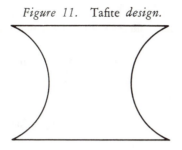

are two toned instruments about nine feet long, played in pairs by men who dance from house to house. Unlike the *aougufi*, which is performed in the plaza in the late afternoon, the *ataŋa* players dance from house to house starting in the early morning, and only finish playing when the *aougufi* ends around dusk.

The construction of the *tafite* takes place about a month after the previously described ceremonies begin. The word *tafite* refers generally to any kind of wooden enclosure, including that built over the *anetu*'s grave, a stockade encircling a village (featured in a single Kalapalo myth and not presently built in the Upper Xingu), and a fence around a garden built to keep out foraging peccary.

Several days before the *tafite* is to be built, a set of rituals is performed which have almost no meaning for the Kalapalo, except that "they are for the *anetu* who is buried." In fact, during my stay in Aifa only two people, a brother and sister, actually knew how these rituals should be performed, and the people who were asked to participate (mainly kinsmen and affines of the two senior *anetaw*) did so with much embarrassment and joking, as they performed in public something which appeared ridiculous to them. This set of rituals includes single pairs of individuals of the same sex walking in figure eight movements over the grave. These movements appear to represent the *tafite*. First, two men are instructed to walk over the grave waving *kejite* leaves. This is repeated by two women. Next, the men wave the leaves about, then rub them over their body and armpits, and finally place them on the grave. Then, two other women walk about clacking pieces of gourds and breaking them over the grave area. Still others must whistle while walking, and finally, pretend to blow their noses into their hands over the grave. No one, including Apihu, who directed these activities, could tell me what they meant.

The next day, all the women of the village are led by a female *anetu* to the new grave, which they sweep clean of the leaves and bits of gourd left from the previous ceremony. The women place this debris in gourd containers and throw it away at the edge of the village. After they have finished sweeping the grave site, they break the gourds into tiny bits and toss them on top of the debris they have discarded.

A few days after this ceremony, the men are called out to gather the logs of *weigufi*, used both in constructing the *tafite* and (later) in making posts which represent the dead *anetaw* during the *egitsu* proper.[4] The logs have already been cut by the deceased's kinsmen, and the surviving *anetaw* direct the men of the

---

[4] Note that this same wood was used by Kwatiŋï to form the bodies of the wives of Nitsuegï. The Kalapalo often call it *i anetu*, "chief of the trees."

village to bring these in from the forest. The building of the *tafite* takes place on the following day, after which the men are given fish and manioc bread in payment for their labor.

The *tafite* is not regarded with special reverence, nor even minimally shunned by adults or children. Dogs walk freely through it without being chased away, and infants occasionally defecate in the area without provoking undue comment.

The night before an *egitsu* performance, visiting groups enter the forest around the host village, being directed to the camping areas where they are to stay by the *tiñi* who had originally invited them. Later, the visitors enter the village cheering and circling the plaza, where, under a rudimentary shelter constructed in front of the *kuakutu* (or if the dead *anetu* was *kagutu oto*, in place of the *kuakutu* which was torn down after he or she died) are the *egitsu* posts. These are sections of *weigufi* trees, approximately four feet high, which represent dead *anetu*. The designs painted on them indicate whether the person represented was a man or woman, but otherwise all are identically decorated with yellow feather headdresses and cotton belts. In front of each post sit the kinsmen of the deceased before a fire they have built from sections of the *tafite* constructed over the recently dead *anetu*'s grave. As the guests enter the village, these kinsmen begin wailing as if mourning for their dead relative. Pieces of wood from their fires are snatched up by the men as they dance by, and are taken back to the campgrounds to light the guests' fires. While this is going on, the *aougufi* is being sung by specialists who stand behind the *egitsu* posts.

Throughout the performance of *egitsu*, the deceased, or rather, their shadows, are supposed to be watching, drawn to the village of the living by the wooden representations of their former physical selves and the singing of *aougufi*. For this reason, it is the duty of shamans (who may also be the *aougufi* singers) to prevent them from actually "entering" the posts and thereby returning to life. To this end tobacco smoke is blown over the wooden figures, discouraging the dead from appearing before their assembled relatives, which would result in the deaths of all concerned.

The next morning the guests decorate themselves with urucu and feather ornaments. Then, the same two *tiñi* who have invited them appear, signifying it is time for the group to enter the village. In contrast with the preceding night, this entrance is formal and orderly.

In the center of the plaza before the *egitsu* posts sit the host *anetaw*, and sitting around the plaza are other groups which had previously entered the village. Each group is assigned a place in the plaza by the *tiñi* who had originally invited them. Stools are placed in readiness for representatives of groups which have not yet entered. Upon their arrival, the *tiñi* lead the guest *anetaw* by the hand to these seats, then return to where their own representatives are seated. The guest *anetaw* seat themselves, and behind them women and young children of their group settle on the ground. Then the men of the guest village enter the plaza, cheering and waving their ornaments, dancing around the village circle, and advancing and retreating towards other visiting groups that are already seated. Finally, they stand behind their own representatives.

On most occasions when strange men arrive at a village, be they formally invited or not, they must wrestle all of the male residents.[5] Similarly, when men from several villages come together to participate in a ceremony, wrestling takes place. Thus wrestling is one of the most important events on these occasions because all the groups must wrestle one another. In fact, the importance of wrestling as a dominant activity is apparent to the Kalapalo themselves, who often refer to their active participation in an intervillage ceremony as "going to wrestle."

Wrestling is seen by the Kalapalo as a competitive sport, and each village takes pride in men who are champions in this activity. The matches begin with each senior *anetu* calling out his village's champions. These men wrestle each other first. Then, individuals from each village group challenge one another until each of the men who has come to the event has had a turn with everyone else. Younger men of seclusion age are encouraged to wrestle with champions in order to gain experience themselves. The *anetaw* make sure everyone has had a chance; they must often urge the less skillful members of their groups to more actively participate. Only men who are affines (especially *ifotisofo*) refrain from competing with one another. When the wrestling ends, the hosts are expected to formally greet their guests one by one. The guests, in turn, acknowledge this greeting, but in a perfunctory manner.

In organizing these formal bouts, the host *anetaw* are most evident, urging their men to wrestle and calling out visitors from each guest village to participate. The guest *anetaw* in turn urge their men to accept challenges, seeing that every person has had a chance to wrestle the hosts. The wrestling ends when everyone has taken turns; then the men go to bathe and (they hope) to meet their lovers who await them along the path to the bathing place.

The next phase of the ceremony is the playing of *ataŋa* flutes by two men from each village, who dance around the village with young women of the host group. During this event, which lasts several hours, the guest *anetaw* remain in the plaza where they had first been asked to sit by the *tiñi*. While these flutes are being played, a *mazope* is led out to distribute toasted piqui seeds to the guest representatives. She walks to each group with one hand on the shoulder of the host *anetu*, followed by her mother. The contrast of the fully decorated young girl and the unkempt, unpainted adult woman is striking. Without touching the *anetaw* of the visiting groups, the *mazope* ladles a small amount of seeds from a gourd and places them before each man. This distribution represents the piqui which has been earlier given in payment by the sponsors to the performers of the preliminary events, and thus demonstrates to the visitors that the *egitsu* has been properly sponsored and paid for.

If the *egitsu* is given in conjunction with ear piercing, that afternoon the men of all the villages join arms with the young boys who are to undergo the ritual, and sing the songs associated with that event. During this dance, each man links arms with his *ato* from another village, and thus no two men from the same local group are next to one another. In this final event, the men who were formerly opposed

Stages in the Egitsu: *(a) During the construction of a* tafite, *the men pause to receive food payment donated by the dead* anetu's *kinsmen. The fish and manioc bread will be distributed by three* anetaw *(two men scratching, and man in center, rear).* Enumï, *the son-in-law of one of these* anetaw, *continues to work while the others relax.*

(b) Bïjïjï and Apihu watch members of their village group dance around egitsu *posts at the start of the ceremony in the Awïtï village.*

(c) The Awïtï sponsor calls his village's champions to the plaza, where they kneel prior to wrestling the guests.

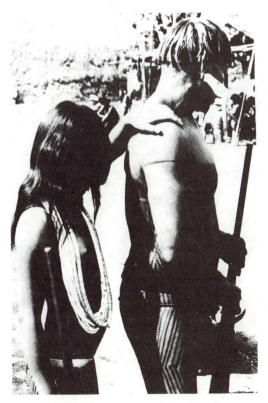

(d) Mazope, led by egitsu sponsor, distributes piqui seeds to visiting anetaw. Both are painted in special egitsu design.

(e) *Kuikuru* atana *players dance with Awitï women.*

(f) *At end of* egitsu, *the visitors sing ear piercing songs while dancing with the boys who are to undergo the ordeal. Note the sponsor's son in center, wearing feather headdress.*

and competitive during wrestling and *ataŋa* playing, and who were spatially separated in their location at the edge of the plaza during the earlier events, are now united in a ceremonial expression of Upper Xingu male solidarity.

Late that afternoon the posts representing dead *anetaw* are pulled up, thus ending their ceremonial significance. The *aougufi* singers use them as seats, until toward dusk the young boys of the village roll them into the nearest body of water, usually the bathing area.

The form of the *egitsu* is, as I noted earlier, partially "explained" by several myths which specify in historical terms the origin of certain of its elements, particularly the *aougufi* songs, the practice of constructing posts to represent the dead, and the invitation of outsiders to participate in the climactic events. However, these myths do not associate any of the same practices with the *anetaw* status itself. Furthermore, a number of ritual elements are left unexplained, even historically; for example, the Kalapalo cannot explain why the *tafite* are built. However, these unexplained elements are not disturbing to the Kalapalo. What is most important to them is the fact that several village groups participate in a ceremony during which they are opposed and competitive. It seems as if the ability of different village groups to participate in the event and to act out the various rituals which comprise the *egitsu* is more significant than any "meaning" which each specific ritual might have.

The *Uluki*

The intervillage trade ceremony, or *uluki*, contrasts in several ways with the *anetaw* ceremonies. First, only two village groups participate in the *uluki*. Second, the ceremony is organized privately by two *anetaw* who are senior representatives of their villages, and no messengers are sent. The date is fixed during an informal meeting between the two representatives. Thus the event is dependent to a great extent upon the amiable relationships between individuals of different village groups; if prominent persons in one group are suspected of witchcraft practices by another group, the latter will resist asking them to an *uluki*. Third, although any member of the guest village can join the ceremony, the implication of the invitation is that the *anetaw* and his faction are the only ones who are specifically asked to come. Finally, unlike *anetaw* ceremonies, during the *uluki* the visitors are housed and fed in the host village, thus emphasizing the friendly relationships between the two groups. The *uluki* is therefore a medium of intervillage factional alliances.

When the visitors arrive at the host village, the plaza is deserted; the men of the village are gathered inside the *kuakutu*, prepared to wrestle the male visitors. The guests formally enter the plaza in a single file, led by their *anetaw*. They wait for a few moments before the *kuakutu*, until the host *anetaw* emerge from their houses, carrying stools for the guest representatives to sit on. The latter sit before the *kuakutu* in front of the rest of their group, then the senior host *anetu* begins his speech of welcome. First, he calls to the other *anetaw* of the village to join him in the plaza. When they have done so, each begins to recite a speech directed at the members of their own village group. Together the *anetaw* urge their fellow villagers to be generous towards their guests, the men to fish, and the women to make manioc bread for them. Here again, as with other *anetaw* speeches, the words are almost unintelligible, and the intent is clearly not to convery a verbal message. Rather, the *anetaw* seem to be "legitimizing" the ceremony by their presence in the plaza.

After these speeches the senior host representative calls to the women living in the house in which the visitors will stay (this usually being the largest house or one in which few persons are living). The senior woman (or women) of that house then walks to the plaza and agrees to the *anetu's* formal suggestion that the guests live in her house. Then wives or adult daughters of the senior *anetu* bring *telisiñi* for the guests to drink.

The next event is a wrestling match between the male hosts and the guests. As during the *ipoñe* ceremony, the champion wrestlers from each village compete first, then all the other men of the two groups. When the wrestling has ended, the *uluki* itself begins.

The guests sit once more before the *kuakutu*, while their male hosts stand facing them. Women of the host village sit watching from in front of their houses, and do not participate. The senior guest *anetu* formally opens the trading by presenting an item of value on the ground before him. This item is something which can be readily accepted by the hosts, for example, fine eagle or parrot tail feathers for fletching arrows or decorating headdresses. The senior host *anetu* picks up whatever is offered, walks to his house, and returns with an equally fine object, such as a well-made pair of serving gourds. These are placed on the ground by the host and picked up by the first man. A second guest *anetu* then offers another item, again by placing it on the ground; this is received by another host *anetu* who trades an item of his own in return. The third pair of *anetaw* trade in the same fashion. The representatives continue trading until they have nothing more to offer, but they always present items which are of sufficient worth to be unquestionably "tradeable." The items are neither too expensive to buy on the spot (as are shell ornaments, hardwood bows, jaguar claw necklaces, toucan feather headdresses, and very large ceramics, which are usually bought and sold under private arrangements), nor too cheap to be considered of any real value. The *anetaw* present such things as fine arrows, large quantities of beads, large balls of newly twined cotton string, newly made urucu, large bottles of piqui oil, packages of salt, fishing line, and boxes of .22 ammunition. After they have presented everything they wish to trade, they urge other members of their group to contribute. At first, the things offered are much the same as those presented by the *anetaw*, for the more wealthy members of the community are avid participants. However, as poorer individuals begin to trade, the items which appear are of markedly less value. Small ceramics, individual strings of beads, a few fish hooks, a small spool of fishing line, arrows, small balls of urucu, small gourd containers, feather arm bands, earrings, and similar objects of minor importance are presented. Although these things are perfectly acceptable during the *uluki*, they are presented more often than not with the aim of receiving things of equivalent (or, with luck, greater) value. Specific objects are often requested (especially by the guests), things of lesser value rejected, and the guests sometimes refuse to accept an item they consider an unfair trade. There is an undercurrent of resentment and stinginess at this point, as the men initiating a trade receive items in exchange which appear of less value to them. Because the hosts are not supposed to reject anything presented by their guests, the *anetaw* are kept

busy suggesting to individuals that they accept what is offered. The host *anetaw*
attempt to keep up the semblance of generosity as long as possible, but as the *uluki*
continues and the rich have traded away most of their possessions, the burden begins to fall upon poorer men. There is less interest now in trading for the sake of
trade, for these men are unable or unwilling to part with the few objects they own.
Unlike rich men, who continually receive items as payment for services they perform, and who can thus expect a continual influx of material goods, others, especially
those who are young or of low status, cannot expect to obtain replacements for
their possessions in the near future, and thus are reluctant participants. Usually they
remain in the background, occassionally offering some small item for trade, but they
only accept proffered items when an *anetu* affine requests them to do so.

At the end of the *uluki* proper, the host representative conduct the visitors to
the house in which they will stay; inside they hang up the hammocks of the guest
anetaw, after which the rest of the visiting group may tie theirs in place. Then,
after they have bathed, the guests are fed with fish and manioc bread especially
prepared for them. For the rest of the afternoon, the guests lie about the house,
gossiping among themselves. If they have relatives, *ato*, or *ajo* in the village, and
can speak one another's language, there is considerable communication between
hosts and guests, but if they have few ties or speak different languages, there is
almost none.

At night, the male hosts dance from house to house singing while their guests
are asked by *ifï* to join the *kagutu* players.

The second day, one of several dance and song combinations is performed,
lasting from the early morning until dusk. Whatever the performance, it has no
inherent connection with the *uluki*. Like all secular ceremonies, those performed
after the *uluki* have little meaning for the participants outside of the pleasure of
dancing and the connection with a particular person who sponsors it. When the
performance ends, the *anetaw* of the visiting group step before the house in which
they are staying. Their host counterparts face them, according to their comparable
ages. The guests then simultaneously state in a formal speech their intentions of
returning home the next day. The hosts in turn ask them to stay, in order that the
members of their village group can fish for them. After the speeches, which are
often unintelligible to the *anetaw* of each village, gifts (or promises thereof) are
exchanged between them. These consist of the most expensive material items,
including large ceramics, shell ornaments, and toucan feather headdresses. After
the exchange of presents, the men relax and each pair tries to converse. When they
speak the same language there is no problem, but men who cannot understand one
another exchange trite comments in Portuguese, such as "How are you?" and "Are
you well?"

Later that day, the guests walk from house to house receiving gifts from their
hosts, an event known simply as *ifulundako*, "they are walking around." This occurs
not only after the *uluki*, but on any occasion (except mourning) when visitors
are in the village. In the afternoon, before preparing to leave for their own village,
the guests walk in pairs or, if a husband and wife attend, in family groups around
the village circle. As they enter a house, they are greeted by the household leader,
asked to sit on stools (if male), and presented with gifts by the individual mem-

The Uluki: *(a) Kalapalo* anetaw *formally recognize the arrival of their Yawalipiti* uluki *guests.*

(b) Men of Kuikuru and Kalapalo groups wrestling.

(c) In the Kuikuru village, a host anetu *accepts harpy eagle feathers presented by the Kalapalo representatives, Apihu, Bijiji, and Yafula. A second Kuikuru* anetu *is seen at the left, walking to his house with parrot tail feathers, for which he will return with a set of finely made gourd containers. On the right, three village leaders who are not representing their groups stand away from the rest of the men, waiting to take part in the trading.*

bers of the group. Those who have represented their villages during a ceremony, or who are lucky to have many *ato* and relatives in the host group, receive a great many small gifts (such as arrows, cloth, soap, razor blades, ammunition, and beads) which together amount to a considerable increment in personal wealth. Those with few relatives or young men of low status usually end up with a small number of presents, though it is extremely rude for visitors to be allowed to leave a household without having been given something. The Kalapalo say that certain individuals are notorious for coming to a village "for no reason," simply to receive gifts in this fashion, and there is considerable resentment (especially on the part of poorer young men) when several successive groups of visitors have depleted a village's resources. However, after a ceremony it is perfectly acceptable for guests to do this, and considerable prestige is conferred on hosts who display a proper level of generosity.

Early the next morning, the guests leave the village. As they walk through the plaza to the path leading out of the village, they are greeted and sent on their way by the host *anetaw*. In the future, perhaps a year or two later, they will expect their hosts to visit them for another *uluki*. In the meantime, they will have hosted and been guests at *uluki* with other villages.

The *Ifagaka* Ceremony

The *ifagaka* or spear throwing ceremony is held by the Kalapalo to be a Trumai ritual, introduced by that group to the rest of the Upper Xingu villages. Today, whatever meaning it originally had for the Trumai has become lost, and it is now performed in commemoration of a dead *anetu*, under the sponsorship of his son who has succeeded him. It is an entirely self-contained event which is apparently never performed in conjunction with other *anetaw* ceremonies, yet like the *egitsu* and *ipoñe*, it emphasizes the opposition of local groups, who are in the end united by a ritual of solidarity during which the ideals of *ifutisu* are demonstrated.

The *ifagaka* ritual, like other *anetaw* ceremonies, is begun in each of the competing villages several months before the main event in the host group. A set of songs and dances is performed, during which spears and spear throwers are prominently displayed by each man. A dummy is erected in the plaza, and at the end of each day's performance, one by one the men throw their spears at it, uttering a mocking insult aimed at an individual of the host group.[6] On the day of the ceremony, these events are repeated in the host village. The insults, when understood by the persons at whom they are directed, are taken quite seriously and thus an explicitly aggressive tone is present from the very beginning of the ceremony. Following these mocking insults, the village groups come together in a dance during which the *ifagaka* songs are sung once more. The village representatives, however, are seated formally at the edge of the village circle, where they passively watch the performance. After the singing has finished, the two opposing teams begin a second set of songs, ending with a confrontation in which the two groups aggressively charge at one another. Then the *anetaw* of each group, who have been watching nearby, charge into the melee to prevent physical abuse. After the groups have been separated, two bundles of poles are placed at each end of a narrow space on either side of which are the men of each team. Experts from each side pair up, each man taking a turn at hitting his opponent with a spear thrown from his spear thrower. The purpose is to hit the man on the thigh before he can jump behind the barrier. Next the champions from each village are paired against each other, but without the benefit of a shield behind which to jump. No village is considered the winner of these events, only individuals, but as with wrestling during other kinds of intervillage ceremony, the individual winners confer prestige upon their group. At the end of this contest, the spears and spear throwers are ceremoniously burned by the *anetaw* of the participating villages. Finally, the *ifagaka oto* distributes food to the participants.

In this ceremony, village groups are opposed in a kind of mock battle, making use of special equipment which is never used on other occasions. The hostility of local groups is not merely symbolic, however, for the insults which precede the contest engender bad feelings between the competitors. The rituals of opposition are constantly in danger of exploding into overt physical aggression, and only the

[6] Many of these insults seem to employ the use of animal imagery. For example, the following were recorded at a particular *ifagaka*: "K., he is like a rooster. When he comes to the Post, he walks behind his wives, who are like hens running before him"; "The Yawalipiti *anetu*, he eats mules"; "W., he is like an armadillo" [that is, is impotent].

presence of the village representatives prevents it from happening. In keeping with the aggressiveness of the event, in which individuals are explicitly opposed in both the mocking preliminaries and the contest itself, male decoration is considerably more individualistic than in other ceremonies. However, despite the aggressive opposition of both individuals and village groups, the final event of the ceremony is a symbol of the normally peaceful relationships between them, for here the two ideals of pacificity and generosity are once again openly displayed.

SUMMARY: THE VILLAGE REPRESENTATIVE AND UPPER XINGU SOCIETY

During *anetaw* ceremonies and the *uluki*, the *anetaw* of both the host and guest villages act as formal representatives of their groups. Rather than initiate action and influence others who are present, in such situations their behavior is extremely controlled and stylized, to the extent that they are considerably more passive than the other members of their respective groups. Often, they must sit quietly and observe the performances; at best (as sponsors), they make speeches which mark stages in the ceremony, but which do not convey any coercive message to the onlookers.

Although considerable time and energy is expended by a host group during the preliminaries to *anetaw* ceremonies, most elements of the ritual are without much significance to the performers. Only during the climactic performance, when village groups are explicitly displayed against one another in a relationship of opposition, do the ceremonies seem to take on real meaning to the participants. This opposition is expressed in various ways, according to the event, including explicit physical competition (wrestling, spear throwing) and spatial distinctions (especially when groups are seated at great distances from each other at the edge of the plaza). However, the emphasis on local group distinctiveness is, during other phases of the event, mitigated by rituals which unite them through the expression of commonly held ideals, namely generosity and pacificity. Thus, several types of exchange, including assistance in the performance of the ceremony in return for food payment, the giving of gifts by hosts to guests, and ultimately the reciprocity inherent in reversing the host–guest roles on future occasions, all serve to stress the fact that the groups are in reality units which form a true society—a society which is founded in what the Kalapalo know as *ifutisu*.

Glossary

ENGLISH TERMS

Affine: A relative by marriage.

Bride-service: A set of obligations which a newly engaged or married man must fulfill toward the kinsmen of his bride-to-be or wife.

Bride-wealth: Objects which are given to the bride's kinsmen by the kinsmen of the groom, representing the giving of rights to her person and her children by the former to the latter.

Culture: A system of conceptual categories, symbols, definitions, and rules for behavior which are commonly understood by a group of people.

Descent: A principle by which persons who are kinsmen are classed together as a result of their common relationship to an ancestor-figure.

Endogamy: A rule which specifies marriage within a category of persons.

Exchange system: A set of rules for the transference or circulation of things, including spouses, material objects, and the performance of specific duties.

Exogamy: A rule which specifies marriage outside a category of persons.

Filiation: The relationship of parent and child.

Kindred: A category of persons who are related to a specific individual through both of his parents, regardless of sex, but who are not necessarily related to one another.

Kinsman: A person who is related to an individual as a result of their parentage. How "parent" is defined varies according to the particular culture in question. Therefore, some anthropologists claim there is no universal definition of "kinship."

Nuclear family: A man, his wife, and their children.

Polyandry: The practice wherein a woman is married to more than one husband simultaneously.

Polygyny: The practice wherein a man is married to more than one wife simultaneously.

Relationship of opposition: A reciprocal or interdependent relationship between two or more like units which are also conceived as being in some way different from one another.

Social structure: The analytical model of a society constructed by the anthropologist.

Society: The systematic behavior of people who have a common culture.

Symbol: Anything which stands for a concept or concepts commonly understood by a group of people. The content or form of the symbol is not necessarily related to its meaning.

Unmarked category: A category which is labeled by a term used also to name a more inclusive taxon. The unmarked category is a member of a set, other members of which are labeled by different terms. These other categories are *marked* categories.

KALAPALO TERMS

In some cases, these words can be used to represent both singular and plural meaning. The definitions given below are those which correspond most closely to the meanings emphasized in the book.

ago: Affines; a group of people living in the same household or village as the speaker; living things (in general).

ajo: A man or woman who is an extramarital sex partner or "lover."

anetu: A village representative; the exclusive leader or head of a category of beings.

ato: A man or woman who is a "friend."

egitsu: A ceremony commemorating dead village representatives.

fuati: A shaman; that is, one who makes contact with monsters for the purpose of curing or divining.

ifagaka: The spear throwing contest.

ifi: A ceremonial specialist, (literally, "maker").

ifutisu: Peaceful, generous behavior; respect.

iñikogo: "Fierce" Indians; Indians who are not members of Upper Xingu society.

iṇikogu: Property.

ipoñe: The boys' ear piercing ritual.

itologu: Pets.

itseke: Monsters.

itsotu: Unpredictably violent behavior.

kagaifa: non-Indians.

kagutu: Ceremonial trumpets forbidden to the sight of women.

kejite: Aromatic leaves used in making contact with *itseke*.

kifi oto: A revenge magician (literally, "master of the revenge charm").

kuge: Human beings; people of Upper Xingu society.

kwifi oto: A witch (literally, "master of the darts").

mazope: A girl in puberty seclusion.

oto: A sponsor; a patron; the owner of an object.

otomo: A group of persons who are related to an individual or thing in some specific way; for example, the members of a village group, or a person's kindred.

tiñi: Ceremonial messengers (literally, "those who go to ask").

tuwąkita: A medical practice in which, after fasting, a person drinks a large quantity of liquid, then forces it up in order to promote good health.

uṇalï: A boy in puberty seclusion [literally, "person being housed"].

References

Agostinho da Silva, Pedro, 1972, "Information concerning the Territorial and Demographic Situation in the Alto Xingu," in *The Situation of the Indian in South America*, pp. 252–283. Geneva: World Council of Churches.

Askew, G. P., D. J. Moffatt, R. F. Montgomery and P. L. Searl, 1970, "Soil Landscapes in North Eastern Mato Grosso," *The Geographical Journal*, 136 (pt. 2):211–227.

Basso, Ellen B., 1970, "Xingu Carib Kinship Terminology and Marriage: Another View," *Southwestern Journal of Anthropology*, 26:402–416.

———, 1973, "The Use of Portuguese in Kalapalo (Xingu Carib) Encounters. Changes in a Central Brazilian Communications Network." *Language in Society*, 2 (no. 1): 1–19.

Beals, Alan R., and Bernard J. Siegel, 1967, *Divisiveness and Social Conflict: An Anthropological Approach.* Stanford, Calif.: Stanford University Press.

Carneiro, Robert L., 1956–1957, "La Cultura de los Indios Kuikurus del Brasil Central. I-La Economia de Subsistencia," *Runa* 8 (pt. 2):169–185.

———, 1956–1958, "Extramarital Sex Freedom among the Kuikuru Indians of Mato Grosso," *Revista do Museu Paulista*, n.s. X:135–142.

———, 1961, "Slash and Burn Cultivation among the Kuikuru and its Implication for Cultural Development in the Amazon Basin," in *The Evolution of Horticultural Systems in Native South America: Causes and Consequences*, ed. by Johannes Wilbert. *Antropologica*, supplemento no. 2, pp. 47–67. Caracas, Venezuela: Sociedad de Ciencias Naturales La Salle.

Chagnon, Napoleon A., 1968, *Yanomamö: The Fierce People.* New York: Holt, Rinehart and Winston, Inc.

Dole, Gertrude E., 1956–1957, "La Cultura de los Indios Kuikurus del Brasil Central. II-La Organizacion Social," *Runa* 8 (pt. 2):185–202.

———, 1956–1958, "Ownership and Exchange among the Kuikuru Indians of Mato Grosso," *Revista do Museu Paulista*, n.s. X:125–133.

———, 1960, "Techniques of Preparing Manioc Flour as a Key to Culture History in Tropical America," in *Man and Cultures: Selected Papers of the Fifth International Congress of Anthropological and Ethnological Sciences*, ed. by Anthony F. C. Wallace, pp. 241–248. Philadelphia: University of Pennsylvania Press.

———, 1966, "Anarchy Without Chaos: Alternatives to Political Authority among the Kuikuru," in *Political Anthropology*, ed. Marc Swarz *et al.* Chicago: University of Chicago Press.

Galvão, Eduardo, and Mario F. Simoes, 1965, "Notícia Sôbre os Indios Txicão, Alto Xingu," *Boletim do Museu Paraense Emílio Goeldi*, n.s. Antropologia, No. 24.

Greenberg, Joseph, 1966, *Language Universals.* The Hague: Mouton.

Gregor, Thomas, 1970, "Exposure and Seclusion: A Study of Institutionalized Isolation among the Mehinacu Indians of Brazil," *Ethnology*, 9:235–250.

Holmberg, Allan R., 1969 (reissued 1985), *Nomads of the Long Bow.* Prospect Heights, IL: Waveland Press, Inc.

Kay, Paul, 1966 (reissued 1987), "Comments on Colby," in *Cognitive Anthropology*, ed. by Stephen Tyler. Prospect Heights, IL: Waveland Press, Inc.

Lévi-Strauss, Claude, 1969, *The Elementary Structures of Kinship.* Boston: The Beacon Press.

Maybury-Lewis, David, 1965, *The Savage and the Innocent*. Cleveland: The World Publishing Company.

————, 1967, *Akwê-Shavante Society*. New York: Oxford University Press.

Meyer, Hermann, 1898, "Im Quellgebiet des Schingu. Landschafts und Volkerbilder aus Centralbrasilien," *Verhandlungen der Gesellschaft Deutscher Naturforscher und Arzte*, 69:135–145.

Murphy, Robert M., and Buell Quain, 1955, *The Trumai Indians of Central Brazil*, American Ethnological Society Monograph No. 24.

Nicholas, Ralph, 1965, "Factions: A Comparative Analysis," in *Political Systems and the Distribution of Power*, ASA Monographs No. 2. London: Tavistock Publications.

Oliveira, Adélia Engracia de, 1968, "Os Indios Juruna e Sua Cultura nos Dias Atuais," *Boletim do Museu Paraense Emílio Goeldi*. n.s. Antropologia No. 35.

Schneider, David M., 1967, "Descent and Filiation as Cultural Constructs," *Southwestern Journal of Anthropology*, 23:65–73.

Steinen, Karl von den, 1886, *Durch Central Brasilien*. Leipzig.

————, 1894, *Unter den Naturvolkern Zentral-Brasiliens*. Berlin.

Villas Boas, Orlando, and Claudio Villas Boas, 1970. *Xingu-os Indios, seus Mitos*. Rio de Janeiro: Zahar Ed.

Recent books on the Kalapalo by Ellen Basso:

1985   A Musical View of the Universe. Kalapalo Myth and Ritual Performances (University of Pennsylvania Press)

1987   In Favor of Deceit. A Study of Tricksters in an Amazonian Society. (University of Arizona Press)

LIBRARY OF MOUNT ST. MARY'S COLLEGE EMMITSBURG, MARYLAND

JUN 9 1992